HUMAN SURVIVAL AND CONSCIOUSNESS EVOLUTION

Edited by STANISLAV GROF

with the assistance of MARJORIE LIVINGSTON VALIER

Human Survival and Consciousness Evolution

State University of New York Press

Published by
State University of New York Press, Albany

For information, address State University of New York
Press, State University Plaza, Albany, NY 12246

Library of Congress Cataloging-in-Publication Data

Human survival and consciousness evolution.

Includes index.
1. Man. 2. Consciousness. 3. Human evolution.
4. Human evolution—Religious aspects. I. Grof,
Stanislav, 1931-   . II. Valier, Marjorie
Livingston.
BD450.H865 1987   128   87-7118
ISBN 0-88706-527-9
ISBN 0-88706-528-7 (pbk.)

10 9 8 7 6 5 4 3 2 1

Contents

INTRODUCTION
    Stanislav Grof   vii
ONE   *Human Survival: A Psycho-Evolutionary Analysis*
    Roger Walsh   1
TWO   *Transpersonal Vision*
    Frances Vaughan   9
THREE   *The Transformed Beserk: Unification of Psychic
Opposites*
    Marie-Louise von Franz   18
FOUR   *On Getting to Know One's Inner Enemy: Transformational
Perspectives on the Conflict of Good and Evil*
    Ralph Metzner   36
FIVE   *Modern Consciousness Research and Human Survival*
    Stanislav Grof   57
SIX   *Individuality: A Spiritual Task and Societal
Hazard*
    John Weir Perry   80
SEVEN   *Thoughts on Mysticism as Frontier of Consciousness
Evolution*
    Brother David Steindl-Rast   93
EIGHT   *Jesus, Evolution, and the Future of Humanity*
    John White   119
NINE   *The Buddhist Path and Social Responsibility*
    Jack Kornfield   135

TEN   *Transition to a New Consciousness*
       Karan Singh   144
ELEVEN   *The Darkness of God: Theology After Hiroshima*
       James Garrison   151
TWELVE   *The Incomplete Myth: Reflections on the "Star Wars"*
Dimension of the Arms Race
       Michael E. Zimmerman   177
THIRTEEN   *Laying Down A Path in Walking: A Biologist's Look*
at a New Biology and Its Ethics
       Francisco J. Varela   204
FOURTEEN   *Pacific Shift: The Philosophical and Political*
Movement from the Atlantic to the Pacific
       William Irwin Thompson   218
FIFTEEN   *Space-Age and Planetary Awareness: A Personal*
Experience
       Russell L. Schweickart   239
SIXTEEN   *Near Death Experiences: Implications for*
Human Evolution and Planetary Transformation
       Kenneth Ring   251
SEVENTEEN   *The Omega Project*
       Kenneth Ring and Alise Agar   271
EIGHTEEN   *Death, The Final Stage of Growth*
       Elisabeth Kübler-Ross   274

CONTRIBUTORS   287

INDEX   293

Introduction

Contemporary humanity has the dubious privilege of being in a role that is unique and unprecedented in the history of our planet. We are the first species that has developed the potential to commit collective suicide and to destroy in this catastrophic act all the other species and life on earth. It is a sad irony that this situation has been made possible by rapid advances of science and technology, two forces that Western peoples have long considered to be reliable means of creating a bright and happy future for the world.

In a certain sense, modern science has fulfilled this promise. It has made discoveries that have the potential to solve most of the problems that plague humanity; it can ameliorate diseases, poverty and hunger, create renewable and inexhaustible supplies of energy, and generate resources that enable an average person to have a living standard that in earlier times was reserved only for a privileged few. Within a few centuries, science has made astonishing break-throughs and has radically transformed our everyday life. It has been able to release the energies of the atom, build jet airplanes faster than sound and spacecraft that can travel beyond the limits of our solar system, explore the depths of the oceans, transmit sound and color pictures all over the globe and across cosmic space, and decipher the genetic code.

However, all these promising discoveries and inventions have failed to create the desired sorrow-free future. As a matter of fact, the shadow side of the rapid advances of science is becoming more evident every day. The greatest scientific triumphs—atomic energy, electronics, space-age rocketry, cybernetics, laser light, and the miracles of modern chemistry and bacteriology have backfired and turned into a menace of unimaginable proportions.

Surrounded by all the miraculous technology approaching science fiction, humanity seems to be farther away from a happy and sorrow-free existence than ever before. As a matter of fact, the most technologically advanced countries show a rapid increase in emotional disorders, suicidal rate, criminality, and drug abuse. The prospect of a glorious future has been replaced by a set of highly plausible dismal scenarios.

The most drastic and apocalyptic of these doomsday scripts is, of course, radical extermination of life on this planet by an atomic war and the following radioactive winter. While this nightmarish vision of a possible nuclear holocaust permeates our lives as a perpetual threat, there are other scripts that are already well under way. Although less obvious and dramatic, they are insidiously unfolding in the middle of our daily existence and could in the long run lead to similar consequences.

We can mention here, above all, the industrial pollution that already endangers life and health of the population in many areas of the world. Beside such dramatic manifestations as acid rain, toxic dumps, smog, pollution of water, soil and air, and dying of forests (Waldsterben), there is also the invisible danger of all the pollutants that we ingest every day with our food—preservatives, dyes, artifical sweeteners, hormones, pesticides, herbicides, and disinfectants. We can add to these threats the unsolved problem of the radioactive waste and the danger of nuclear accidents, so dramatically illustrated by the disasters at Three-Mile Island in the United States and Chernobyl in the U.S.S.R. And there are also several less imminent doomsday scenarios, such as possible loss of planetary oxygen by reckless deforestation and poisoning of the ocean plankton and other flora, destruction of the ozone layer of the earth, increase of temperature and melting of polar ice, the specter of AIDS, and possible disastrous consequences of genetic engineering.

In view of the dangerous situation in the world, it seems extremely important to understand the roots of the global crisis and to develop effective strategies and remedies to relieve it. Most of the existing approaches focus on factors of historical, political, or economic nature, that are symptoms of this crisis rather than its causes. Similarly, the

measures that are being undertaken reflect this superficial understanding and are nothing but extensions of the strategies that generated this crisis in the first place. As such, they offer very meager
hope for a successful resolution.

Human Survival and Consciousness Evolution focuses on an aspect
of the global crisis that has received in the past much less attention,
although it is clearly of paramount significance—the role that the
human psyche and human nature have played in this unfortunate
development. In the last analysis, the problems we are facing are
not economical, political, or technological in nature. Considering the
available resources and the progress of science, problems of hunger,
poverty, and most disease-related deaths in the world are unnecessary. There is also no real need for senseless plundering of nonrenewable reserves and polluting of vital resources. There exist means
and technological know-how for feeding the population of the planet,
guaranteeing reasonable living standards for all, combatting most
diseases, reorienting industries to inexhaustible sources of energy,
and preventing pollution.

What stands in the way are factors intrinsic to human nature and
personality. Because of them, unimaginable fortunes are wasted in
the insanity of the arms race, power struggles, and pursuit of "unlimited growth" and unlimited wealth of select individuals and groups.
These forces prevent a more appropriate division of resources among
individuals, classes, and nations as well as reorientation of ecological
priorities that are vital for continuation of life on this planet. As
Mahatma Gandhi so poignantly pointed out, there is no real shortage
in the world; there is enough to satisfy everybody's need, but not
everybody's greed.

Those who have tried to analyze these problematic forces in the
human nature have often referred to a dangerous schism that seems
to exist in modern humanity. It has been described in many different
ways—as an imbalance between the precipitous intellectual development and emotional maturation of the human race, disproportional
evolution of the neocortex in relation to the archaic parts of the
brain, interference of instinctual and irrational forces with the rational
processes, excessive influence of masculine instrumental thinking and
suppression of feminine intuitive sensitivities, and many others.

Some also emphasize the negative role of mechanistic science and
of the Newtonian-Cartesian paradigm that have portrayed human

beings as nothing but biological machines and highly developed animals. This position justifies the Darwinian concept of the "survival of the fittest" and endorses self-assertion, ambition, and reckless competition as essentially healthy tendencies reflecting the true nature of human beings. Mechanistic science has in general created a fragmented and biased world-view that is incapable of discovering the absolutely vital need for, as well as potential for, complementarity, synergy, and cooperation.

Modern consciousness research and transpersonal psychology brought a fresh and optimistic perspective into this problem area. According to this view, the factors in human nature that have created the crisis in the world are not fatally connected with the instinctual nature of human beings and with the hardware of the human brain. Human beings are in a difficult and crucial stage of consciousness evolution and have the potential to reach eventually undreamt of levels of emotional, intellectual, and ethical development. In acient times, this was dramatically expressed by the Neoplatonist Plotinus, who described mankind as "poised midway between the gods and the beasts." Modern versions of the same idea can be found in the writings of Sri Aurobindo, Teilhard de Chardin, Gopi Krishna, and Ken Wilber.

Transpersonal psychology does more than just throw new light on the problem of the world crisis. It also describes a wide spectrum of techniques by which we can accelerate consciousness evolution in ourselves and others. These range from ancient spiritual practices of the Oriental and Western mystical traditions to Jungian psychology, and clinical or laboratory methods of experimental psychiatry. They make it possible to confront and integrate the shadow aspects of one's personality, to transcend the indentification with the body and the ego, and to connect with the transpersonal domains of one's psyche—the Self and the collective unconscious. The experiences of oneness with other people, nature, and the Universe then lead to increased tolerance, capacity to love, development of deep ecological concerns, and a tendency to seek one's wellbeing in harmony with that of others.

Human Survival and Consciousness Evolution brings together original contributions of a number of prominent representatives of the transpersonal movement who address the problem of the global crisis from their unique individual perspectives. The psychological presentations include the paper by psychiatrist Roger Walsh who gives a brief analysis of the current world situation and emphasizes its potential as an evolutionary catalyst. Psychologist Frances Vaughan offers a concise description of transpersonal psychology and its goals and discusses how its understanding of the healing process can be applied to the situation in the world.

The world-known Jungian analyst Marie-Louise von Franz uses in her article the historical example of the Swiss saint, Brother Niklaus von Flue, to show that Western civilization has dissociated and disowned the shadow aspect of the archetypal figure of Christ and has been paying great toll for it in the form of detrimental returns of the repressed. However, like Brother Niklaus, modern humanity can confront, transform, and integrate the inner Berserk.

Similarly, consciousness researcher Ralph Metzner emphasizes the integration of the opposites—good and evil, male and female, and human-beast—as a means of transformation of potentially dangerous aspects of the human psyche. Psychiatrist Stanislav Grof draws in his paper on three decades of his research on nonordinary states of consciousness. Like the previous two authors, he emphasizes that violence in the world has important transbiographical roots. His special interest is in the task of confronting destructive emotions connected with the biological birth process, transcending them and mediating access to the transpersonal domains of the psyche. Jungian analyst John Weir Perry has discovered in his work with individuals experiencing acute psychotic states that many problems of the world reflect a misunderstood and misdirected impulse to become a fully individualized human being (Great Man), an ideal which was first realized historically in the person of ancient sacred kings in different parts of the world. In modern times, this process of individuation can and has to be internalized in the form of transformative experiences, rather than acted out in a concretized way. While the internalized individuation is conducive to greater social conhesion, harmony, and loving bonds among people, its concretized form is divisive and has destructive consequences for society.

A similar situation exists in relation to religion. True spirtuality, found in the mystical branches of the great religions, such as the Christian mystics, the Sufis, and the Kabbalists, is based on deep realization of the unity underlying all humanity and the entire phenomenal world; insights of this nature transcend race, color, culture,

and church affiliation. The misunderstanding of mythology and religious symbolism as historical and geographical references that char-
acterizes most mainstream religions leads to exclusivity and to religious antagonism, chauvinism, and wars.

Brother David Steindl-Rast explores in his paper the nature of
mysticism. He points out with extraordinary clarity how a unifying
mystical experience can become divisive when it turns into dogmatism, moralism, and ritualism of mainstream religions. The resulting fundamentalist trends then contribute significantly to the crisis
in the world. John White then specifically focuses on Christianity,
distinguishing its genuine and vital core and original meaning from
later distortions and accretions. Psychologist and meditation teacher
Jack Kornfield shows how correctly understood spirituality does not
lead to selfish withdrawal from the world and indifference to its
problems, but to compassion and social responsibility. Karan Singh
combines his profound knowledge of Indian scriptures and his ex-
pertise as a modern politician to outline his vision of a comprehensive
program that could help to meet the challenges of the global crisis.

Another group of papers in the book focuses on the interface
between modern technology, spirituality, and depth psychology. Jim
Garrison, using a Jungian approach, explores the archetypal images
underlying the problems of the nuclear age and discusses the impact
of Hiroshima and Nagasaki on the consciousness and ethics of modern
humanity. Michael Zimmerman uses a depth-psychological approach
in his analysis of another major issue of our times, the expensive
and dangerous "Star Wars" Strategic Defense Initiative (SDI). Biologist
Francisco Varela brings to the problem of the world crisis interesting
insights drawn from his work in information and system theory and
artificial intelligence. In his brilliant analysis of the trends of conceptual evolution in Western society, William Irwin Thompson out-
lines his idea of the "science of compassion," synthetizing most
advanced scientific thinking and the best of the ancient spiritual
traditions of the East into a holistic planetary vision. Apollo astronaut
Russell Schweickart illustrates in his account of the mystical experience he had while observing the Earth from an orbiting spaceship
the impact that space technology might have on humanity's development toward planetary consciousness.

Two papers in the book bring in insights from the ultimate teacher,
death. Thanatologist Kenneth Ring explores the global implications

of his study of near-death experiences. He believes that their transformative potential is an important indication that humanity is heading to a higher evolutionary stage described by Teilhard de Chardin as Omega Point. Elisabeth Kübler-Ross, world famous pioneer in research of death and dying then closes the volume with her reflections on death as the final stage of growth.

The ideas expressed in *Human Survival and Consciousness Evolution* are exciting and bring new hope into the serious and grim situation we are all facing. Whatever questions one might have about the feasibility of inner transformation of humanity and consciousness evolution as a world-changing force, it might well be our only real hope for the future.

STANISLAV GROF

CHAPTER ONE

Human Survival: A Psycho-Evolutionary Analysis

ROGER WALSH, M.D., PH.D.

The great experiment in consciousness, human evolution, now stands at a precipice of its own making. That same consciousness which struggled for millions of years to ensure human survival is now on the verge of depleting its planet's resources, rendering its environment uninhabitable, and fashioning the instruments of its own self-annihilation. Can this consciousness (we) develop the wisdom *not* to do these things? Can we foster sufficient self-understanding to reduce our destructiveness, and mature rapidly enough to carry us through this evolutionary crisis? These are surely the most crucial questions of our time, or of any time. Today we face a global threat of malnutrition, overpopulation, lack of resources, pollution, a disturbed ecology, and nuclear weapons. At the present time, from fifteen to twenty million of us die each year of malnutrition and related causes; another six hundred million are chronically hungry, and billions live in poverty without adequate shelter, education, or medical care (Brandt, 1980; Presidential Commission on World Hunger, 1979). The situation is exacerbated by an exploding population that adds another billion people every thirteen years, depletes natural resources at an ever-accelerating rate, affects "virtually every aspect of the earth's ecosystem (including) perhaps the most serious environmental development . . . an accelerating deterioration and loss of the resources essential for agriculture" (Council on Environmental Quality, 1979, p. 32). Desertification, pollution, acid rain, and greenhouse warming are among the more obvious effects.

Overshadowing all this hangs the nuclear threat, the equivalent of some twenty billion tons of TNT (enough to fill a freight train four million miles long), controlled by hair-trigger warning systems, and creating highly radioactive wastes for which no permanent storage sites exist, consuming over $660 billion each year in military expenditure, and threatening global suicide (Schell, 1982; Sivard, 1983; Walsh, 1984). By way of comparison, the total amount of TNT dropped in World War II was only three million tons (less than a single large nuclear warhead). The Presidential Commission on World Hunger (1979) estimated that $6 billion per year, or some four days worth of military expenditures, could eradicate world starvation. While not denying the role of political, economic, and military forces in our society, the crucial fact about these global crises is that all of them have psychological origins. Our own behavior has created these threats, and, thus, psychological approaches may be essential to understanding and reversing them. And to the extent that these threats are determined by psychological forces within us and between us, they are actually symptoms—symptoms of our individual and collective state of mind. These global symptoms reflect and express the faulty beliefs and perceptions, fears and fantasies, defenses and denials, that shape and misshape our individual and collective behavior. The state of the world reflects our state of mind; our collective crises mirror our collective consciousness.

Attempts to deal with global crises solely by traditional economic, political, or military means will certainly have limited success. If efforts to deal with nuclear weapons, for example, focus solely on establishing equal stockpiles, the underlying psychological forces that fuel the arms race will go untouched. To cure, or at least produce significant long-term inprovement, demands more than symptomatic treatment. It demands not just food for the starving and reduction of nuclear stockpiles, but also psychological understanding and personal sacrifice. Developing understanding may be one of the most urgent tasks facing our generation and may determine the fate of all future generations.

We have clearly created a world situation that demands unprecedented psychological and social maturation if we are to survive. Until now, we have been able to cover or compensate for our psychological shortcomings. We have been able to consume without fear of depletion, discard wastes without fear of pollution, bear children without fear of overpopulation, and fight without fear of extinction. We have been able to act out our psychological immaturities rather than having to understand and outgrow them, to indulge our addictions rather than resolve them, and to revolve through the same neurotic patterns rather than evolve out of them. But if the world is a stage, it is now no longer big enough for us to continue playing out our psychological immaturities. It is time for us to grow up, and we ourselves have created the situation which may force us to do so.

This growing up that is now demanded of us, this psychological maturation, this development of consciousness, is a form of evolution. For evolution is of both bodies and minds, of matter and consciousness (Wilber, 1981). "Evolution is an ascent towards consciousness," wrote Teilhard de Chardin, and this view has been echoed by Eastern thinkers such as Aurobindo (1963, p. 27), who said that "evolution of consciousness is the central motive of terrestrial existence" and that our next evolutionary step would be "a change of consciousness." This means conscious evolution—a conscious choosing of our future, driven by necessity but steered by choice (McWaters, 1981). Aurobindo said, "Man occupies the crest of the evolutionary wave. With him occurs the passage from an unconscious to a conscious evolution" (Elgin, 1980). This is not only evolution but it is the evolution of evolution.

Because this psychological maturation is demanded of us, our global crises may function as an evolutionary catalyst. And from this perspective, these current crises can be seen not as an unmitigated disaster but as a challenge, a push to new evolutionary heights. They can be seen as a call to each and every one of us, both individually and collectively, to become and contribute as much as we can. This perspective gives us both a vision of the future and a motive for working toward it.

Is this image idealistic? Yes, indeed it is! But this is by no means bad. Our situation seems to demand nothing less, and idealistic images can be very helpful if used skillfully. Unfortunately, our usual use of ideals is far from skillful. We tend to regard them as hopelessly unattainable, and we either scoff or give up in despair; or we use them as excuses for punishing ourselves when we fail to attain them. Either approach only ensures more pain and failure.

A skillful way to use ideals is to see them not just as goals that must be reached, but as guiding images or visions that provide signposts and directions for our lives and decisions. Such images attract us to actualize them and ourselves. This is the way we must view the evolutionary image; we must not automatically dismiss it as hopelessly idealistic. Rather, we need to see the possibilities it offers for guidance and direction, for escaping our current quandary, and for realizing our human potential. Humanistic, transpersonal, Jungian, Eastern, and some existential psychologists agree that the challenge of individual maturation and evolutionary advance must be a major human motive. "The basic actualizing tendency is the only motive which is postulated in this system," said the great humanistic psychologist Carl Rogers (1959).

To fulfill this demand may be deeply rewarding. Failing to fulfill it may result not only in a lack of growth, but in a particular kind of psychological suffering, a kind which often goes unrecognized. For when these actualizing needs go ungratified, their effects are subtle, existential, and therefore less easily identified. "In general, they have been discussed through the centuries by religionists, historians, and philosophers under the rubric of spiritual or religious shortcomings, rather than by physicians, scientists, or psychologists: (Maslow, 1971). Maslow called them "metapathologies" and described examples such as alienation, meaninglessness, and cynicism, as well as various existential, philosophical, and religious crises. These are the very symptoms that have increasingly plagued Western societies in recent decades (Yalom, 1980) and that contribute to the growing sense of social unrest. The very immaturities and failures of psychological growth from which our global crises stem are surely central to the prevailing psychological malaise of our time.

A perspective that views these global crises as a potential evolutionary catalyst may help in several ways. Research shows that when people face a life-threatening crisis they feel a desperate need to restore self-esteem by attempting to regain mastery of the situation and by finding some sense of meaning in it (Taylor, 1983).

An evolutionary view meets these needs well. It provides a sense of meaning on a grand scale—a scale that encompasses the totality of contemporary threats, includes individuals and the entire species, and transcends all traditional, national, and political boundaries. It enhances self-esteem by seeing our current situation, not as final proof of human inadequacy and futility, but rather as a self-created challenge to speed us on our evolutionary journey. It motivates us to regain mastery of the situation and demands that we fulfill our individual and collective potential far more than at any time in history. It also provides an antidote to the metapathologies of purposelessness and alienation that have been growing in developed countries during recent decades.

> By their own theories of human nature, psychologists have the power of elevating or degrading that same nature. Debasing assumptions debase human beings; generous assumptions exalt them. (Allport, 1964)

The evolutionary perspective provides a meaningful and inspiring view of our contemporary predicament and exalts human nature at the same time.

This perspective has dominated human thought and action during other periods of great transformation. Analyses of the few truly major transformations of human self-image throughout history suggest that they all combined a broad synthesis of knowledge with an evolutionary view of human kind (Mumford, 1956). Great thinkers such as Plato and Thomas Aquinas, who sparked transformations, said that the first order of business for humanity is to align ourselves with this evolution. But where will this evolution take us? What is our destiny in the universe? To answer this is to go beyond objective facts and to state our personal philosophy, our faith, and our worldview.

The two extreme world-views are probably represented by materialism and *the perennial philosophy*, the central core of understanding common to the great religions. The materialistic perspective suggests that life and consciousness are accidental by-products of matter, and that their evolution is driven by the interplay of random events and the instinct for survival. The purpose of human life and evolution is solely what humanity decides it is.

The perennial philosophy, which lies at the heart of the great religions and is increasingly said to represent their deepest thinking (Huxley, 1944), suggests that consciousness is central and its development is the primary goal of existence. This development will culminate in the condition variously known in different traditions as enlightenment, liberation, salvation, *moksha*, or *satori*.

The descriptions of this condition show remarkable similarities across cultures and centuries (Walsh & Vaughan, 1980). Its essence is the recognition that the distortions of our usual state of mind are such that we have been suffering from a case of mistaken identity. Our true nature is something much greater, an aspect of a universal consciousness, Self, Being, Mind, or God. The awakening to this true nature, claimed a Zen master, is "the direct awareness that you are more than this puny body or limited mind. Stated negatively, it is the realization that the universe is not external to you. Positively, it is experiencing the universe as yourself" (Kapleau, 1965). A different description can be found in almost any culture. Typical is the claim by an Englishman that to realize our true identity is to "find that the I, one's real, most intimate self, pervades the universe and all other beings. That the mountains, and the sea, and the stars are a part of one's body, and that one's soul is in touch with the souls of all creatures" (Harman, 1979). Nor are such descriptions the exclusive province of mystics. They have been echoed by philosophers, psychologists, and physicists (Wilber, 1984). "Out of my experience . . . one final conclusion dogmatically emerges," said the great American philosopher William James (1960). "There is a continuum of cosmic consciousness against which our individuality builds but accidental forces, and into which our several minds plunge as into a mother sea."

From this perspective, evolution is a vast journey of growing self-awareness and a return to our true identity (Wilber, 1981). Our current crises are seen as expressions of the mistaken desires, fears, and perceptions that arise from our mistaken identity. But they can also be seen as self-created challenges that may speed us on our evolutionary journey toward ultimate self-recognition.

Which world-view is correct? Are we solely survival-driven animals or are we also awakening gods? How can we decide? Both world-views give answers which are similar and different: similar in that they both tell us to research and explore, different in the emphasis of our exploration. The world-view of materialism says to explore the physical universe and thereby ourselves; the perennial philosophy says to explore our own minds and consciousness and thereby the universe.

In practical terms, it is crucial that we do both. Our survival and our evolution require that we deepen our understanding of both the universe within and the universe without (Walsh, 1984). We are challenged to choose and create our destiny. That challenge demands that we relinquish our former limits and be and become and contribute all that we can. It calls on us to play our full part in the unfolding human drama that we ourselves have created and asks that we choose, both individually and collectively, something entirely new: conscious evolution.

> In conclusion, hard material necessity and human evolutionary possibility now seem to converge to create a situation where, in the long run, we will be obliged to do no less than realize our greatest possibilities. We are engaged in a race between self-discovery and self-destruction. The forces that may converge to destroy us are the same forces that may foster societal and self-discovery. (Elgin, 1980).

REFERENCES

Allport, G. W. (1964). The fruits of eclecticism: Bitter or sweet. *Acta Psychologica, 23,* 27–44.

Aurobindo, A. (1963). *The future evolution of man.* India: All India Press.

Brandt, W. (1980). *North south: A program for survival.* Cambridge, MA: MIT Press.

Council on Environmental Quality. (1979). *The global 2000 report to the president.* Washington, D.C.: U.S. Government Printing Office.

Elgin, D. (1980). The tao of personal and social transformation. In R. Walsh & F. Vaughan (Eds.), *Beyond ego: Transpersonal dimensions in psychology* (p. 253). Los Angeles: J. P. Tarcher.

Harman, W. (1979). An evolving society to fit an evolving consciousness. *Integral View,* 14.

Huxley, A. (1944). *The perennial philosophy.* New York: Harper & Row.

James, W. (1960). In G. Murphy & R. Ballou (Eds.), *Psychical research* (p. 324). New York: Viking.

Kapleau, P. (1965). *The three pillars of Zen.* Boston: Beacon Press, 143.

Maslow, A. H. (1971). *The farther reaches of human nature* (pp. 316–317). New York: Viking Press.

McWaters, B. (1981). *Conscious evolution: Personal and planetary transformation.* San Francisco: Institute for the Study of Conscious Evolution.

Mumford, L. (1956). *The transformations of man.* New York: Harper Brothers.

Presidential Commission on World Hunger. (1979). *Preliminary report of the presidential commission on world hunger.* Washington, D.C.: U.S. Government Printing Office.

Rogers, C. (1959). A theory of therapy, personality, and interpersonal relationships as developed in the client-centered framework. In S. Koch
(Ed.), *Psychology: The study of a science: Formulations of the person and
the social context: Vol. 3* (pp. 184–256). New York: McGraw-Hill.

Schell, J. (1982). *The fate of the earth.* New York: Knopf.

Sivard, R. (1979, 1981, 1983). *World military and social expenditures.* Leesburg,
VA: World Priorities.

Taylor, S. (1983). Adjustment to threatening events: A theory of cognitive
events. *American Psychologist, 38,* 1161–1173.

Walsh, R. (1984). *Staying alive: The psychology of human survival.* Boulder,
CO: Shambhala.

Walsh, R., & Vaughan, F. (Eds.). (1980). *Beyond ego: Transpersonal dimensions
in psychology.* Los Angeles: J.P. Tarcher.

Wilber, K. (1981). *Up from Eden.* New York: Doubleday.

Wilber, K. (Ed.). (1984). *Quantum questions: The mystical writings of the world's
great physicists.* Boulder, CO: New Science Library/Shambhala.

Yalom, I. (1980). *Existential psychotherapy.* New York: Basic Books.

RELATED READING

Shapiro, D., & Walsh, R. (Eds.). (1984). *Meditation: Classic and contemporary
perspectives.* New York: Aldine.

Smith, H. (1976). *Forgotten truth.* New York: Harper & Row.

Walsh, R., & Shapiro, D. (Eds.). (1983). *Beyond health and normality: Explorations of exceptional psychological well-being.* New York: Van Nostrand.

Wilber, K. (1977). *The spectrum of consciousness.* Wheaton, IL: Quest.

Wilber, K. (1980). *The atman project.* Wheaton, IL: Quest.

Wilber, K. (1983). *A sociable god: a brief introduction to a transcendental
sociology.* New York: McGraw-Hill.

CHAPTER TWO

Transpersonal Vision

FRANCES VAUGHAN, PH.D.

THE TRANSPERSONAL PERSPECTIVE

Transpersonal psychology was born from the shared vision of a group of psychologists who saw that the predominant psychological theories of the time were too narrow to do justice to the full spectrum of human potentiality. The *Journal of Transpersonal Psychology*, now in its sixteenth year of publication, was originally established to publish theoretical and applied research, original contributions, and empirical papers that expanded the field to include psychological inquiry into self-actualization, values, states of consciousness, transcendental phenomena and concepts related to these experiences and activities. Gordon Allport (1964) wrote:

> By their own theories of human nature, psychologists have the power of elevating or degrading that same nature. Debasing assumptions debase human beings; generous assumptions exalt them.

The work of pioneers in the field of consciousness research such as Charles Tart (1969, 1975a, 1975b), Stanislav Grof (1975), Elmer and Alyce Green (1977), and Ken Wilber (1977), contributed to legitimizing this field in the 1970s. In recent years, interest in the psychological investigation of states of consciousness and experiences of transcendence, previously the province of philosophy and religion, has been growing. Definitions of mental health have gradually expanded to include optimal states of consciousness. Thus a more encompassing view of human nature and psychological development has evolved, and consciousness has become a central focus for

9

psychologists concerned with health and well-being (Walsh & Shapiro, 1983).

Since optimum psychological health is inextricably interwoven with other aspects of well-being, from a transpersonal perspective wholeness depends on a balanced integration of physical, emotional, mental, existential, and spiritual levels of consciousness (Vaughan, 1986). Health is not a static condition that is achieved once and for all, but a dynamic ongoing process of optimum functioning and relational exchange at all levels.

"Transpersonal" means, literally, beyond the personal. As the study of human development beyond the ego (Walsh & Vaughan, 1980), transpersonal psychology affirms the possibility of wholeness and self-transcendence. Transcendence is explored as manifested in and through personal experience. A transpersonal view of human relationships recognizes that we exist embedded in a web of mutually conditioned relationships with each other and with the natural environment. Any attempt to improve the human condition must therefore take global, social, and environmental issues into account.

In the past, attention to inner development and consciousness was considered a luxury for a few individuals who could afford to seek personal liberation or who chose to renounce the world. Today, however, we are acutely aware that no one can escape our collective destiny, and humanity as a whole must acknowledge its responsibility for the welfare of the planet. Since all major threats to human survival are now human-caused, attention to psychological and spiritual development has become a social necessity (Walsh, 1984). As human beings, we have the power to destroy the world, but will we find the wisdom to preserve it? The great religious and spiritual traditions all teach that the source of wisdom lies within us, and it is human consciousness that holds the key to the fate of the earth. Carl Jung (1969) was one of the first to call attention to the centrality of consciousness in human development. He wrote that

> in the history of the collective as in the history of the
> individual, everything depends on the development of
> consciousness. This gradually brings liberation from
> imprisonment in "agnoia," "unconsciousness," and therefore is
> a bringer of light as well as of healing.

We can no longer afford to ignore the necessity for both inner work and outer work. Both are necessary if we are to make wise and informed decisions affecting the quality of our lives. The interdependence of the healthy person and the healthy society becomes apparent in exploring the common ground of biological, psychological, and spiritual experience underlying cultural diversity. We are shaped by our environment, but we are also the shapers of that environment.

Appreciating the diversity of approaches to healing and personal growth that are available today can contribute to a better understanding of different values among different cultures and different levels of consciousness within each culture. Understanding the common purpose underlying different approaches to spiritual practice can also deepen our appreciation of the universality of transpersonal experience. Recognizing the unity as well as the diversity of human experience can also help us find the path best suited to our particular needs.

PERCEPTION, KNOWLEDGE AND WISDOM

Perception that focuses on particular objects of consciousness and splits the world into subject and object can be distinguished from vision that sees the context in which objects exist as well as the relationships between them. Transpersonal vision allows simultaneous awareness of unity, diversity, and interconnecting relationships. Thus, a primary function pertaining to the transpersonal domain has been called vision/logic (Wilber, 1980), emphasizing the complementarity of intuitive vision and reason. Knowledge of the transpersonal domain depends on the integration of empirical, rational, and contemplative perceptions of reality, not on the substitution of one for another.

Perceived solely with the eye of reason, transpersonal vision may appear to be ephemeral or illusory. Perceived intuitively, however, it may appear to be more real or fundamental than rational conceptual constructs that attempt to explain whatever lies beyond the boundaries of current understanding. Huston Smith (1982) states that

> to those who, their hearts having been opened, can see with
> *its* eye (the Sufi's *"eye of the heart,"* Plato's "eye of the soul"),
> spiritual objects will be discernible and a theistic metaphysics

will emerge. The final "night vision" which can detect the
awefilled holiness of everything is reserved for those whom
. . . I have called mystics. . . .
The divisions between the levels of reality are like one-way
mirrors. Looking up, we see only reflections of the level we
are on; looking down, the mirrors become plate glass and
cease to exist. On the highest plane even the glass is
removed, and immanence reigns . . . looking up from the
planes that are lower, God is radically transcendent . . .
looking down, from the heights that human vision can to
varying degrees attain, God is absolutely immanent.

The clarity of this inner vision depends on self-awareness and
intuitive insight. Concepts can either help or hinder the process of
awakening this level of consciousness that dissolves boundaries and
offers transcendent insight. Depending on how they are used, concepts can be either stepping stones or obstacles to vision. They serve
a purpose in communication, but vision transcends rational understanding. Great spiritual teachers are individuals of great vision who
can use concepts to communicate their insight and wisdom to others.

When inner vision is ignored or obscured, one may be caught by
illusions that constrict awareness of reality. Inner vision is a gift that
requires only attention for recognition. The light that is necessary
for vision is ever-present, but anything one fears to see becomes an
impediment to clear vision.

Enlightenment, as a goal of the spiritual path, is partly a result of
awakening vision. Discussing the question. *What is Enlightenment?*,
John White (1985) writes as follows:

Enlightenment is understanding the perfect poise of being-
amid-becoming.
The truth of all existence and all experience, then, is none
other than the seamless here-and-now, the already present,
the prior nature of that which seeks and strives and asks:
Being. *The spiritual journey is the process of discovering and
living that truth.* It amounts to the eye seeing itself—or rather,
the I seeing its Self. In philosophical terms, enlightenment is
comprehending the unity of all dualities, the harmonious
*com*posite of all *op*posites, the oneness of endless multiplicity
and diversity. In psychological terms, it is transcendence of all
sense of limitation and otherness. In humanistic terms, it is

understanding that the journey is the teaching, that the path and the destination are ultimately one.

Knowledge of the past, like knowledge of the future, depends on selective perception that is subject to change with any shift in perspective. Past and future do not now exist anywhere except in the mind; all of the past and all of the future are included in the full awareness of the present. Any spiritual path can serve as a means of awakening consciousness when truth is the goal.

Traditionally the spiritual path leads through dreams and illusions to knowledge, liberation, and enlightenment, and the awakened mind comes to know itself in wholeness. The goal may be apprehended as unity consciousness, or the truth of existence as intuited by clear vision, free from the constricting distortions of partial perceptions. Vision can give a sense of direction to the journey, intuiting the completion before it is attained.

Wisdom, in contrast to knowledge gathered by empirical or rational investigation, is an attribute of one who, by virtue of inner vision, understands the nature of illusion and duality. Wisdom becomes available when we see things as they are. Our task is to remove the obstacles to awareness that limit and distort perception.

Vision can be a resource of inexhaustible abundance and unlimited possibility that informs the mind with boundless creativity. Vision sees time and eternity, emptiness and form, consciousness and its objects. Transpersonal vision gives access to an inner source of guidance and inspiration that transcends narrow personal perceptual frames. It is renewed, rather than depleted, by being shared. Illumination of vision occurs naturally when the mind is at peace. An empty mind and open heart become the matrix of wisdom wherein all possibilities may be conceived.

HEALING AND WHOLENESS

As the journey of a thousand miles begins with a single step, healing the whole begins with healing ourselves, our relationships and our world. Our inherent capacity for self-healing is empowered when we awaken to the vision of unity consciousness. We are challenged to see ourselves whole, free from egocentric attachment to form or outcome.

For the first time in history, humanity is confronting the necessity of seeing the world as a whole. Spirituality must also be addressed in global terms. An awareness that transcends cultural distinctions may be essential to human survival. The healing vision that sees beyond appearance and duality to the unity of spirit does not require belief in a personal deity; it does require a willingness to be aware, moment by moment, of what is true in our shared experience.

The desirability of sharing experiences, not just doctrines and ideas, is gradually becoming accepted. If we are to become persons of global vision, self-knowledge must deepen into awareness of universal spirituality. Abraham Maslow said that self-actualizing people are always involved in something beyond themselves (Maslow, 1971).

The wisdom needed for healing the world cannot be taught by words alone. It must be discovered within and applied in relationship. As we grow toward wholeness we may become more aware of our shared psychological and spiritual resources. Any situation may be perceived as an opportunity to heal the mind that generates conflict while caught in the illusion of separateness. A mind possessed by illusions can be healed when it awakens to transpersonal vision.

As we become conscious of wholeness, we can more effectively participate in the cocreation of our future. If we would participate in co-creating a future different from the past, a future that could heal the earth, we must begin by envisioning possibilities. Ken Wilber (1981) has suggested the following:

> For those who have matured to a responsible, stable ego, the next stage of growth is the beginning of the transpersonal, the level of psychic intuition, of transcendent openness and clarity, the awakening of a sense of awareness that is somehow more than the simple mind and body. To the extent that it does start to occur, there will be profound changes in society, culture, government, medicine, economics. . . .
> [This] will mean a society of men and women who, by virtue of an initial glimpse into transcendence, will start to understand vividly their common humanity and brother/ sisterhood; will transcend roles based on bodily differences of skin, color, and sex; will grow in mental-psychic clarity; will make policy decisions on the basis of intuition as well as rationality, will see the same Consciousness in each and every

soul, indeed, in all creation, and will start to act correspondingly; will find mental psychic consciousness to be transfigurative of body physiology, and adjust medical theory accordingly; will find higher motivations in men and women that will drastically alter economic incentives and economic theory; will understand psychological growth as evolutionary transcendence, and develop methods and institutions not just to cure emotional disease but foster the growth of consciousness; will see education as a discipline in transcendence, body to mind to soul, and regear educational theory and institutions accordingly, with special development; will find technology an appropriate aid to transcendence, not a replacement for it; will use mass media, instant telecommunication, and human/computer linkages as vehicles of bonding-consciousness and unity; will see outer space as not just an inert entity out there but also as a projection of inner or psychic spaces and explore it accordingly; will use appropriate technology to free the exchanges of the material level from chronic oppression; will find sexuality to be not just a play of reproductive desire but the initial base of kundalini sublimation into psychic spheres—and will readjust marriage practices accordingly; will see cultural national differences as perfectly acceptable and desirable, but will see those differences on a background of universal and common consciousness; . . . will realize fully the transcendent unity of all Dharmakaya religions, and thus respect all true religious preferences while condemning any sectarian claim to possess "the only way"; will realize that politicians, if they are to govern all aspects of life, will have to demonstrate an understanding and mastery of all aspects of life—body to mind to soul to spirit. . . .
In short, a true Wisdom Culture will *start* to emerge. . . .

The vision of a world that is healed and whole, that provides a supportive environment for humanity and all other forms of life, is a possible dream. We must dare to dream of the qualities and values that are needed for healing and well-being. Everyone is given opportunities for service and creative participation. The challenge of our time is for each of us to do our part in creating a world we would want for everyone. If we fail to choose our future, we may not have one. The state of the world, reflecting the state of our collective mind, indicates that we are badly in need of healing. Will we awaken in time to the vision of wholeness that points the way to continuing creative participation in sustaining life on earth? Consciousness has, by necessity, become both the object and the instrument of change.

We must learn to apply what we know about healing ourselves to healing the world, and empower ourselves and each other in cocreating peaceful evolutionary alternatives to self-destruction. This is not a task that can be undertaken by anyone alone. We can no longer afford to wait for a heroic leader to rescue us. We have learned the hard way that evil cannot be conquered in battle. Conflict perpetuates the problem. It is, rather, our capacity for vision and self-transcendence that must be recognized if present danger is to be transformed into opportunity for renewal. If we persist in our folly of wishful thinking and blaming others for our predicaments, we may forfeit the chance to grow into wisdom.

It is not impossible to envision a world where we can learn to live in harmony, in the light of the perennial wisdom of the great traditions. As we awaken from the dream of being isolated entities in a fragmented universe where individual thoughts, feelings, and actions make no difference, we see that our destiny is shared.

By perceiving the unity of opposites we may begin to envision the emergence of a global spirituality concerned with the welfare of the whole rather than with particular forms of religious practice. A shared dream of healing and wholeness is no more improbable than others that we collectively entertain.

Each one of us has a unique function in healing the whole. We can discover it by awakening the transpersonal vision and seeing things as they are. We have the capacity to turn problems into challenges and to encourage others to manifest a vision of wholeness. We can no longer afford to pretend to be children playing while the home we inhabit is being destroyed. We must acknowledge our responsibility for the world as it is and for choosing to change. In sharing a vision that transcends present limitations and inspires creative imagination, we become the visionmakers and healers of our time. As we learn to shift the focus of our attention from the part to the whole, from the content to the context, we begin to expand limited perception and awaken vision.

Awakening transpersonal vision does not impose a new image on reality or provide ready answers to questions of the way-seeking mind. It does allow each of us to see for ourselves what is true. We cannot be satisfied with lies and illusions. We can delude ourselves temporarily, but true vision is not deceived. At times we may ask others for guidance, but ultimately we must learn to see for ourselves. Facing our collective challenge calls for a willingness to witness the pain of the human condition, to open our hearts and to heal the wounds of deprivation—physical, emotional, mental, and spiritual. Let us begin by envisioning peace and healing within and among ourselves, that we may extend it in the world.

REFERENCES

Allport, G. W. (1964). The fruits of eclecticism: Bitter or sweet. *Acta Psychologica, 23*, 27–44.

Green, E., & Green, A. (1977). *Beyond biofeedback*. New York: Delacorte.

Grof, S. (1975). *Realms of the human unconscious*. New York: Viking.

Jung, C. G. (1969). Four archetypes (R. F. C. Hull, Trans.) In *The Collected Works of C. G. Jung, Vol 9, Part I* (2nd ed., p. 272). Princeton, NJ: Princeton University Press, Bollingen Series XX.

Maslow, A. (1971). *The farther reaches of human nature*. New York: Viking.

Smith, H. (1982). *Beyond the post-modern mind*. New York: Crossroads.

Tart, C. (Ed.). (1969). *Altered states of consciousness*. New York: John Wiley.

Tart, C. (1975a). *States of consciousness*. New York: E. P. Dutton.

Tart, C. (Ed.). (1975b). *Transpersonal psychologies*. New York: Harper and Row.

Vaughan, F. (1986). *The inward arc*. Boston: Shambhala/New Science Library.

Walsh, R. (1984). *Staying alive: The psychology of human survival*. Boston: Shambhala/New Science Library.

Walsh, R., & Shapiro, D. (Eds.). (1983). *Beyond ego: Transpersonal dimensions in psychology*. Los Angeles: J. P. Tarcher.

White, J. (Ed.). (1985). *What is enlightenment?* Los Angeles: J. P. Tarcher.

Wilber, K. (1977). *The spectrum of consciousness*. Wheaton, IL: Theosophial Publishing House.

Wilber, K. (1980). *The atman project: A transpersonal view of human development*. Wheaton, IL: Theosophical Publishing House.

Wilber, K. (1981). *Up from Eden: A transpersonal view of human evolution*. New York: Doubleday.

CHAPTER THREE

The Transformed Berserk:
Unification of Psychic Opposites

MARIE-LOUISE VON FRANZ, PH.D.

At the core of the relationship between individual transformation and social responsibility is the problem of psychic opposites. For, as Carl Gustav Jung once pointed out, "there always will be the two standpoints: the standpoint of the social leader who, if he is an idealist at all, seeks salvation in a more or less complete suppression of the individual, and the leader of minds who seeks improvement in the individual only." These two types "are necessary pairs of opposites which keep the world in balance."[1] Examples of social leaders with or without a feeling of responsibility for their people are to be found everywhere in the limelight of the mass media. Therefore, I will try to describe in more detail an opposite example by choosing our only Swiss saint, Brother Niklaus of Flüe, a conscious leader of souls. He was a deeply introverted, solitary hermit who worked only to improve himself and yet became, all the same, *the* political savior of Switzerland.

Niklaus of Flüe was born on March 21, 1417, in the so-called "Flüeli," the slopes above Sachseln (Unterwalden), the son of an honorable local farmer, Heinrich von Flüe, and his wife, Emma Ruberta. The fifteenth century was a time in which the Catholic church was in a state of decay, corruption, and full of inner dissension, a fact which led many individuals to concentrate more on the search for inner guidance. Politically it was also a bad time in Switzerland, for the original Swiss mountain communities (Urkantone) were completely bled to death and disintegrated by the bad habit of its male youths to run away from home and fight in foreign military services

18

(the so-called Reislaufen). Saint Niklaus himself did not take part in such mercenary activities, but we find his name on the lists of several warlike expeditions of his own country.

Apparently, he even became a captain but was said to have always tried to prevent unnecessary massacres and destruction. Around 1447 (when he was thirty years old) he married Dorothea Wyss and, in the course of time, they had ten children. From 1459 until 1462 he functioned as a judge and a member of the Council of Unterwalden. As a judge he often had to witness injustices and cases of bribery, which evoked in him deep indignation and disgust for all worldly occupations. Once, while in court, he had a vision of fire flowing out of the mouth of an unjust judge.

When he was about forty five years old, he began to suffer from a deep depression, with feelings of resistance against his family and a longing to devote himself completely to his inner religious vocation. His friend, Heiny am Grund, the local priest of Kriens, advised him to do some regular prayer-exercises, but that was not very helpful. Finally Klaus managed to get the agreement of his wife (he was then about fifty years old) and left home with the intention of wandering into the unknown world as a sort of religious mendicant pilgrim.

But several incidents and an important vision he had near the Swiss border impelled him to return home. There, with the help of his friends and relations, he built a little hermit's cell about 250 meters from his home beside a deep shadowy creek called the Ranft, and he stayed there for the rest of his life, fasting almost completely, with the exception of receiving the host. He had many visionary states and slowly acquired such fame as a saintly healer and counselor that often up to six hundred people were waiting around his cell to have a word with him.

When Klaus was sixty four years old, he became involved in the famous political incident of the meeting (Tagsatzung) and treaty of Stans on December 22, 1947. A conflict had exploded between some of the more democratic rural original Cantons (Urkantone) and the new, more aristocratically ruled town Cantons. A declaration of civil war was impending. At this moment the priest of Kriens, Heiny am Grund, ran through the whole night to Klaus's hermitage in Sachseln and begged Klaus to speak to the warring parties. Klaus agreed to address the two camps; he simply admonished the Swiss to keep

peace, to accept the two new town Cantons but not to expand their
territory too far, and to settle their fight with a treaty. However, he
suggested that if they were attacked, they should defend themselves
valiantly. And such was the authority of Klaus that they unwillingly
but humbly obeyed him and settled their quarrel. Had there been a
war, Austria and France would have interfered and walked in, and
Switzerland would most certainly have disappeared from the map
forever. All of this is not legend, but hard historical fact.

The content of the message Klaus delivered was in itself not very
special; it was in a way just common sense, something that any old
farmer could have said. What had such an unusual effect was the
awe in which everyone held him. Later, Klaus became a counselor
of dukes and ambassadors in many other political affairs, and thus
actually achieved what Master Kung Fu-tse (Confucius) tried to do
in China but failed on account of more unfavorable circumstances.
But let us now turn to the deeper question: What is really behind
such an unusual effect? In my view, an important vision of Niklaus
of Flüe reveals more about this question. The following text is the
description of this vision:

It seemed to him (to Brother Klaus) that a man resembling a pilgrim
came to him. He had a stick in his hands, a hat with its brim folded
down like a wanderer's hat, and a blue coat. And Klaus realized
inwardly that the man came from the East or from far away. Though
the pilgrim did not say so, Klaus knew that he came from *where
the sun rises in summertime*. Then he stood before Klaus and sang
the word: "Alleluja." When he began to sing, his voice reverberated
and everything between heaven and earth sang with him. And Klaus
heard three perfect words coming from a place of origin and then
they were shut away like with a snapping lock. When he heard
these three words he could only speak of one word. When the pilgrim
had finished his song, he asked Brother Klaus for an alm. Klaus
suddenly had a penny in his hand which he dropped into the hat
of the pilgrim. And this man (Klaus?) had never known before what
a great honor it is to receive a gift of money in one's hat.

And Klaus wondered who the pilgrim was and where he came
from. The Wanderer said: "I came from there," and did not want
to say any more. Klaus stood before him and looked at him. In that
moment he (the pilgrim) changed shape; he no longer had a hat on,
but had a blue or greyish vest and no coat. He was a noble, good-

looking man, so that Klaus looked at him with pleasure and desire. His face was brownish, which gave him a noble look, his eyes black like a magnet, his limbs of eminent beauty. Though he had his clothes on, Klaus could see his limbs through them. As Klaus stared at him, the Wanderer looked at him too. In that moment great miracles happened: the mountain Pilatus crumbled and became completely flat and the earth opened up so that Klaus felt as though he could see the sins of the whole world. He saw a lot of people and behind them appeared the Truth, but all the people turned their backs to it and in their hearts he saw a great disease, a tumor as big as two fists. This tumor was selfishness, which seduces people so much that they cannot stand the man's (the Truth's) glance, which to them was like fire so that they ran about in great confusion and shame and finally ran away, but the Truth remained.

And then his (the pilgrim's) face changed like a "Veronica" and Klaus felt a great desire to see more of him. Then he saw him again as he had been before, but his clothes had changed and he stood before him as if he had on a bearskin, a vest and bearskin leggings. The fur was interspersed with golden sparks, but Klaus saw clearly that it was the skin of a bear. The bearskin suited him very well, so that he (Klaus) saw that it was of special beauty. As he stood before him, so nobly in his bearskin, Klaus realized that he wanted to leave. He asked: "Where do you want to go?" He answered: "I will go up the country," and he did not want to say more. When he left, Klaus stared after him and saw that the bearskin shone as when someone moves a well-cleaned sword and one can see its reverberations on the wall. And he thought that this was something hidden from him. When the Wanderer had gone about four steps away he turned around, took off his hat and bowed to Klaus. Klaus realized that there was such great love in the Wanderer for him that he was quite smitten and confessed that he had not earned such love and then he saw that this love was in him. And he saw that his spirit, face, eyes, and his whole body was full of loving humility, like a vessel brimful of honey. Then he saw the Wanderer no more, but he was so satisfied that he did not desire anything more. It seemed that everything there is between heaven and earth had been revealed to him.

This great vision would need many hours of interpretation, but here I can only point out some essential aspects of it. This pilgrim is obviously an image of what Jung has called the Self (in contrast to the ego) that is Klaus's eternal inner spiritual core, something like the "inner Christ" in the writings of the mystics. But though the pilgrim sings the Biblical word "Allelujah" (praise to God), his clothes clearly characterize him as Wotan, a Germanic god of War, Truth, Ecstasy, and of shamanic wisdom. According to some myths, Wotan was always walking about as a wanderer visiting people, wearing a grey-blue coat and a wide-brimmed hat and looking very aristocratic with flaming eyes. Other myths describe that he could constantly change his shape; therefore he was often called Svipall, the changing one, or Grimmir, the masked one, or Tveggi, the two-fold one. In Klaus's vision, he comes from the place of sunrise, the symbolic place from which new illuminations and revelations from the collective unconscious arise. This connection is reflected in the saying that something "dawns on us."

Later in the vision, the wanderer appears as personified Truth behind the backs of people. Wotan too had the epithet "Sannr"- true. He was said to have second sight and could open all mountains and "see and take what was in them" (Snorri Sturluson). Seen in a Christian context, the Holy Ghost is the Spirit of Truth, but here it is strangely blended with the old Germanic God of Ecstasy, Love, and Spiritual Devotion. This pilgrim conveys to Klaus a feeling of knowing everything between heaven and earth, that is, he imparts to Klaus what Jung called the "absolute knowledge" of the unconscious, which is typical for many experiences of the Self.

But even more, he conveyed to Klaus a feeling of infinite love, described as a vessel brimming over with honey. This motif of the honey reminds one of a verse in the Brhadaranyaka-Upanishad, which runs: "The Self is honey of all beings and all beings are honey of this Self. Likewise, this bright immortal person is this Self and that bright immortal person, the Self (both are madhu-honey). He indeed is the same as that Self, that Immortal, that Brahman, that All."[2] "And verily the Self is the lord of all beings, the king of all beings. And as all spokes are contained in the axle and in the felly of the wheel, all beings and all those Selfs (of earth, water, etc.) are contained in the Self."[3] Madhu-honey meant here, as Max Müller explains, an objective complete interdependence or interconnectedness of all things, the same that Jung would call "objective love," in contrast to ordinary subjective love, which is full of ego projections and desires.

But the most amazing and unorthodox motif in this vision of Brother Klaus is the bearskin that the pilgrim wears. It is a detail which again points to Wotan who, among other titles, was called *hrammi*—bear's paw, as the god of the berserkers. In the Old Testament the bear represents the dark side of Jahweh, and in Nordic shamanism the bear is the most frequent "helping spirit" or ally of the shaman. In most northern countries of Europe, the bear was so sacred in former times that one only spoke of him as "the Father," "the Holy Man," "the Holy Woman," "the Wise Father," or "the Goldfoot."

For the old Germans to wear a bearskin means to be a beriserkr— a berserk. Going berserk was the parapsychological gift inherited in certain Germanic warrior families. It was a divine ecstasy, a kind of "holy rage." Such people were said to faint and fall to the ground as though they were dead, while their soul left their body in the form of a bear and was then seen raging in the battle, killing all enemies, but, sometimes by mistake, also their own people. The basic mood in going berserk was called *grimr*, which translates as "anger." To go berserk was also called "hamfong," which means changing one's skin or shape and also shadow or ally (Schutzgeist). To sum this up, the bear aspect of the holy pilgrim in Klaus's vision is the dangerous, uncanny animal shadow of the Self.

Jung writes in a letter about this very vision: a "man charged with *mana*, or numinous man, has theriomorphic attributes, since he surpasses the ordinary man not only upwards but also downwards."[4] The vision of the berserk shows the figure of the inner Christ in two forms: "1. as a pilgrim who, like the mystic, has gone on the *peregrinatio animae*; 2. as a bear whose pelt contains the golden luster." The latter alludes to the "new sun" in alchemy, a new illumination. And Jung continues: "The meaning of the vision may be as follows: On his spiritual pilgrimage and in his instinctual (bear-like, i.e., hermit-like) subhumanness Brother Klaus recognizes himself as Christ. . . . The brutal coldness of feeling that the saint needed in order to abandon his wife and children and friends is encountered in the subhuman animal realm. Hence the saint throws an animal shadow. . . . Whoever can suffer within himself the highest united with the lowest is healed, holy, whole. The vision is trying to show him (Klaus) that the spiritual pilgrim and the Beriserkr are both Christ, and this opens the way to forgiveness of the great sin which holiness is." Later in his life Klaus had a frightening vision of God's wrath, "because this wrath is aimed at him, who has betrayed his nearest and dearest and the ordinary man for God's sake."

The Christ-Berserk of Brother Klaus's vision thus unites irreconcilable opposites, subhuman wildness and Christian spirituality, the rage of the warrior and Christian *agape*—love of mankind—and only because Klaus had given space to this inner figure in himself was he able to unite the opposites outside, to convince his countrymen to keep peace instead of getting swept away into civil war.

In order to understand how this actually works we must consider certain basic facts of depth psychology. Let us look at the situation depicted on the diagram.

The outermost dots, A, A, A, represent the *ego consciousness* of human beings. Below is a psychic layer, B, B, B, which represents the sphere of the so-called *personal unconscious*, which is that psychic layer that Freud discovered: the sphere of forgotten and repressed

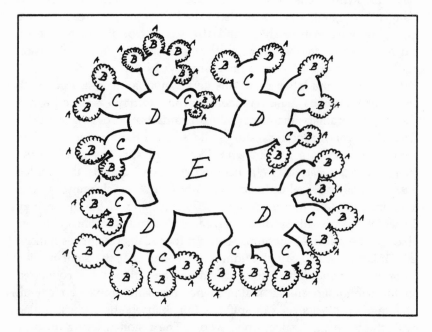

Figure 1. Diagram showing the structure of the unconscious. A—ego consciousness, B—personal unconscious, C—group unconscious, D—unconscious of large national units, E—universal archetypal structures.

memories, desires, and impulses. Below it comes the layer, C, C, C, which is a kind of *group unconscious*, as it manifests in family therapy or group therapy; it contains the common reactions and complexes of whole groups, clans, tribes, etc. Below it we have D, D, D, which would be the *common unconscious of wide national units*. We can, for instance, see that Australian or South American Indian mythologies form such a wider "family" of relatively similar religious motifs which, however, they do not share with all of mankind. An example would be the motif of catching and weakening a demonic figure of the sun, a motif that we find in the Far East but not in the West. Finally, the center circle, E, would represent the sum of those *universal psychic archetypal structures* that we share with the whole of mankind, such as the archetypal idea of mana, the hero, the cosmic god-man, the mother earth, the helpful animal, or the trickster figure, which we find in all mythologies and all religious systems.

Whenever an individual works on his own unconscious he invisibly affects first the group (when he reaches C); and if he goes even deeper, he affects the large national units (layer D), or sometimes even all of humanity (layer E). Not only does he change and transform himself but he has an imperceptible impact on the unconscious psyche of many other people. That is why Kung Fu-tse (Confucius) said: "The superior man abides in his room. If his words are well spoken, he meets with assent at a distance of more than a thousand miles."[5]

The collective unconscious is actually like an atmosphere in which we are all contained and by which we are affected. One of the most important images in E, the common center, is the image of a god-man or cultural hero, which we find practically in all cultural communities (Christ, Osiris, Avalokiteshvara); let us call it the symbol of the *Anthropôs*. In contrast to various gods, ghosts and demons, who symbolize the more autonomous special impulses in the collective psyche, Anthropôs represents *that* aspect of the collective unconscious which appears *integrated in man as his specific cultural consciousness or religion*.

There seems to exist a basic law in the development of religious cultural communities—the periodic falling apart and decay or renewal and reunion of its elements. In principle, all single instinctual drives, such as sexual impulses, aggression, power, or self-preservation, have a physiological and a symbolic, that is psychological or spiritual, aspect. On an archaic level these two aspects work completely together; that means that the ritual and physical activities and their representatives are one. But in the course of historical development these two aspects often tend to get separated; then the ritual and religious doctrines become only rigid spiritual formalisms against which the physiological instincts revolt. This is a situation of conflict that is needed for the development of higher consciousness. But the conflict can also go too far and become destructive. This then requires reconciliation of the opposites. Such a situation calls for an anamnesis of the original man, the archetype of man as the Anthropôs, who is at the core of all great religions. In the idea of a *homo maximus*, the Above and Below of creation are reunited.[6]

The Christ-Berserk in Klaus's vision is such a spontaneous emergence of a complete Anthropôs figure which complements the official incomplete image of Christ. But this vision of Christ as a berserk overflowing with Eros is not an isolated image turning up in an unusual individual, but it reaches back and is connected with a long hidden historical continuity. There exists, as Jung has shown, an unofficial development of the Christ-figure within the whole of Western Christian culture in its two thousand-year-old tradition. In this book *Aion*,[7] Jung points out that in the Apocalypse (5, 6) a lamb appears, with seven horns and eyes, a monstrous figure not at all resembling the sacrificial lamb that is traditionally associated with Christ. It is praised as victor in battle (17, 14) and as the "lion of the tribe of Judah" (5, 5). It looks therefore, as if at the end of time a certain shadow aspect of Christ returns and reunites with his figure, a shadow that Christ had cast away before. If one compares the ecclesiastical image of Christ with that of God in the Old Testament, he does not seem to incarnate that God completely. Jahweh himself is of infinite goodness, just as he shows infinite cruel rage and vengefulness; in contrast, Christ incarnates only the former aspect. This probably is the reason why he himself predicted that, in a process of reversal, the figure of Antichrist would rise at the end of the Christian aeon. However, the demonic ram of the Apocalypse is not an Antichrist figure, it is rather a reborn or reformed or completed Christ symbol, in which certain dark vengeful aspects are integrated rather than split off.

Perhaps this is a partial return to Jewish ideas of a belligerent messiah, born out of an anti-Roman resentment. The Christian answer to the realization of the good-evil double nature of God was first unequivocal: God is only good and Christ, his incarnation in man, is only good too. From approximately the year 1000 of the Christian era, this symbolic religious answer became doubtful. The problem of evil became more and more urgent. There existed in this respect two possibilities: the first of these was the official idea that an anti-Christian movement would arise and undo, on a grand scale, all of the cultural and moral achievements Christ had brought forth. A second possible development was also brought up from the unconscious; this was the idea to complete the figure of Christ into a good *and* evil figure—a true union of opposites.

In his *Answer to Job*[8] Jung proposed that in the Apocalypse one could see an image of this second development. There appears a woman with a crown of twelve stars on her head who is persecuted by a dragon. She gives birth to a male child but, subsequently, they are both carried away and disappear in heaven. This seems like a vision of a reborn Christ-figure, the anticipation of the collective unconscious of a more complete symbol of Self which is no longer split into a good and an evil half.

This idea of a more complete Christ-figure also haunted the minds of many medieval alchemists. Their "philosophers' stone," which they likened to Christ, was not just exclusively good; he was a union of opposites. And more than that, he also united spirit and matter, as well as man and animal. He was not only a savior of souls like Christ, but a savior of the whole of the nature of the macrocosm.

If we look at the outer history of our Western Christian civilization, this union of opposites has not, or at least not yet, been realized. On the contrary, Europe is split between the so-called Christian Western half and the openly anti-Christian Eastern half; large parts of the rest of the world then side with one or the other. The openly anti-Christian spiritual development in Europe began in the Renaissance, that is, in the time of Brother Klaus. It is, therefore, amazing to consider that at that very time, quite independently and spontaneously, Klaus's unconscious brought up a Christ-figure who, like the alchemical stone, *unites the opposites*. The dark aspect is a berserk, harking back to the pagan Germanic tradition. If we consider what that Wotanic German berserk did in the Second World War, we can realize what terrible destructiveness this means when it is autonomous and no longer united with its opposite. Jung called World War II a Wotanic experiment and remarked that apparently we are now preparing for still another Wotanic experiment, but this time on a worldwide scale. Such an explosion is only possible if the berserk shadow, that is, aggression, remains autonomous and is not integrated within the inner totality of man.

In confining himself, in his desperate depression, to his hermitage in the Ranft, Brother Klaus forced his shadow to remain within, where it became amalgamated with the inner Christ in him. It is worth noting: *We* cannot integrate such divine powers of aggression in our ordinary selves. All that hopeful benevolent talk about integrating one's aggression is nonsense. We can only, through our efforts and suffering, bring forth an integration of these forces within the Self. In other words, we can only integrate our own personal shadow, but not the collective shadow of the Self, or the dark side of the godhead.

However, by suffering to the absolute extreme under the problem of opposites and by accepting it within ourselves, we can sometimes become a place in which the divine opposites spontaneously come together. That is what obviously happened to Brother Klaus; his vision showed him that in the Self the divine opposites had become one and this united figure was now overflowing with honey, that is, with love. It is a love which emanates from the total, the individual man, and not from his different complexes or impulses.

Interesting parallels to this process can be found in alchemical writings. In a way that greatly resembles Klaus's vision of the cosmic berserk filled with honey, many alchemists praised their philosopher's stone as a living being emanating "rose-colored blood" or "hue" which has a healing effect on its surroundings. This is one of the strangest images that can be found in the alchemical texts. The Paracelsist, Gerald Dorn, says, for instance, about the philosopher's stone: (The philosophers) "called their stone animate because, at the final operations . . . a dark red liquid, like blood, sweats out drop by drop. . . . And for this reason they have prophesied that in the last days a most pure (*putus* = genuine, unalloyed) man, through whom the world will be freed, will come to earth and will sweat bloody drops of a rosy or red hue, whereby the world will be redeemed from its Fall. In like manner, too, the blood of their stone will free the leprous metals and also men from their diseases. . . . In the blood of this stone is hidden its soul, which is in his blood."[9] Another alchemist, Henricus Khunrath, mentions the same blood as that of a "lion lured forth from the Saturnine mountain."[10] There we have, like the bear in Klaus's vision, a lion from the "Saturnine mountain," also a wild animal which comes from the places of darkness and depression, but brings forth the healing blood of love. The same Khunrath also speaks elsewhere of that "rose-colored Blood . . . that flows forth . . . from the side of the innate Son of the Great World," that is, of an intracosmic Christ-figure who is the "Healer of all imperfect bodies and men."[11] Unlike the Biblical Christ, he is not only a savior of men, but also like the alchemical Christ, or Lapis, a healer of all nature.

"It seems," writes Jung, "as though the rose-colored blood of the alchemical redeemer was derived from a rose mysticism that penetrated into alchemy. It expresses a certain kind of *healing Eros*. This Eros emanates from the *homo totus*, the cosmic man whom Dorn called *putissimus* = unalloyed. This most pure or most true man must be no other than what he is . . . he must be entirely man, a man who *knows and possesses everything human and is not adulterated by any influence or admixture from without*." He will appear, according to Dorn, only "in the last days." "He cannot be Christ, for Christ by his blood has already redeemed the world. . . . It is much rather the alchemical savior of the universe, representing the still unconscious idea of the whole and complete man, who shall bring about what the sacrificial death of Christ has obviously left unfinished, namely the deliverance of the world from evil. . . . His blood is a psychic substance, the manifestation of a certain kind of Eros which unifies the individual, as well as the multitude, in the sign of the rose and makes them whole."[12]

In the sixteenth century the Rosicrucian movement began, whose motto, "per crucem ad rosam," was anticipated by the alchemists. Such movements, Jung points out, [13] "as also the emergence of the idea of Christian charity with its emotional overtones, are always indicative of a corresponding social defect which they serve to compensate. In the perspective of history, we can see clearly enough what this defect was in the ancient world; and in the Middle Ages as well, with its cruel and unreliable laws and feudal conditions, human rights and human dignity were in a sorry plight." And, we can add, so were the social conditions of Brother Klaus's time. It seems, therefore, that this berserk full of honey, which is Eros, turned up in his vision because, as we know, Klaus worried very much

about the social injustices and cruelties which occurred in his surroundings.

But what kind of love could this be? As Jung stresses, love taken
in itself is useless without a certain amount of understanding. "And
for the proper use of understanding a wider consciousness is needed,
and a higher standpoint to enlarge one's horizon. . . . Certainly love
is needed . . . but a love combined with insight and understanding.
Their function is to illuminate regions that are still dark and to add
them to consciousness. . . . The blinder love is, the more it is
instinctual, and the more it is attended by destructive consequences,
for it is a dynamism that needs form and direction."[14] We can see
this when mothers love their children so much that they suffocate
them, or collectively when, out of love, we try to develop so-called
undeveloped countries by brutally imposing upon them our ideas
and technology. Out of so-called love, innumerable crimes and
destruction have been brought upon man, and the more sentimental
love is, the more brutal the shadow that follows it. By contrast, in
the symbol of the berserk-Christ, the brutal shadow (the bear aspect)
is integrated into the human figure and thus no longer acts autonomously behind its back.

The whole problem is an ethical one; it is a problem of differ-
entiating our feelings. Western civilizations of late have one-sidedly
developed extroverted thinking and sensation in their technology,
and introverted sensation-thinking in their theoretical studies. Intuition is also not quite suppressed because it is needed for finding
new creative ideas. But feeling and the whole world of Eros, love,
is in a sorry plight indeed. I even think that at present everything
depends on whether we succeed in developing our feeling and social
Eros or not.

It is psychologically impossible to say what Eros is, for it is an
archetypal power far beyond our comprehension. At the bottom of
it—if we observe it from an empirical angle—there seems to lie a
participation mystique, what Jung called archaic identity. It is an
unconscious conformity of collective ideas or feeling values. On it
is based the general assumption that what is good for us is also
good for the other, that I have the right to correct other people, and
that altogether the other person is basically like myself. This is an
original, basic, gregarious, instinctive bond among all men, but it
can even extend to animals, plants, and other outer objects. Even

Christian love of one's neighbor or Buddhistic compassion are ultimately based on this deep-rooted instinctual condition. The symbolic image of the Anthropôs, or divine man, contains this aspect insofar as he is mythologically often spoken of as the basic material from which the whole cosmos was made, like the Purusha in India, P'an ku in Chinese mythology, the giant Ymir in the German genesis, Gayomart in Persia, or Osiris-Rê in Egypt. The Judaeo-Christian figure of the first Adam and the second Adam (Christ) also have this aspect. According to certain Midrashim, for instance, Adam was first a cosmic giant in whom all the souls of mankind "were united, like strands in a wick." And Christ has the same function in relation to the Christian community; we are all supposedly brothers and sisters "in Christ."

The phenomenon of archaic identity does not, however, sufficiently take into account that there are also great differences among all human beings. They manifest in archaic conditions in tribal wars between different groups of people and sometimes even in chaotic social conditions where everybody fights everybody, as was the case in certain times of interregnum, as J. G. Fraser has shown. This fact of inevitable personal tensions and hostilities forces us to recognize that other people are sometimes different and that they do not always behave according to our expectations. This leads to a phenomenon which Jung calls *the taking back of projections*, that is to wake up to the realization that certain of our assumptions and judgements about other people are not true for them, but only for ourselves. Such a realization is still very rare and I think we are only now at the very beginning of this wider realization. Especially where there are really great differences, as for instance between man and woman, or between far-away ethnic groups of people and us, the search for and the realization of projections is of paramount importance.

Only when projections are withdrawn, does *relationship*, as contrasted with archaic identity, become possible; however, this presupposes psychological knowledge. We have embassies in foreign countries which are supposed to provide us with such psychological knowledge. How poorly that still works is unfortunately well-known. In all pluralistic, democratically organized societies there is an attempt to somehow regulate the cooperation of different groups and individuals without forcing them to adhere completely to the rules of archaic collective identity. In contrast to the latter, *relationship* includes the idea of a *certain distance*. Jung writes: "one of the most important and difficult tasks in the individuation process is to bridge the distance between people. There is always a danger that the distance will be broken down by one party only (intruding into the other's realm of concerns), and this invariably gives rise to a feeling of violation followed by resentment. Every relationship has its optimal distance, which of course has to be found by trial and error."[15] We are still probably aeons away from realizing such a state of free mutual interrelatedness among all human beings. A profound respect for the real"otherness" of the other being or ethnical group is needed as well as the intimacy of a feeling of identity. But even this is not yet the ultimate stage of possible development. It is obvious that on the surface (outer lines of our model) this would cause too great a fragmentation or isolation of the conscious individual egos. There exists another stage, however, which I would like to call a *personal connection of fate through the Self with selected people*. It is like a return to the first stage but on a higher, more conscious level. It is a relationship with the Self in the other person, with her or his totality and oneness of opposites. Only love and not mind can understand the other person in this way. This form of love, Jung writes, "is not transference and it is more primitive, more primeval and more spiritual, than anything we can describe. That upper floor is no more you or I, it means many, including yourself and anybody whose heart you touch. There is no distance, but immediate presence. It is an eternal secret—how shall I ever explain it?"[16]

One could perhaps say that it is a *timeless connection in eternity* which, however, in *this* world, in our space-time, appears as that mysterious something which makes any deep real encounter of two human beings possible. It occurs when, meeting somebody for the first time, one has the feeling that one has "known" the other for all eternity, and this is not an error, as it is sometimes on account of ordinary archaic identity, but it proves to be true. This kind of relationship can appear between people of the same sex, as for instance in the "eternal" relationship of certain masters with their pupils, but more frequently in the love between man and woman, who represent the greatest opposites among mankind. According to Jung, this latter problem of relationship lies at the *core* of all problems of modern mankind. Either we can bridge these opposites within ourselves or we will contribute to the explosion of wars outside.

Personal love is the only existing compensation for the fragmentation—even atomization—of modern society. In it the image of the
Anthropôs might reappear again and with it "the Truth" behind
people's backs, as Klaus saw it in his vision.

Brother Klaus was not at all weak and sentimental. In his consultations, he unhesitantly uncovered the lies and hidden sins of his
clients, but at the same time he did this always with a twinkle of
humor in his eyes and with helpful warmth. Since these are characteristics of a good therapist, Jung has said that Klaus should be
made the patron saint of psychotherapy. It was somehow the personified Truth of his vision of the bearskin pilgrim which acted
through him. His love or warmth was always directed towards the
individual before him, for the relationships of an individuated person
are always unique—*from one unique being to another unique being.*
Only within such relationships can our soul come alive and can the
transpersonal Self be constellated. With it (as the berserk-Christ figure
shows) a certain inner dualism in the Self is united into one.

I am convinced that if Brother Klaus had not had this berserk
figure behind him he could not have appeased the meeting of Stans.
This berserk is a visible image of that invisible authority which
emanated from him and made the warring parties settle their conflict.
In this way Klaus achieved politically more than any ruler or am-
bassador could have done. He is a wonderful example of how
individual transformation and universal responsibility can be united.
Naturally, Brother Klaus is a unique example, which we cannot simply
choose to imitate. In everybody's inner evolution these opposites of
individual transformation versus collective responsibility take on a
different form and nuance.

In the *I Ching*,[17] in the first chapter on the creative principle, there
is one line which refers to this problem. It is the fourth line, which
runs: "Wavering flight over the depths. No blame." and the Comment
runs:

> A place of transition has been reached, and free choice can
> enter in. A twofold possibility is presented to the great man:
> he can soar to the heights and play an important part in the
> world, or he can withdraw into solitude and develop himself.
> He can go the way of the hero or that of the holy sage who
> seeks seclusion. There is no general law to say which of the

two is the right way. Each one in this situation must make a
free choice according to the inner law of his being. If the
individual acts consistently and is true to himself, he will find
the way that is appropriate for him.

Compared to such holy sages as Lao-tse or Chuang-tse, Brother
Klaus is less only as the figure of a retired hermit. In the first half
of his life, he took part in all the activities of ordinary outer life;
only when an inner call found him, did he leave the world. At first,
he tried arduously to "imitate Christ" and practice the Christian love
of one's neighbor, but then the berserk—a deeply introverted fierce
need to follow his own inner truth—overcame him. And what was
perhaps the greatest miracle was that the people around him did
not interpret this as madness. Some theologians tried to criticize him
for leaving his family, but the general public all around him and
mostly the people of Unterwalden stood up for him and saw in his
retirement the sign of a divine call and not a sign of social madness
or irresponsibility. I think this comes from the honey-Eros aspect of
the berserk pilgrim figure that these people must have felt in him.

Returning to our sketch, the central sphere of the collective unconscious is in most religions represented by an Anthropôs figure,
a symbol of a god-man or cosmic man. Thus the berserk represents,
in a paradoxical way, the greater personality of the Self of Brother
Klaus and simultaneously the Self of the whole collective. In this
latter aspect it was and still is today a *living archetype*. During World
War II, some Swiss regiments had a collective vision of Brother Klaus
standing at the Swiss border towards Germany, spreading his arms
out to protect Switzerland from being invaded by Hitler. The greater
achetypal core of Klaus is, in this way, still alive today in Switzerland.

Modern zoologists like Konrad Lorenz and innumerable psychologists write today about the problem of aggression and how to
integrate, abreact, or suppress it. Brother Klaus's vision shows us
how he *really* succeeded in integrating and transforming it. Then it
is no longer what we call aggression but rather a clearly defined
separateness and firmness of the individual which succeeds in remaining steadfastly in "himself" and does not succumb to group or
mass suggestions. In many collective panic situations in a nation,
everything depends on whether or not some individuals can keep

their heads and not succumb to the general paranoiac emotion. That, according to Jung, is the only way to avoid war.

This is still clearly a very remote goal for humanity and in the meantime nations and groups will inevitably go on fighting each other. But one thing seems sure to me: we have reached a point in history where the differentation of Eros has become of paramount importance, because the world has become so small that we *have* to realize we are all in the same boat.

Presented at the Eighth Conference of the International Transpersonal Association (ITA) on *Individual Transformation and Universal Responsibility*, August 27–September 2, 1983, in Davos, Switzerland.

NOTES

1. Jung, C. G. (1975). Letter of October 19, 1934. In G. Adler & A. Jaffé (Eds.). *Letters, Vol. I*. Princeton, NJ: Bollingen Series XLV, Princeton University Press.
2. Brhad Aranyaka Upanishad, II. 54, p. 116. (1900). (M. Müller, trans.). Oxford: Clarendon Press.
3. Ibid.
4. Jung, C. G. (1975). Letter on W. Christ. In *Leters, Vol. I*.
5. The *I Ching* or *Book of Changes*, chapt. 62. (1950). (R. Wilhelm, trans.) Princeton, NJ: Bollingen Series XIX, Princeton University Press.
6. Jung, C. G. (1955). Mysterium coniunctionis. In *Collected works, Vol. XIV*. Princeton, NJ: Bollingen Series XX, Princeton University Press.
7. Jung, C. G. (1951, 1954). Aion. In *Collected works, Vol. IX, 1. 2*. Princeton NJ: Bollingen Series XXM, Princeton University Press.
8. Jung, C. G. (1958). Answer to Job In *Psychology and religion: West and east. Collected works, Vol XI*. Princeton, NJ: Bollingen Series XX, Princeton University Press.
9. Jung, C. G. (1967). Alchemical studies, para 381. In *Collected works, Vol. XIII*. Princeton, NJ: Bollingen Series XX, Princeton University Press.
10. Jung, C. G. (1967). Alchemical studies, para. 383.
11. Ibid., para. 384.
12. Ibid., para. 390.
13. Ibid., para. 391.
14. Ibid., para. 391.
15. Jung, C. G. (1975). *Letters, Vol. I*, p. 53ff.
16. Ibid., p. 298.
17. Op. cit.

CHAPTER FOUR

On Getting to Know One's Inner Enemy: Transformational Perspectives on the Conflict of Good and Evil

RALPH METZNER, PH.D.

The shadow, the id, the beast, the devil, the monster, the adversary—these are some of the many names of a psychological complex that is present in all human beings. We can regard it as a psychic image that functions as an inner opponent, our opposite, with whom we struggle and argue throughout our lives. To reconcile this opposition has been recognized as a central challenge on the part of individuation, or self-transformation. Ancient wisdom of East and West and modern transpersonal philosophy and psychology affirm that getting to know these opposites, seeing them as aspects of our being, is essential to growth and wholeness. C. G. Jung, following Nicholas of Cusa, referred to this as the *coincidentia oppositorum*, "the co-incidence of opposites"—the acceptance and reconciliation of two polarized facets of our nature. According to Nicholas, the dualities in opposition, existing throughout all of Nature, including human nature, are the wall that makes God invisible to man."

The *good/evil* or *good/bad* judgment is often superimposed on other dualities. When superimposed on the duality of male and female, we get sexist attitudes of women as inferior and men superior, or the reverse. When superimposed on the duality of human and animal, we get images of monsters, dragons, beasts, and fear of our own and others' bestial impulses and passions. When this judgment is superimposed on religious, racial, cultural, or national difference, we get bigotry, racism, chauvinism, and the prejudices that separate and antagonize—the in-group versus the out-group, or the notorious *us* versus *them* (Russians/Americans, Nazis/Jews, blacks/whites, etc.).

The *good/bad* or *good/evil* judgment is often superimposed on the duality of spirit and matter, or spirit and body, or Spirit and Nature. The spiritual realm of the human being is then regarded as *good*, *light*, or *higher*; and the material world, the realm of Nature and the body is seen as *inferior, dark, fallen* or *sinful*. Sometimes, paradoxically, the superimposition is reversed: The Self, or Spirit, is identified with the shadow—it is feared or hated. This happens when we deny or reject our higher nature, the spiritual aspect of our being. Paul Ricoeur, in his book, *The Symbolism of Evil* (1967), has even suggested that evil is always essentially connected to the sacred; that it is an inverse reflection of the sacred. I suggest a more limited view. For individuals who have an image of God as a punitive, terrifying, or judgmental deity, an encounter with the divine or higher Self may well be traumatic and overwhelming. We see this kind of ego-annihilating encounter portrayed in the story of Job, or of Jacob wrestling with the angel, or of Saul on the road to Damascus, being struck blind by God.

Our task of transformation in relation to these dualities is integration: We must bring about a coexistence of the opposites—the male and the female balanced in a wholeness that transcends both; the human and the animal integrated in a peaceful inner friendship or alliance; the self and its shadow come to terms. We must make friends with the inner enemy; or, if not friends, then at least, and at first, we must get to know our inner adversary. We must get to the point where we can truthfully say, with the Roman poet Terentius, "nothing that is human is alien to me" (*nil humanum mihi alienum*).

Throughout history people have experienced this entity that we call evil in many different ways. A common thread is the recognition that something is wrong. A mistake has been made or something horrible has occurred, or something uncanny, something that threatens reality. This wrong must be corrected or dealt with in some way.

Our feeling of wrongness or mistakenness derives from our capacity for judgment. According to Judaic-Christian mythology, the result of eating the fruit of the Tree of Knowledge of Good and Evil was precisely that Adam and Eve, and all humanity descended from them, acquired this power of judgment.[1] While the ability to make discriminative judgments is undoubtedly essential to survival, and hence not something to be eliminated or suspended, spiritual traditions have consistently pointed out that this judging tendency is also one of the chief obstacles to a development of clear understanding. Judgment, especially prejudgment, contracts and distorts our perception, as expressed in Christ's parable about the beam in our eye, to which we are oblivious while we are judging the mote in someone else's eye. According to the Jewish Kabbalah, evil occurs when the function of discrimination or judgment (*Gevurah*) is separated from its natural complement—loving kindness or mercy (*Hesed*). The implication is that discriminative judgment must be integrated with kindness or compassion for this opposite to be transformed.

We must discuss various experiences that human beings have had of evil, and the processes involved in its transformation. In the first section *On Integrating the Shadow*, we consider Jung's metaphor for the dark, evil, or destructive aspect of the psyche, and how this transformative integration is brought about. In the second section we look at the notion that the dark or evil side of our nature is what the conscious self-concept finds unacceptable; the transformational challenge is *Accepting the Unacceptable*. As described in the third section, *From Denial to Affirmation*, that which has been denied, negated, repressed, has to be brought into our awareness and recognized. In the fourth section, *Purification and Elimination*, we explore the imagery of evil as sin, corruption, defilement, and how this can be transformed. Then, in the section entitled *From Inner Warfare to Inner Peace*, we explore different approaches to the understanding and resolution of inner conflict and opposition. The final section, *On Facing One's Demons*, examines the experiential reality behind the many myths of demons, devils, and evil spirits.

There is a difference between the judgment *good/bad* and the judgment *good/evil*, athough they have in common that they are both judgments imposed on experience. The judgments we make are a function of our conditioning—of cultural and familiar values that we have accepted. The difference is that *bad* suggests that something is useless, worthless, inferior—to be ignored, or eliminated, or possibly changed and made better. We are not horrified by something we think of as bad. Evil, on the other hand, is much more dynamic.

It is a force or tendency that actively opposes the good, that tries to destroy, negate, tear down, kill. It frightens and horrifies us. Traditionally it was said that the devil, the embodiment of evil, opposes everything we do towards enlightenment, or tries to block our approach to the realm of Spirit, Self, and God.

ON INTEGRATING THE SHADOW

The shadow, in Jung's psychology, is described as a "dark" (meaning unconscious) aspect of the personality. It has an emotional charge and presents a significant moral opposition to the ego-personality. Integrating the shadow is regarded as an essential step in the process of individuation. We must be able to recognize and acknowledge the existence in ourselves of dark, destructive tendencies.

A much more difficult task confronts us when, as is often the case, the dark aspects within are not recognized, and the intense, primitive feelings are projected onto other people in our environment. They, the others, then are the ones who are bad, evil or dangerous; this permits us to maintain unconsciousness of our own dark aspects. As Jung wrote, "projections change the world into the replica of one's own unknown face."[2] The projections need to be withdrawn: we need to "own" our shadow, so that its destructive impact can be neutralized within our own psyche. This is undoubtedly one of the most difficult and elusive problems we may encounter in our self-examination, or in psychotherapy.

The principal reason for working on integrating the shadow aspect in ourselves is that we cannot recognize it for what it is when it is bound up in projections. This was Jung's analysis of the phenomenon of Hitler and the Germans: Because the German people denied the existence of the shadow aspect within themselves, they did not recognize the incarnation of the collective shadow represented by Hitler (C. G. Jung, 1970). Many thousands of Germans, including Jews, simply refused to believe what they heard about concentration camps. And yet clearly, for a person to be susceptible to being influenced by the collective shadow, as the Germans were influenced by Hitler, there has to be some correspondence in the individual's psychic constitution. We must have within us some of that same tendency. It is this personal correspondence that makes us vulnerable to infection by the collective shadow as expressed by psychopathic demagogues or propagandists. We need to make ourselves immune to the propaganda of evil.

More current examples of this phenomenon can be found in the political rhetoric of East and West. Some American politicians and journalists foster the image of the Russians as the "enemy" (the word "evil" has even been used about them), which means that we deny the same behavior and attitudes in ourselves; and Russians, of course, similarly see in us only capitalist warmongers. The dangerous consequences of such delusional projections to the peace and stability of the entire world are painfully obvious.[3]

It may seem unbelievable, but it is a fact that opposites, such as black and white, metaphorically represent the individual and his or her inner opponent; they may occur as symbols in dreams and altered state experiences and can create conflict. For example, to a member of the white race, black may symbolize *bad* or *evil*. It must be remembered that we are dealing with the symbolic language of the psyche, in which any form or pattern can be used to stand for any other form or pattern.

The most immediate conclusion of practical value for self-transformation that one could draw from this metaphor is that each of us needs to discover how we symbolize to ourselves the aspect of our personality referred to as the shadow. In some of us it might be a black or dark person; in others it might be a white person; in yet others, a beast. Their effect on us is what defines these images: They frighten, threaten, attack, violate, and oppose us in every way. Those images we find ourselves avoiding or trying to suppress are precisely the ones we must bring into the light of awareness.

ACCEPTING THE UNACCEPTABLE

While it is probably true for most people that the "shadow" is a kind of aggregate of destructive, violent, and aggressive impulses, this need not always be the cast. For example, a professional killer or psychopathic sadist who consciously and intentionally indulges in destructive or murderous actions, is not expressing the shadow side. Such an individual has no difficulty accepting and expressing feelings of murderous hatred, and this behavior is not the opposite of any conscious purpose or conscience in their psyche.

For such people, values are reversed, and they cannot recognize or express feelings of tenderness, compassion or kindness. What is in the shadow, in the darkness of unconsciousness, are the good feelings and impulses. For transformation to take place in these people, there must be an integration of these good feelings.

We all clearly differ in which of our traits and qualities we regard as unacceptable. For some it may be sexuality, for others aggressiveness, for yet others, laziness or inertia. One person's shadow may be quite innocuous and acceptable to another. What makes some part of our nature *shadow* is not its destructiveness per se; it is the fact that we are unconscious of this aspect. That which is consciously unacceptable to us, yet lives somehow in the unconscious layers of the psyche, is what causes problems.

Thus, in some ways, the notion of something unacceptable, and therefore hidden, is perhaps more appropriate than the symbol of the shadow (something dark). One may have a feeling of rejection or exclusion toward some part of the psyche—some thought, feeling, or impulse. This part is excluded from awareness, and from the conscious sense of self, or identity. This alien element is rejected, split off, separated from awareness, not acknowledged. In the process of individuation it must be acknowledged and assimilated. For wholeness, we need to accept the unacceptable—a paradoxical challenge indeed!

It is quite likely that this process of splitting off or rejecting may have an influence in the formation of diseases such as cancer. It has been suggested, on the basis of evidence such as the fantasy processes of cancer patients, that in some cases the disease represents a kind of congealing of a split-off negative emotional charge such as anger, grief, fear, or some other feeling that is found incompatible with the dominant self-image.[4]

The work of R. D. Laing on what he calls "the divided self" has clearly described the process of splitting off parts of oneself, or one's self-image, in psychosis. Such splitting may take the form of a *false self* versus a *true self*, or a *good self* versus a *bad self*. Laing cites examples of psychotic patients who experience themselves as machines or robots, or objects, or animals, or monsters—something nonhuman or antihuman (Laing, 1969).

I would like to suggest the term *schizon* as an alternative for shadow in instances where we are dealing with an experience of

rejecting or excluding an aspect of our nature. The splitting-off of
the schizon can be seen as a defensive reaction, similar in intent to
projection of the shadow onto another person. We separate that part
of ourselves because we find it unacceptable to the ego, to our
conscious self-image. That part of our identity is sent into internal
exile. The schizon, like the shadow, is perceived as a threat to the
ego; it is feared, avoided, hated, or denied and ignored.[5]

Beside projecting our unacceptable side onto others, another common way of dealing with it is to hide it in the unconscious recesses
of the psyche, isolating it from awareness. Freud, who discovered
this mechanism, called it repression—in German, *Verdrängung*, literally "a pushing away." In the Basque culture, the word for this
unacknowledged part of our nature that causes us to behave in
violent and destructive ways is *oshua*, which means "the hidden"
(A. Arrien, personal communication). The well-known myth of King
Minos, who had an elaborate labyrinth built in order to hide the
monstrous, devouring Minotaur, gives expression to this theme. The
folktale of Bluebeard, who murdered his spouses and kept their
skeletons hidden in a closet, to which he forbade entry, is another
metaphor for this process; this is the prototype of the well-known
"skeleton-in-the-closet" motif.

We want to hide this unacceptable part, this schizon, from ourselves, but we are rarely able to hide it completely from others,
because others do not necessarily have the same difficulty in seeing
this aspect of our character. For example, if I have a self-image that
does not allow me to express rage, then I will defensively hide every
urge to express it openly. I will be unconscious of the feeling of
rage, and of my (nonverbal) expression of it. Other people, however,
are not likely to be invested in my image of myself as being without
rage, and they will perceive my feelings.

This situation is symbolized in the Old Testament story of Cain
and Abel. After the murder of Abel, Cain complains that he now
has to hide from the world. But he also wears the mark of the
murderer. Hiding draws attention to itself. The Jewish *midrashim* tells
us that after the murder of Abel, the eye of God, or in some versions,
the voice of God, followed Cain all over the world. This is the eye,
or voice of conscience, from which we cannot hide because it is the
eye of the Self within. From the point of view of the little self, the

ego-personality, this is the guilty conscience, the vengeful or punitive super-ego.

The eye of God (of Self) sees everything that we are and do. But in relationship to others we want to hide the schizon, the antihuman behavior, because we cannot face it and we do not want others to see it. Traditionally, in religious mythology, the *face* of evil is unimaginable and is not to be perceived. This may well underlie the use of masks or disguises by practitioners of evil, such as Inquisitors, torturers, or the KKK. The "Star Wars" film epics, with mythic insight, show Darth Vader, the personification of evil, wearing a metallic, inhuman mask. The mask turns the perpetrators of evil into faceless nonpersons. They are not recognized, hidden in the shadows of darkness and concealment, just as our own unacceptable side is hidden in the unconsciousness of the *shadow*, or the psychic exile of the *schizon*.

For the process of transformation, the symbolism of both *shadow* and *mask* underscores the importance of awareness and recognition. That which is hidden in the shadow or behind the mask, in the depths of our own psyche, must be seen and identified. I cannot integrate some aspect of myself unless and until I can recognize it for what it is. By recognizing and identifying evil, we neutralize its power, which is based on concealment and masking. This is as true of collective manifestations of evil as it is of the individual's intrapsychic process. If there had been more Germans able and willing to call attention to the genocidal death camps of the Nazis, that particular holocaust might not have gone as far as it did. The one thing that can stop state-endorsed torture and murder is to expose it to the eyes of the world: to document and call attention to it, as the work of the Amnesty International organization has demonstrated.

As a way of making this theme more concrete and personal, I offer the following exercise in self-awareness: Ask yourself what about yourself you most want to hide. What thought or impulse do you have that you least want anyone else to know about? Try accepting the possibility that you might do that, or be like that. To face the shadow, or the hidden evil side of our psyche, requires courage and inspires humility. It requires courage because the dark face is terrifying and destructive. It inspires humility because our self-image and self-esteem are definitely diminished by such a confrontation.

FROM DENIAL TO AFFIRMATION

The question naturally arises as to why it is apparently so difficult for human beings to transform their negative complex, when all that is needed is to recognize it, identify it, and understand it. The reason for the difficulty is what Western psychology call unconsciousness, and Indian traditions call *avidya*, ignorance, not-knowing. These threatening elements of the psyche remain unconscious and unknown precisely because we deny that we have them. This points up the important role of denial and negation in the splitting off of these factors, and their repression into unconsciousness.

It was Sigmund Freud who first pointed out that repression, the pushing of something into the unconscious, involves a process that is an exact analogy to the linguistic function of negation.[6] Denial and repression say "no" to the impuse, or thought, or wish that is being repressed or defended against. In the situation referred to earlier, where we see someone behaving in a way that we consciously regard as bad or evil, we are likely to think (and perhaps say), "I could never do that." In other words, the thought or impulse is denied. This created a kind of split-off area of consciousness referred to as the unconscious, to maintain that negation and denial. Repression and denial, repeated countless times in the process of growing up and living, create a system of inhibitions and prohibitions, defensive walls, that can end up being a kind of prison of the mind.

We all know the young child, the three- or four-year-old that we once were, and partly still are, who vehemently announces "No, I won't." This is normal resistance and negation, the ego exercising its power to set its own limits. In relation to spiritual development, the function of negation and resistance is metaphorically associated with the devil. In Goethe's *Faust*, Mephistopheles introduces himself as "the spirit who always says 'no' " (*der Geist der stets verneint*). Psychologically, when we attempt, through denial, to impose our own ego-will on the ever-changing life process, we are, in a way, playing the same game as the devil.

This process, experienced mentally as negation, emotionally as rejection and exclusion, and perceptually as a hiding and concealing, is a stoppage, a blocking of life-energy flow. The sum of these blocks and holding patterns that hinder life-energy flow was symbolized by Wilhem Reich as the *armor*—the character armor which is also a muscular armor. According to Reich, the function of this armor is to defend the ego against unacceptable impulses, to block or negate the experience and the expression of these impulses.

The armor functions as a kind of prison from which we try to break out. Reich was impressed by the extent to which the armoring process leads to reactions of rage and violence, as the armored individual unconsciously tries to break through the defensive armoring. In this attempt there is an immense concentration of destructive rage, precisely the kind of behavior that we would traditionally attribute to the devil and regard as opposed to the life force. This is why Reich concluded that the armor was the source of man's diabolical violence. "I seriously believe that in the rigid, chronic armoring of the human animal, we have found the answer to the question of his enormous destructive hatred . . . we have discovered the realm of the devil" (Reich, 1949).

Another perspective on the role of denial and negation in the conflict of good and evil tendencies can be obtained by considering the nature of lying. In European Christian theology and folklore, one of the devil's common modes of operating was to sow seeds of doubt, to question, to suggest that perhaps it was not so. In this way, the devil was the slanderer, undermining people's faith and belief in divine reality. Denying the existence and sovereignty of God and the saving efficacy of the Holy Ghost was regarded as the most serious, unpardonable sin, inspired of course by the devil, the "one who always denies."[7]

We typically experience the conflict between good and evil tendencies in our nature as a kind of struggle between yes and no. A part of us affirms life and another part of us denies it. Freud identified this struggle between yes and no as the struggle between the sexual and agressive impulses of the animal-like id and the rational, human ego. He argued that it was a necessary and inevitable consequence of civilized existence. The experience of doubt is another yes versus no situation: When we are in a state of doubt, we are "of two minds" about something. One part of us believes it, says yes to it; another part denies it, says no.

We can see that denial per se is not necessarily evil or destructive. If the impulse is *bad* or destructive, then denying it and inhibiting it may well be the path of the *good*. In the most basic terms, the word *no* sets a limit, it defines a situation. Any form or pattern has

a limit or boundary. That boundary says no to a further expansion
of the process within that form. So the no is necessary to set a limit
to the yes. In the struggle between them we experience the chronic
split in our nature. And we also generate the energy for the process
of transformation.[8]

I recommend the following exercise in awareness: Observe what
it is you often find yourself denying. What are you saying no to in
yourself? The exercise becomes a transformative one if we then accept
those things as part of our experience. To accept them does not
mean we act out the baser impulses; rather, we accept the fact that
we experience them and that they exist. We can say yes to the
feeling or impulse while saying no, setting limits, to its expression
where not appropriate. Thus both sides are acknowledged.

PURIFICATION AND ELIMINATION

A variation on the theme of something in us being dark like a
shadow, or being split off like a schizon, is the common image that
something in our nature is covered with dirt, or polluted, or tainted,
and needs to be purified. People who have a strong puritanical
upbringing are particularly susceptible to this metaphor. In dreams,
meditations, or psychedelic experiences, they may find themselves
dealing with issues of defilement, pollution and the corruption of
the flesh.

There are many examples of this particular metaphor in the New
Testament. Insane or obsessed individuals were said to be inhabited
by "unclean spirits." Jesus drove unclean spirits out of a man and
into a herd of pigs. Our sins are compared to stains on the radiant,
pure soul. The soul must be "washed in the blood of the lamb," to
remove the stain of original sin. This metaphor for evil or sin is
linked to ancient purification taboos and practices.

There are basically two possible postures that we adopt in relationship to something that we find in ourselves or in others that we
regard as polluted or impure: either we want to purify and cleanse
it, or we want to excrete and eliminate it. I propose that the biological
excretion of fecal waste may be the organic and experiential basis
for the judgment of *bad* in the child. What is excreted is bad for the
body, and young children, through instinct or learning, come to
regard excrement as bad, worthless, to be eliminated. This may also

explain why children and adults, in moments of anger, refer to bad things or events as "shit."

In some individuals, and in some cultures, the judgment that something is bad and therefore to be eliminated becomes a judgment that it is evil and therefore to be feared and condemned. There exists a fairly widespread association of the functions and organs of excretion with evil and the devil that has never been satisfactorily explained.[9] The great reformer Martin Luther, for example, habitually referred to the devil as something black and filthy, and he uses homely German anal terminology (*bescheissen*, etc.) to describe his recommended attitude toward the devil.

In some Christian paintings of Hell or the Last Judgment, the devil, chief of the demons, is shown excreting sinners through his anus. In some branches of Hindu mythology, the origin of evil is explained as emanating from certain parts of the body of the creator, Brahma, whether it be the penis, or most often, the anus. In one mythic cycle, human beings are seen as having been created as the excretions of Brahma. Some children believe that babies come from defecation.

According to his metaphor, then, something that is evil or bad is a blemish, pollution, or feces. It should be eliminated before it corrupts the organism or psyche in which it is found. This is essentially the peculiar rationale that underlay the Nazis' bizarre theories of racial purity. This grotesque and genocidal perversion should not cause us to overlook the valid principle that waste matter or toxins in any organism or system, if retained, become pathological and must therefore be eliminated for the preservation of health and normal functioning of that system.

The alternative to elimination of something putrid and rotten is purification. Purification and elimination can be regarded as two principal means for dealing with corrupt elements in the psyche. As such, they are aspects of the general process of integrating the shadow and reconciling the opposites.

FROM INNER WARFARE TO INNER PEACE

In some of our experience, the duality of good and evil is felt as a defensive stand-off, a separation, a gulf, a rejection. We are unconscious of the shadow aspects, blind to our faults, we want to separate from that in us which we feel is rotten. In other phases of our experience, there is a more active struggle or conflict going on. We may love and hate simultaneously, or feel both attraction and aversion toward the same object or person. We may be in turmoil as our fears and inhibitions struggle with impulses of lust or aggression. In meditative states, or dreams, or psychedelic visions, we may witness what seems like a clash of opposing tendencies in our psyche, like armies battling in the night.

The task of personal transformation is to turn this inner warfare to inner peace. We need to come to terms with "enemies," both inner and outer. The clashing opposites must be reconciled. Forces, tendencies, and impulses that are locked in seemingly endless conflict must learn to coexist. I used to believe one had to make friends with the inner enemy, the shadow self. I now feel that making friends is perhaps not necessary, that this "other side" of our nature may always stay in opposition to our true nature. We may want to keep this figure, to function as what Castaneda's Don Juan calls a "worthy opponent," for warrior training. But we need to understand this enemy. Making friends with the inner enemy may be possible. Getting to know him or her is essential.

All spiritual tradition agree that the seeds of warfare, the violent, destructive forces are within us, as are the peaceful, harmonizing forces. A Hindu teacher, Swami Sivananda, writes, "the inward battle against the mind, the sense, the subconscious tendencies (*vasanas*), and the residues of prior experiences (*samskaras*), is more terrible than any outward battle" (Perry, 1971, p. 397). A text by one of the fathers of the Eastern Church, from the Philokalia, states, "there is a warfare where evil spirits secretly battle with the soul by means of thoughts. Since the soul is invisible, these malicious powers attack and fight it invisibly" (Perry, 1971, p. 410). The good Christian, in order to be saved, is exhorted to battle temptations, to ward off demonic invaders and harmful external influences. A poem by the Persian Sufi Rumi states: "We have slain the outward enemy, but there remains within us a worse enemy than he. This *nafs* (animal self, or lower self) is hell, and hell is a dragon. . . ." (Perry, 1971, p. 397). I cite this imagery because it illustrates how widespread, across many religious traditions, is this symbolism of inner warfare.

As a psychologist, I have been investigating the many metaphors used to describe the transformation process in order to determine their origin.[10] I pose the question: How does the feeling of being in a state of inner conflict arise in us in the first place? And I suggest partial answers to this question from three different perspectives: the personal/developmental, the evolutionary/historical, and the theological/mythical.

The *personal/developmental basis* for the experience of conflict may very well be (in part) the phenomenon of sibling rivalry in early childhood. Competition between brothers and sisters for the attention and approval of the parents and other adults is extremely common. This competitive attitude may be maintained into adulthood and carried over into personal and work relationships with peers. Alternatively, it may be internalized, so that one feels that there is an inferior and superior self-image competing and struggling with each other. The founder of gestalt therapy, Fritz Perls, called this the conflict between top dog and underdog.

There are numerous myths about bitter and protracted competition between rival brothers, such as Cain and Abel, or Osiris and Seth, and stories about hostile sisters, such as Cinderella, or the daughters of King Lear, that illustrate this theme of sibling competition. From the perspective of the psychology of transformation, we interpret such stories as referring to an internal process. Both the good sibling and the wicked sibling are aspects of our own nature. In the words of the English Boehme disciple William Law, "You are under the power of no other enemy, are held in no other captivity, and want no other deliverance but from the power of your own earthly self. This is the murderer of the divine life within you. It is your own Cain that murders your own Abel."[11]

In addition to its childhood origin in sibling rivalry, this theme of inner conflict also has probable *evolutionary* and *historical* antecedents—the age-old, long-continuing struggles between tribes and societies for territory and economic survival. The cutthroat competition of the haves and the have-nots is a deeply ingrained factor in the consciousness of the human race. Whether humanity, as a species, can transform this territorial and economic competition into peaceful and cooperative coexistence is perhaps our most difficult challenge.

Going even further back into mammalian evolution, one could speculate about the possible residue in human genetic memory of the millions of years of competitive interaction between predators and prey. The ecologist Paul Shepard has argued that the predator carnivores developed a different sort of consciousness, a different kind of attention from the prey herbivores, related to their different lives of hunting or escaping (Shepard, 1978). Predator intelligence is searching, aggressive, tuned to stalking and hunting. Prey intelligence is cautious, expectant, tranquil, but ready for instant flight. I suggest that these different styles of awareness, these opposing modes of relating, form a kind of substrate to the human experience of aggressors (predators) and victims (prey). Do we not still hunt, prey on and victimize our fellow humans for survival? Do we not still, in the paranoid mode, vigilantly watch for threats, prepared to flee or defend?

In the human imagination, the encounter with the shadow is often experienced as a confrontation with a dangerous beast. When the ideal-ego feels attacked by a monster who emerges out of the unconscious, it feels like a victim. Transformation involves realizing that this ideal-ego is also the beast, the aggressor, the predator. We are both the hunter and the hunted. When we realize this, then the two can make peace—first within, and then in external relationships. In the final days, when planetary transformation is completed, according to ancient prophecies, "the lion and the lamb shall lie down together"; erstwhile victims and aggressors will coexist peacefully.

The third perspective on the origin of the inner conflict is *theological/mythical*. Many ancient mythologies offer a cosmic story of the world inherently split by discord and strife. Heraclitus said: "War (of opposites) is the father and king of all." In the Zoroastrian religion of ancient Persia, competition between the forces of light and darkness was given a most dramatic expression: Here we find the myth of the long-drawn struggle, and alternating rulership of the world between Ahura-Mazda, the Light Creator, and Ahriman, the Prince of Darkness. This Zorastrian conception of a fundamental cosmic dualism undoubtedly had a profound influence on both the Jewish and the Christian religions. The Manichaeans and Gnostics were particularly affected by this myth, with their strong emphasis on the fundamental duality of the Creator and the parallel duality of the created cosmos.[12]

In this complex of conflict and warfare, made up of personal, evolutionary, and mythological elements, we find the story of man's inhumanity to man—destructiveness, violence, cruelty, sadism, intentional injury, and violation of another's physical or psychological integrity. Recalling the earlier discussion of judgment, I offer the following perspective on these manifestations of human evil: They represent a combination of judgmentalism with violent rage. The judgment is expressed and acted upon in a destructive and aggressive way. Those who are judged *bad*, or *evil*, or *opposite*, are attacked and destroyed.

To put it another way, the judgment that is rendered serves as a rationalization for the naked expression of rage. The rationalization may be literary or aesthetic, as with the Marquis de Sade; or it may be spuriously racial or genetic, as with Hitler's genocidal holocaust; or it may be religious, as with the torturers of the Inquisition—the pattern is everywhere the same. The conflict of the judge-persecutor with the judged victim is perhaps the most vicious of all the warring opposites we know. This variant is also played out within the psyche: We are ourselves the punitive judge (in Freudian terms, the super-ego) *and* the punished victim of persecution (psychologically, the guilt-ridden ego).

For transformation to take place, we need to learn to become wise, impartial judges of ourselves, not punitive, vindictive judges. And again, we must start by realizing that the opposing enemies, the clashing and competing forces, are all within—both the judge and the accused, the jailor and the prisoner, the executioner and the condemned.

On Facing One's Demons

In traditional and contemporary folk religions, demons are the relatives of the devil—they are personifications of evil forces, of alien and destructive influences and impulses. They are definitely regarded as something outside of us, something not-self. In primitive or native cultures, living in a state of "participation mystique" with Nature, demons, like giants, often represent the destructive, violent energies of hurricanes, storms, lightning, wildfires, avalanches, floods, earthquakes, or volcanic eruptions. By inventing or imagining living beings, whether spirits or demons, who guide these forces, their terrifying character is somehow made more tolerable.

Conversely, our own inner states may at times feel to us to be out of control, like the forces of Nature. We then find it natural to describe these inner states as analogous to these forceful aspects of Nature. We speak of someone as a "tempestuous character," or of being in a "stormy mood," or "flooded with grief," or having a "volcanic explosion" of temper. Our inner life, like Nature around us, seems at times to be dominated by violent, clashing energies that seem alien and overwhelmingly powerful to us. This is one aspect of the experience of the demonic.

In the East, both Hindu and Buddhist mythology offers a somewhat different perspective on demons, or *asuras*, also known as "angry gods," or "titans." In many myths, the *asuras* are seen as playing a kind of counterpart role to the good gods, or *devas*. They are the opponents of the gods, analogous to a kind of cosmic Mafia, with values opposite to those of normal humans and gods. In the Buddhist *Wheel of Life*, which symbolically portrays six different types of lives one can be born into, the world of *asuras* is one of the six worlds, one possibility for existence. Buddhists say these demons are dominated by feelings of pride, jealousy, and anger, and are engaged in perpetual competitive struggle and conflict.

From a psychological point of view, we are in this world of demons when we are dominated by feelings of pride, jealousy, anger, and competitive struggle. The mythic picture of the *asuras* is shown to us as a kind of reminder of how our feelings, our thoughts, and our intentions create the kind of reality in which we live. The chaotic, murderous existence of the demons and of humans dominated by demons, is an external consequence of an inner state.[13]

In Western culture, the concept of demon has an interesting history. For the Greeks and Romans, the "daimon" (Latin "genius") was not evil at all but was a protective spirit, a divine guardian, something like what later European folklore called the "guardian angel." Socrates was wont to say that he would converse with his *daimon* in order to obtain guidance. It is only under the later influence of Christianity that the word demon came to connote something malevolent or destructive. As is well known, Christianity tended to turn old pagan gods such as Pan and Dionysus into devils or demons.[14]

Generally speaking, there appears to be a much greater tendency in the Western, Judaic-Christian tradition to polarize good and evil as absolute opposites. Only the three monotheistic religions have a concept of an evil deity—the devil or Satan, who opposes God and the spiritual aspirations of human beings. In the Asian traditions and in the Egyptian and Greek polytheistic religions, we more often find a pluralistic view that accepts a multitude of different perspectives and states of being of various origins and values. And although there may be numerous harmful spirits, demons, and enemies, there is not one personification of all evil. There are gods of death—Hades, Pluto, Yama, Mara—but these are not like the devil or Satan.

The figure of Satan, at least in Western culture, has all the traits and qualities that are part of our shadow or unacceptable side. He is the liar, the slanderer, the destroyer, the deceiver, the tempter, the one who brings guilt and shame, the adversary, the unclean and dark one, who denies and negates everything that enlarges and enhances life, who opposes everything that we value and hold most sacred.[15]

In Jungian terms, the devil represents or embodies the collective shadow of the entire Western Judaic-Christian civilization. He is an amalgamated projection of the shadow image of all the thousands and millions of individuals who have believed in him through the centuries. As with other projections, by attributing dark impulses and feelings to the devil, someone not-self, one is relieved of any responsibility for them—as expressed in that most classic of all excuses, "the devil made me do it." Satan exists in the same sense that the ancient gods and goddesses exist and live in the psyches of individuals who express their qualities and characteristics, whether consciously or unconsciously. The legion of forms and names that the devil can take, the many variations on this theme of clashing opposites, are a tribute to the creative imagination of human beings.

This is the multifarious figure whose features can be detected somewhere behind the persona-mask of every man and woman. It is the beast that haunts every beauty, the monster that awaits every hero on his quest. But if we recognize, acknowledge, and come to terms with it, a great deal of knowledge formerly hidden, unconscious, in the shadows, becomes conscious. When we recognize this devil as an aspect of ourselves, then the shadow functions as a teacher and initiator, showing us our unknown face, providing us with the greatest gift of all—self-understanding. The conflict of opposites is resolved into a creative play of energies and limitations.

NOTES

1. Modern psychobiological research suggests that this kind of primitive emotional value judgment may be mediated by the mid-brain, or limbic

system, also known as the "mammalian brain," which controls emotional reactions of "fight or flight" in animals and humans. See Carl Sagan's *The Dragons of Eden* (New York: Ballantine Books, 1977) and Melvin Konner's *The Tangled Wing* (New York: Holt, Rinehart & Winston, 1982), for a discussion of the emotions and the limbic system in the brain.

2. C. G. Jung, "The Shadow," in *Aion* (Collected Works, Vol. 9, II, Bollingen Series XX. Princeton University Press, 1968), p. 9. Other significant discussions of the nature of evil, from a Jungian perspective, may be found in Edward Edinger's *Ego and Archetype* (New York: Penguin Books, 1972); and in *Archetypes*, by Anthony Stevens (New York: Quill, 1983). Two other books that have influenced my thinking on this subject are Ernest Becker, *Escape from Evil* (New York: Free Press, 1976), and David Bakan, *The Duality of Human Existence* (Chicago: Rand McNally, 1966).

3. There are some hopeful signs that the divisiveness of this kind of delusional projection and paranoia is beginning to be understood and discussed. In early 1983, a conference was held in San Francisco, called "Faces of the Enemy," on the perceptions by Russians and Americans of each other. See *The Tarrytown Letter* (Tarrytown, NY, 10591), No. 38, April 1984; and *Evolutionary Blues* (Box 40187, San Francisco, CA 94140), especially the interview with Robert Fuller.

4. See a most interesting paper by Philip Lansky, M.D., "Possibility of Hypnosis as an Aid to Cancer Therapy," in *Perspectives in Biology and Medicine*, Vol. 23 (3), Spring, 1982. If this view is correct, it would help explain the otherwise mysterious processes of "remission" that sometimes occur, as well as the sometimes healing effects of imagery processes in cancer, pioneered by Dr. Carl O. Simonton. Different individuals would have different capacities to accept the unacceptable parts of their nature, and this would affect healing and recovery.

5. What I am calling "schizon" here, to draw attention to the split-off character of this psychic fragment, is called by Jung, and Freud, a "complex." Jung writes, "We can take it as moderately certain that complexes are in fact 'splinter psyches.' " (C. G. Jung, "A Review of the Complex Theory," in *The Structure and Dynamics of the Psyche (Collected Works, Vol. 8*, Bollingen Series XX, Princeton University Press, 1969), pp. 96-98.

6. In his paper "Negation," first published in 1925, Freud wrote that "a repressed image or thought can make its way into consciousness on condition that it is *denied.*" S. Freud. *General Psychological Theory*, New York: Liveright Publishing Co., 1935., pp. 213-214.

7. The English word "devil" comes from the Latin *diabolus*, which in turn is derived from the Greek *diaballein*, to slander or lie, literally "to throw (*ballein*) across (*dia-*)." In English folk-speech we have the interesting phrase "to put something over" on someone, meaning to lie or trick them—which still reflects this etymological origin.

8. The Russian teacher G. I. Gurdjieff made a strong case for the notion that the conflict of opposites within human consciousness, the struggle between "yes" and "no," generates a kind of friction, and this friction

provides an energy necessary for "work on oneself." (P. D. Ouspensky, *In Search of the Miraculous.* New York: Harcourt, Brace & Jovanovich, 1965), pp. 32-33.

9. Norman O. Brown devoted a major portion of his study of psychoanalysis and history—*Life Against Death* (Middletown, CT: Wesleyan University Press, 1959)—to an exploration of the meanings and implications of anality. W. D. O'Flaherty, in *The Origins of Evil in Hindu Mythology* (Berkeley: University of California Press, 1977), discusses Indian myths that see humans as emitted from the anus of Brahma, the Creator. Stanislav Grof, in his *Realms of the Human Unconscious* (New York: E. P. Dutton, 1976), has described excremental visions in LSD therapy that derive from memories of the birth experience. In his paper "Perinatal Origins of Wars, Totalitarianism, and Revolutions: (*Journal of Psychohistory*, Vol 4., No. 3, Winter, 1977), Grof applies his LSD findings to the phenomena of the concentration camps. The folklorist Alan Dundes, in his book *Life is Like a Chicken Coop Ladder*, has examined and presented German folklore and literature for evidence of anality as a trait of the German national character, with significant implications for an understanding of the Nazi holocaust.

10. Ralph Metzner, *Opening to Inner Light—The Transformation of Human Nature and Consciousness* (J. P. Tarcher, 1986). My analysis of transformation metaphors has benefited greatly from the philosophical work of George Lakoff and Mark Johnson, *Metaphors We Live By* (University of Chicago Press, 1980), who have made a strong case for the ubiquity of implicit metaphors in everyday speech and thought.

11. Quoted in A. K. Coomaraswamy, "Who is Satan and Where is Hell?" in *Selected Papers, Vol. 2.*, ed. Roger Lipsey, Bollingen Series LXXXIX, Princeton University Press, 1977.

12. See Mircea Eliade, *History of Religious Ideas, Vol. I*, (University of Chicago Press, 1978), pp. 302-333, for Zoroastrianism, and *Vol. II*, pp. 387-395, for Manichaeism.

13. The Buddhist *Wheel of Life*, which plays a particularly important role in the Tibetan Buddhist tradition, shows a circle divided into six sections, or "worlds." (Francesca Freemantle & Chögyam Trungpa, trans., *The Tibetan Book of the Dead.* Boulder, CO: Shambhala, 1975). These worlds may be regarded as symbolizing (1) different incarnations or lifetimes of human beings, or (2) different personality types, or (3) different states of consciousness that anyone could find themselves in.

14. A. K. Coomaraswamy, in *Selected Papers, Vol. 2* (See note 11), writes "*Agathos* and *Kakos daimons*, fair and foul selves, Christ and Anti-Christ, both inhabit us, and their opposition is within us. Heaven and Hell are the divided images of Love and Wrath *in divinis*, one in God, and it remains for every man to put them together again within himself." An excellent discussion of the concept of *daimon* in classical antiquity, and how this may be understood in terms of depth psychology is in M.-L. von Franz's *Projection and Re-collection in Jungian Psychology: Reflections of the Soul.* (La Salle, IL., Open Court, 1980).

15. The history and meaning of the figure of the devil has inspired numerous studies, of which I mention the following two books by Jeffrey B. Russel: *The Devil—Perceptions of Evil From Antiquity to Primitive Christianity* (Ithaca: Cornell University Press, 1977); and *Satan—The Early Christian Tradition* (Ithaca: Cornell University Press, 1981). A doctoral dissertation with interesting findings was written by Eliot Isenberg, "The Experience of Evil—A Phenomenological Study." (California Institute of Integral Studies, 1983).

REFERENCES

Jung, C. G. (1970). The fight with the shadow. In *Civilization in transition. Collected works, Vol. 10* (pp. 218-226). Bollingen Series XX. Princeton NJ: Princeton University Press.

Laing, R. D. (1969). *The divided self*. New York: Pantheon Books.

Perry, W. N. (Ed.). (1971). Treasury of traditional wisdom, New York: Simon & Schuster.

Reich, W. (1949). *Ether, god and devil* (p. 120). New York: Farrar, Strauss & Giroux.

Ricoeur, P. (1967). *The symbolism of evil*. New York: Harper & Row.

Shepard, P. (1978). *Thinking animals: Animals and the development of human intelligence* (pp. 11-13). New York: Penguin/Viking Books.

CHAPTER FIVE

Modern Consciousness Research and Human Survival

STANISLAV GROF, M.D., PH.D.

One of the most significant implications of modern consciousness research for psychiatry and psychotherapy has been an entirely new status and image of the human psyche. Mechanistic science has portrayed consciousness as an epiphenomenon and product of highly developed matter—the brain. The traditional model of the human psyche that dominates academic psychiatry is personalistic and biographically oriented. It describes the newborn as a tabula rasa (an erased tablet or clean slate) and puts exclusive emphasis on postnatal biographical influences on the individual.

The observations of the last few decades have drastically changed our understanding of the relationship between consciousness and matter and of the dimensions of the psyche. They show consciousness as an equal partner of matter, or possibly even supraordinated to matter, and creative intelligence as inextricably woven into the fabric of the universe. In the light of these new discoveries, the human psyche appears to be essentially commensurate with all of existence. The modern scientific world-view is thus rapidly converging with that of the great mystical traditions of all ages (Huxley, 1944).

I will describe here this new image of reality and of human nature in the light of more than three decades of research of nonordinary states of consciousness that I have conducted in Prague, Czechoslovakia, and in the United States. Although I will focus primarily on the data from my own research, the conclusions are directly applicable to other fields studying human beings that have accumulated observations incompatible with the mechanistic world-view, such as

Jungian psychology, anthropology, laboratory consciousness studies, and thanatology (Grof, 1983, 1985; Ring, 1980, 1984).

The observations and data to which I will refer came from two major sources—approximately two decades of psychedelic research with LSD and other psychoactive substances and ten years of work with various experiential nondrug techniques. Since the issues related to psychedelic drugs belong to the most controversial topics in the world and are associated with many misconceptions, I must emphasize that this work, both in Europe and in the United States, was government-sponsored and medically supervised research conducted in the Psychiatric Research Institute in Prague, Czechoslovakia, and in the Maryland Psychiatric Research Center in Baltimore, Md., respectively. Its various aspects have been descibed in several other publications (Grof, 1976, 1980; Grof & Grof, 1980).

Participants in the psychedelic research programs covered a very wide range, from normal volunteers, through various categories of psychiatric patients, to individuals dying of cancer. The nonpatient population consisted of clinical psychiatrists and psychologists, scientists, artists, philosophers, theologians, students, and psychiatric nurses. The patients with emotional disorders belonged to various diagnostic categories; they included psychoneurotics, alcoholics, narcotic drug addicts, sexual deviants, persons with psychosomatic disorders, borderline cases, and schizophrenics. In the cancer study that included over 150 patients with advanced forms of malignancy, the objective was not treatment of cancer, but relief from emotional and physical pain and change of the attitude toward death through deep mystical experiences induced by psychedelics (Grof & Grof, 1980).

The data are based on more than 4,000 psychedelic sessions that I have conducted personally, and from records of over 2,000 sessions run by my colleagues in Czechoslovakia and in the United States. The two different approaches that were used in this work are called the psycholytic and the psychedelic therapeutic techniques; they differ in their treatment stategies and in their underlying philosophies (Grof, 1980).

The original motive for the use of LSD and other psychedelic drugs was to explore their potential to intensify, deepen, and accelerate the therapeutic process in Freudian analysis. However, when I started using LSD as a therapeutic tool, it became obvious that not only the practice of psychoanalysis but also its theory had to be drastically revised. Without any programming, and against my will, patients were transcending the biographical domain and exploring areas of the psyche uncharted by psychoanalysis and academic psychiatry. Moreover, major therapeutic changes did not occur in the context of the work on childhood traumas that are so much emphasized in psychoanalysis, but followed powerful transbiographical experiences that mainstream psychiatry sees as symptoms of mental illness and tries to suppress by all means.

Since this research involved a powerful mind-altering drug, it is quite natural to question to what extent it is legitimate to use it as a source of data for a psychological theory. There has been a tendency among professionals to see the LSD state as a "toxic psychosis" and the experiences induced by the drug as a chemical fantasmagoria that has very little to do with how the mind functions under more ordinary circumstances. However, systematic clinical research with LSD and related psychedelics has shown that these drugs can best be understood as unspecific amplifiers of mental processes. They do not create the experiences they induce, but activate the deep unconscious and make its contents available for conscious processing. The observations from psychedelic sessions have, therefore, general validity for the understanding of the human psyche.

I have been able to confirm this during the last decade during which my wife Christina and I developed a nondrug experiential technique that we call holotropic therapy (Grof, 1987). It combines controlled breathing, evocative music, and focused body work. In systematic work with this approach, we have been seeing the entire spectrum of experiences characteristic of psychedelic sessions. When the phenomena described in this article can be triggered by something as physiological as hyperventilation, there can be no doubt that they reflect genuine properties of the psyche.

In the experiential work with and without psychedelics, it soon became obvious that the traditional biographical model used in psychoanalysis was superficial and inadequate to describe the broad spectrum of important experiences that became available through these techniques. It was necessary to create a new model of the psyche that would be much more extensive than the one generally accepted in academic psychiatry. In addition to the biographical-recollective level, the new cartography includes the perinatal realm

of the psyche focusing on the phenomena of birth and death, and
the transpersonal domain.

The experiences of all the above categories—biographical, perinatal,
and transpersonal—are quite readily available to most people. They
can be observed in sessions with psychedelic drugs, various forms
of experiential psychotherapy using breathing, music, dance, and
body work, and quite regularly in dreams. Laboratory mind-altering
techniques such as biofeedback, sleep deprivation, sensory isolation
or sensory overload, and various kinesthetic devices (the "witches'
cradle," or the rotating couch) can also induce many of these phenomena (Grof, 1983).

There exists a wide spectrum of ancient and Oriental spiritual
practices that are specifically designed to facilitate access to the
perinatal and transpersonal domains. For this reason, it is not accidental that the new model of the psyche shows great similarity to
those developed over centuries or even millennia by various great
mystical traditions.

The entire experiential spectrum has also been described by historians, anthropologists, and students of comparative religion in the
context of various shamanistic procedures, aboriginal rites of passage
and healing ceremonies, death-rebirth mysteries, and trance dancing
in ecstatic religions. Recent consciousness research has thus made it
possible for the first time to seriously review ancient and non-Western
knowledge about consciousness and to aim for a genuine synthesis
of age-old wisdom and modern science.

THE RECOLLECTIVE-BIOGRAPHICAL LEVEL OF THE PSYCHE

For the majority of people, the domain of the psyche that is most
readily available in deep experiential therapy is usually the recollective-biographical level and the individual unconscious. Although
the phenomena belonging to this category are of considerable theoretical and practical relevance, it is not necessary to spend much
time on their description. Most of the traditional psychotherapeutic
approaches have already explored this level of the psyche. There
exists abundant professional literature discussing nuances of psycho-
dynamics in the biographical realm.

The experiences belonging to this category are related to significant
biographical events and circumstances of the life of the individual

from birth to the present. On this level of self-exploration, anything from the life of the person involved that is an unresolved conflict, a repressed memory that has not been integrated, or an incomplete psychological gestalt of some kind, can emerge from the unconscious and become the content of the experience.

ENCOUNTER WITH BIRTH AND DEATH: DYNAMICS OF BASIC PERINATAL MATRICES

As the process of experiential self-exploration deepens, the elements of emotional and physical pain can reach extraordinary intensity. They can become so extreme that the person involved feels that he or she has transcended the boundaries of individual suffering and is experiencing the pain of entire groups of unfortunate people, all of humanity, or even all of life. It is not uncommon that people whose inner processes reach this domain report experiential identification with wounded or dying soldiers of all ages, prisoners in dungeons and concentration camps, persecuted Jews or early Christians, mothers and children in childbirth, or even animals who are attacked by predators or tortured and slaughtered. This level of the human unconscious thus clearly represents an intersection between biographical experiences and the spectrum of phenomena of a transpersonal nature.

Experiences on this level of the unconscious are typically accompanied by dramatic physiological manifestations, such as various degrees of suffocation, accelerated pulse rate, palpitations, nausea and vomiting, changes in the color of the complexion, oscillation of body temperature, spontaneous occurrence of skin eruptions and bruises, or tremors, twitches, contortions, twisting movements and other striking motor manifestations. In psychedelic sessions and occasionally in nondrug experiential sessions or in spontaneously occurring states of mind, these phenomena can be so authentic and convincing that the person involved can believe that he or she is actually dying. Even an inexperienced sitter or witness of such episodes can perceive them as serious vital emergencies.

On the biographical level, only persons who actually have had a serious brush with death would be dealing with the issue of survival or impermanence. In contrast, when the inner process transcends biography, the problems related to suffering and death can entirely dominate the picture. Those individuals whose postnatal life history did not involve a serious threat to survival or body integrity can enter this experiential domain directly. In others, the reliving of serious physical traumas, diseases, or operations, functions as an experiential bridge to this realm. This is particularly true for such biographical situations or events that involve interference with breathing. Thus, reliving of childhood pneumonia, diphtheria, whooping cough, or near drowning can deepen into the reliving of the suffocation experienced at birth.

A profound confrontation with death characteristic of these experiential sequences tends to be intimately interwoven with a variety of phenomena that are clearly related to the process of biological birth. While facing agony and dying, individuals simultaneously experience themselves as struggling to be born and/or delivering. In addition, many of the physiological and behavioral concomitants of these experiences can be naturally explained as derivatives of the birth process. It is quite common in this context to identify with a fetus and relive various aspects of one's biological birth with quite specific and verifiable details. The element of death can be represented by simultaneous or alternating identification with sick, aging, or dying individuals. Although the entire spectrum of these experiences cannot be reduced just to reliving biological birth, the birth trauma seems to represent an important core of the experiential process on this level. For this reason, I refer to this domain of the unconscious as perinatal.

The term perinatal is a Greek-Latin composite word in which the prefix peri- means around or near and the root -natalis denotes relation to birth. It is commonly used in medicine to describe processes that immediately precede childbirth, are associated with it, or immediately follow it; medical texts thus talk about perinatal hemorrhage, infection, or brain damage. In contrast to the traditional use of this word in obstetrics, I am applying the term perinatal to experiences. Perinatal experiences occur in typical clusters whose basic characteristics are related through deep experiential logic to anatomical, physiological, and biochemical aspects of those clinical stages of birth with which they are associated.

In spite of its close connection to childbirth, the perinatal process transcends biology and has important psychological, philosophical, and spiritual dimensions. It would be an oversimplification to interpret it in a mechanistic and reductionistic fashion. Certain important characteristics of perinatal experiences clearly suggest that they are much broader phenomena than simply the reliving of biological birth. Experiences related to the death-rebirth process have important transpersonal dimensions and are conducive to profound changes in the individual's philosophical and spiritual belief system, basic hierarchy of values, and general life strategy.

Deep experiential encounter with birth and death is typically associated with an existential crisis of extraordinary proportions during which the individual seriously questions the meaning of his or her life and existence in general. This crisis can be successfully resolved only by connecting with the intrinsic spiritual dimensions of the psyche and deep resources of the collective unconscious. The resulting personality transformation and consciousness evolution can be compared to the changes that have been described in the context of ancient death-rebirth mysteries, initiation to secret societies, and various aboriginal rites of passage. The perinatal level of the unconscious thus represents an important interface between the individual and the collective unconscious or between traditional psychology and mysticism.

The experiences of death and rebirth that reflect the perinatal level of the unconscious are very rich and complex. Sequences related to various stages and facets of biological birth are typically intertwined or associated with a variety of transpersonal experiences of a mythological, mystical, archetypal, historical, sociopolitical, anthropological, or phylogenetic nature. These tend to appear in four characteristic experiential patterns or constellations. There seems to exist a deep connection between these thermatic clusters and the clinical stages of childbirth.

Connecting with the experiences of the fetus in various stages of the biological birth process functions as a selective stencil which provides experiential access to specific domains of the collective unconscious that involve similar states of consciousness. It has proved very useful for the theory and practice of deep experiential work to postulate the existence of four hypothetical dynamic matrices governing the processes related to the perinatal level of the unconscious and to refer to them as Basic Perinatal Matrices (BPM).

FIRST PERINATAL MATRIX (BPM I.): THE AMNIOTIC UNIVERSE

This important experiential matrix is related to the primal union with the maternal organism—to the original state of intrauterine existence during which the mother and child form a symbiotic unity. If no noxious stimuli interfere, the conditions for the child can be close to optimal, involving security and continuous satisfaction of all needs. The basic characteristics of this experience are transcendence of the subject-object dichotomy, strong positive affect (peace, serenity, tranquillity, and oceanic ecstasy), feelings of sacredness, transcendence of space and time, and richness of insights of cosmic relevance.

The specific content of these experiences can be drawn from situations that share with it lack of boundaries and obstructions, such as identification with the ocean and aquatic life forms or with interstellar space. Images of nature at its best (Mother Nature) and archetypal visions of heavens and paradises also belong to this category. It is important to emphasize that only episodes of undisturbed embryonal life are accompanied by experiences of this kind. Disturbances of intrauterine existence are associated with overwhelming fear, paranoia, and images of underwater dangers, pollution, inhospitable nature, and insidious demons from various cultures.

SECOND PERINATAL MATRIX (BPM II.): THE EXPERIENCE OF COSMIC ENGULFMENT AND HELL

This experiential pattern is related to the very onset of delivery and its first clinical stage. Initially, the intrauterine existence of the fetus is disturbed by alarming chemical signals and later by mechanical contractions of the uterus. The fetus is periodically constricted by uterine spasms, while the cervix is still closed and does not allow passage.

Reliving of the very onset of biological birth is experienced as imminent vital danger and threat of enormous proportions—cosmic engulfment. Overwhelming feelings of free-floating anxiety lead to paranoid ideation and perception. Intensification of this state typically results in the experience of a terrifying vortex or whirlpool sucking the subject and his or her world relentlessly to its center. Frequent experiential variations of this theme are those of being swallowed by an archetypal beast, entangled by a monstrous octopus or python, or ensnared by a gigantic mother spider. A less dramatic form of the same experience is the theme of descent into the underworld and encounter with demonic creatures.

When reliving the first clinical stage of delivery in a fully developed form, the individual faces a situation that can best be described as no exit or hell. He or she feels stuck, encaged and trapped in a claustrophobic nightmarish world, and completely loses connection with linear time. The situation feels absolutely unbearable, endless and hopeless. It seems, therefore, quite logical that these individuals frequently identify experientially with prisoners in dungeons or concentration camps, victims of the Inquisition, inmates in insane asylums, or with sinners in hell and archetypal figures representing eternal damnation. During the deep existential crisis that typically accompanies this state, existence appears as a meaningless farce or theater of the absurd.

THIRD PERINATAL MATRIX (BPM III.): THE EXPERIENCE OF DEATH-REBIRTH STRUGGLE

Many important aspects of this experiential matrix can be understood from its association with the second clinical stage of childbirth. In this stage, the uterine contractions continue, but the cervix is now dilated and allows a gradual propulsion of the fetus through the birth canal. This involves enormous struggle for survival, crushing mechanical pressures, and often high degrees of anoxia and suffocation. In the terminal phases of the delivery, the fetus can experience intimate contact with biological material such as blood, mucus, urine, and feces.

From the experiential point of view, this pattern is rather rich and ramified. Beside actual realistic reliving of various aspects of the struggle in the birth canal, it involves a wide variety of phenomena that occur in typical thematic sequences, and is related with deep experiential logic to anatomical, physiological, and biochemical aspects of the birth process. The most important of these aspects is a sense of being involved in a fight of titanic proportions, sadomasochistic experiences, intense sexual arousal, demonic episodes, scatological involvement, and encounter with fire—all occuring in the context of a determined death-rebirth struggle.

The specific images involve mythological battles of enormous proportions involving angels and demons or gods and Titans, raging elements of nature, sequences from bloody revolutions and wars, images involving pornography and deviant sexuality, violence, satanic orgies and Sabbath of the Witches, crucifixion and ritual sacrifice.

FOURTH PERINATAL MATRIX (BPM IV.): THE DEATH-REBIRTH EXPERIENCE

This perinatal matrix is meaningfully related to the third clinical stage of delivery—to the actual birth of the child. In this final stage, the agonizing process of the birth struggle comes to an end; the propulsion through the birth canal culminates and the extreme buildup of pain, tension, and sexual arousal is followed by sudden relief and relaxation. After the umbilical cord is cut, the physical separation from the mother is complete and the child begins its new existence as an anatomically independent individual. As in the case of the other matrices, some of the experiences belonging here represent an accurate replay of the actual biological events involved in birth, as well as specific obstetric interventions. The symbolic counterpart of the final stage of delivery is the death-rebirth experience.

Paradoxically, while only one step from a phenomenal liberation, the individual has the feeling of impending catastrophe of enormous proportions. This frequently results in a determined struggle to stop

STAGES OF DELIVERY

0   1   2   3

   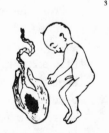

the experience. If allowed to proceed, this experience involves a sense of annihilation on all imaginable levels—physical destruction, emotional debacle, intellectual defeat, ultimate moral failure, and absolute damnation of enormous proportions. This experience of "ego death" seems to entail an instant merciless destruction of all previous reference points in the life of the individual.

The experience of total annihilation and "hitting the cosmic bottom" is immediately followed by visions of blinding white or golden light of supernatural radiance and beauty. It can be associated with astonishing displays of divine archetypal entities, rainbow spectra, or intricate peacock designs. The individual experiences a deep sense of emotional and spiritual liberation, redemption and salvation. He or she typically feels freed from anxiety, depression, and guilt, purged and unburdened. This is associated with a flood of positive emotions toward oneself, other people, and existence in general. The world appears to be a beautiful and safe place and the zest for life is distinctly increased.

The concept of perinatal matrices makes it possible to relate a variety of psychopathological syndromes quite naturally to the anatomical, physiological, and biochemical aspects of the consecutive stages of biological birth. It also reveals new powerful mechanisms of healing and personality transformation that are not available in traditional psychiatry and psychotherapy. These interesting implications of the new model have been discussed in detail in another context (Grof, 1985).

BEYOND THE BRAIN: TRANSPERSONAL DIMENSIONS OF THE PSYCHE

Experiential sequences of death and rebirth typically open the gate to a transbiographical domain in the human psyche that can best be referred to as transpersonal. The perinatal level of the unconscious clearly represents an interface between the biographical and the transpersonal realms, or the individual and the collective unconscious. In most instances, transpersonal experiences are preceded by a dramatic encounter with birth and death. However, there exists also an important alternative; occasionally, it is possible to access experientially various transpersonal elements and themes directly, without confronting the perinatal level. The common denominator of this rich and ramified group of transpersonal phenomena is a feeling that consciousness has expanded beyond the usual ego boundaries and has transcended the limitations of time and space.

In ordinary states of consciousness, we experience ourselves as existing within the boundaries of the physical body (the body image) and our perception of the environment is restricted by the physically and physiologically determined range of our sensory organs. Both our internal perception (interoception) and external perception (exteroception) are confined by the usual spatial and temporal boundaries. Under ordinary circumstances, we can experience vividly and with all our senses only the events in the present moment and in our immediate environment. We can recall the past and anticipate future events or fantasize about them; however, the past and the future are not available for direct experience.

In transpersonal experiences, as they occur in psychedelic sessions, self-exploration through nondrug experiential techniques or spontaneously, one or more of the usual limitations appear to be transcended. Experiences of this kind can be divided into three large categories. Some of them involve transcendence of linear time and are interpreted as historical regression and exploration of the biological, cultural, and spiritual past, or as historical progression into the future. In the second category, experiences are characterized primarily by transcendence of the ordinary spatial boundaries rather than temporal barriers. The third group is characterized by experiential exploration of domains that in Western culture are not considered part of objective reality.

In nonordinary states of consciousness, many people experience very concrete and realistic episodes which they identify as fetal and embryonal memories. It is not unusual under these circumstances to experience (on the level of cellular consciousness) full identification with the sperm and the ovum at the time of conception. Sometimes historical regression goes even further and the individual has a convinced feeling of reliving memories from the lives of his or her ancestors, or even drawing on the memory banks of the racial or collective unconscious. On occasion, individuals report experiences in which they identify with various animal ancestors in the evolutionary pedigree, or have a distinct sense of reliving dramatic episodes from a previous incarnation.

Transpersonal experiences that involve transcendence of spatial barriers suggest that boundaries between the individual and the rest of the universe are not fixed and absolute. Under special circumstances it is possible to identify experientially with anything in the universe, including the entire cosmos itself. Here belong the experiences of merging with another person into a state of dual unity or assuming another person's identity, of tuning into the consciousness of a specific group of people, or of expansion of one's consciousness to such an extent that it seems to encompass all of humanity. In a similar way, one can transcend the limits of the specifically human experience and identify with the consciousness of animals, plants, or even inorganic objects and processes. It is even possible to experience consciousness of the entire biosphere, of our planet, or of the entire material universe.

In a large group of transpersonal experiences, the extension of consciousness seems to go beyond the phenomenal world and the time-space continuum as we perceive it in our everyday life. Here belong numerous visions of archetypal personages and themes, encounters with deities and demons of various cultures, and complex mythological sequences. Additional examples are reports of appearances of spirits of deceased people, suprahuman entities, and inhabitants of other universes. Among the most interesting experiences in this category are visions of abstract archetypal patterns and universal symbols (cross, ankh, yin-yang, swastika, pentacle, or six-pointed star), which are often associated with deep insights into their meaning.

Many people have also described experiences of the energies of the subtle body known from mystical and occult literature—the flow of chi energy through the meridians as they are depicted in ancient Chinese medicine, arousal of the Serpent Power (Kundalini), activation of various centers of psychic energy or chakras, and visions of colorful auras. In its furthest reaches, individual consciousness can identify with cosmic consciousness or with the Universal Mind. The ultimate of all experiences appears to be identification with the Supracosmic and Metacosmic Void, the mysterious primordial emptiness and nothingness that is conscious of itself and contains all existence in a germinal and potential form.

Transpersonal experiences have many strange characteristics that shatter the most fundamental assumptions of materialistic science and of the mechanistic world-view. Researchers who have seriously studied and/or experienced these fascinating phenomena realize that the attempts of traditional psychiatry to dismiss them as irrelevant products of imagination or as erratic fantasmagoria generated by pathological processes in the brain, are superficial and inadequate. Any unbiased study of the transpersonal domain of the psyche has to come to the conclusion that these observations represent a critical challenge for the Newtonian-Cartesian paradigm of Western science.

Although transpersonal experiences occur in the process of deep individual self-exploration, it is not possible to interpret them simply as intrapsychic phenomena in the conventional sense. On the one hand, they form an uninterrupted experiential continuum with bio-graphical-recollective and perinatal experiences. On the other hand, they seem to be tapping directly, without the mediation of the sensory organs, sources of information that are clearly outside of the conventionally defined range of the individual.

The reports of people who have experienced episodes of embryonal existence, the moment of conception, and elements of cellular, tissue, and organ consciousness abound in medically accurate insights into the anatomical, physiological, and biochemical aspects of the processes involved. Similarly, ancestral experiences, racial and collective memories in the Jungian sense, and the past incarnation memories, frequently bring quite specific details about architecture, costumes, weapons, art, social structure, and religious practices of the culture and period involved, or even concrete historical events.

People who experience phylogenetic sequences or identification with existing life forms not only find them unusually convincing and authentic but also acquire extraordinary insights concerning animal psychology, ethology, specific habits, or unusual reproductive cycles. In some instances, these experiences are accompanied by archaic muscular innervations not characteristic of humans, or even by such complex performances as enactment of a courtship dance.

Individuals who experience episodes of conscious identification with plants or parts of plants occasionally report remarkable insights into such botanical processes as germination of seeds, photosynthesis in the leaves, the role of auxins in plant growth, exchange of water and minerals in the root system, or pollination. Equally common is a convinced sense of conscious identification with inanimate matter or inorganic processes—the water in the ocean, fire, lightning, volcanic activity, tornado, gold, diamond, granite, and even stars, galaxies, atoms, and molecules.

There exists another interesting group of transpersonal phenomena that can be frequently validated and even researched experimentally. Here belong telepathy, psychic diagnosis, clairvoyance, clairaudience, precognition, psychometry, out-of-the-body experiences, traveling clairvoyance, and other instances of extrasensory perception. This is the only group of transpersonal phenomena that has been occasionally discussed in the past in academic circles, unfortunately with a strong negative bias.

From a broader perspective, there is no reason to sort out the so-called paranormal phenomena as a special category. Since many other types of transpersonal experiences quite typically involve access to new information about the universe through extrasensory channels, clear boundary between psychology and parapsychology disappears, or becomes rather arbitrary when the existence of the transpersonal domain is recognized and acknowledged.

The philosophical challenge associated with the observations described here—formidable as it may be in itself—is further augmented by the fact that, in nonordinary states of consciousness, transpersonal experiences that correctly reflect the material world appear on the same continuum and are intimately interwoven with others whose content, according to the Western world-view, is not part of objective reality. In this context we can mention the Jungian archetypes—the world of deities, demons, demigods, superheroes, and complex mythological, legendary, and fairytale sequences. These experiences can even impart accurate new information about religious symbolism, folklore, and mythical structures of various cultures about which the person previously had no knowledge.

The ability of transpersonal experiences to convey instant intuitive information about any aspect of the universe in the present, past, and future, violates some of the most basic assumptions of mechanistic science. They imply such seemingly absurd notions as relativity and the arbitrary nature of all physical boundaries, nonlocal connections in the universe, communication through unknown means and channels, memory without a material substrate, nonlinearity of time or consciousness associated with all living organisms (including lower animals, plants, unicellular organisms and viruses), and even inorganic matter.

Many transpersonal experiences involve events from the microcosm and macrocosm—realms that cannot be directly reached by human senses—or from periods that historically precede the origin of the solar system, formation of planet earth, appearance of living organisms, development of the central nervous system, and appearance of *Homo sapiens*. This clearly implies that in a yet unexplained way each human being contains the information about the entire universe or all of existence, has potential experiential access to all its parts, and in a sense is the whole cosmic network, as much as he or she is just an infinitesimal part of it, a separate and insignificant biological entity.

Transpersonal experiences have a very special position in the cartography of the human psyche. The recollective-analytical level and the individual unconscious are clearly biographical in nature. The perinatal dynamic seems to represent an intersection or frontier between the personal and transpersonal. This is reflected in its deep association with birth and death—the beginning and end of individual human existence. Transpersonal phenomena reveal connections between the individual and the cosmos that are at present beyond comprehension. All we can say is that somewhere in the process of confrontation with the perinatal level of the psyche, a strange qualitative Moebius-like shift seems to occur in which deep self-exploration of the individual unconscious turns into a process of experiential adventures in the universe-at-large, which involves what can best be described as cosmic consciousness or the superconscious mind.

As Ken Wilber has demonstrated in his writings (Wilber, 1980, 1983), introducing transpersonal experiences into psychology creates a conceptual bridge between Western science and perennial philosophy. It also throws new light on many problems in history, anthropology, sociology, psychology, psychiatry, philosophy, and comparative religion.

While the nature of transpersonal experience is clearly fundamentally incompatible with mechanistic science, it can be integrated with the revolutionary developments in various scientific disciplines that have been referred to as the emerging paradigm. Among the disciplines and concepts that have significantly contributed to this drastic change in the scientific worldview are quantum-relativistic physics (Capra, 1975, 1982), astrophysics (Davies, 1983), cybernetics, information and systems theory (Bateson, 1972, 1979), Sheldrake's theory of morphic resonance (Sheldrake, 1981), Prigogine's study of dissipative structures and order by fluctuation (Prigogine, 1980) David Bohm's theory of holomovement (Bohm, 1980), Karl Pribram's holographic model of the brain (Pietsch, 1981; Pribram, 1971), and Arthur Young's theory of process (Young, 1976).

The expanded cartography described here is of critical importance for any serious approach to such phenomena as psychedelic states, shamanism, religion, mysticism, rites of passage, mythology, parapsychology, thanatology, and psychosis. This is not just a matter of academic interest; as I have mentioned earlier, it has deep and revolutionary implications for the understanding of psychopathology and offers new therapeutic possibilities undreamt of by traditional psychiatry.

This general description of the new cartography of the human psyche that has emerged from the study of nonordinary states of consciousness leads us to an exploration of its implications for the current global crisis.

PSYCHOLOGICAL ROOTS OF THE CURRENT GLOBAL CRISIS

The observations from modern consciousness research clearly indicate that a psychological approach limited to analysis of biographical factors, such as childhood history, psychosexual traumas, and dynamics of interpersonal relations, is not sufficient for understanding the motivation of human behavior. The biographical events do not represent the primal causes but are conditions for the emergence of deeper forces of a perinatal and transpersonal nature.

The perinatal level of the unconscious and the dynamics of the death-rebirth process represent a repository of difficult emotions and sensations. They function as an important source of various forms of psychopathology and of powerful impulses and motivations of an irrational nature. An individual who is under a strong influence of the negative perinatal matrices approaches life in a way that is not only unfulfilling but also, in the long run, destructive and self-destructive.

People who gain experiential access to the perinatal level of the unconscious typically report that this domain is responsible for what can be called a "rat race" or "treadmill" existence. The perinatal forces tend to introduce into human life an unrelenting drive toward linear pursuit of future goals and insatiable hunger for power, status, fame, and possessions. This is typically associated with an inability to really enjoy the fruits of these pursuits and with general disatisfaction with oneself and one's life. In this context, it is not uncommon that the individual responds to a triumphant accomplishment by depression. This is what Joseph Campbell has described as "getting to the top of the ladder and finding that it was against the wrong wall."

The life experience of a person dominated by perinatal forces is influenced by the memory of the trauma of birth to such an extent that his or her emotions in everyday situations reflect the confinement in the birth canal more than they do the current circumstances. Because of that, the individual never experiences the present moment and the present situation as fully satisfying. Like the fetus who is trying to escape from the clutches of the birth canal into a more comfortable situation, such a person will always expect satisfaction from the achievement of some future goals. Since these goals are, in the last analysis, surrogates for the psychological completion of birth, reaching them never brings the expected satisfaction.

An individual who lives under the spell of the perinatal domain of the unconscious sees existence from the narrow perspective of myself, my family, my religion, my country. From this point of view, other people, groups, and nations are perceived as competitors, the world as a potential threat, and nature as something that has to be conquered and controlled. Although there exist considerable variations in the degree to which this attitude manifests itself in different individuals, this pattern is certainly sufficiently characteristic that most of us recognize it.

On the collective and global scale, this frame of mind generates a philosophy of life that emphasizes strength, competition, and self-assertion, and glorifies linear progress and unlimited growth ("the bigger, the better"). It considers material profit and the increase of the gross national product to be the main criteria of well-being and measures of the living standard. This ideology and the resulting strategies bring humans into a serious conflict with their nature as biological systems and into dissonance with basic universal laws.

Biological organisms depend critically on optimum values: More vitamins, more hormones, more calcium, or more water is not necessarily better than fewer vitamins, fewer hormones, less calcium, and less water. Similarly, higher temperature or blood level of sugar is not better than lower temperature or blood level of sugar. If the largest body size and weight were the goal of evolution, the dinosaurs would still be around and would be the dominant species.

The strategy imposed on the individual by perinatal dynamics is thus unnatural and dangerous. In a universe the nature of which is cyclical, it enforces linearity and the pursuit of unlimited growth. In addition, the resulting approach to existence disregards the ecological imperative and does not recognize the urgent and absolutely vital need for synergy, complementarity, and cooperation.

Moreover, analysis of the experiences and imagery of people who connect with the perinatal level in the context of the death-rebirth process suggests that this domain of the unconscious is an important source of what Erich Fromm called malignant aggression (Fromm, 1973). The emotions and drives originating here find their expression on the individual scale in acts of violence, sadism, criminality, and murder, and on the collective scale in such manifestations of human nature as totalitarian regimes, wars, bloody revolutions, genocide, and concentration camps. The connections between individual, as well as social, psychopathology and the dynamics of perinatal matrices are fascinating and very convincing. I have discussed them at some length in one of my books (Grof, 1985).

However, the observations from modern consciousness research offer more than just fascinating new insights into human problems and a diagnostic contribution to the understanding of the global crisis. They also suggest new possibilities of approaching the dangerous situation in the world in a way that could influence its psychological roots. The clues here come from the study of the changes that occur in those individuals who have successfully confronted and neutralized the perinatal forces and connected experientially with the transpersonal level of the psyche.

Examples can be found in the deep experiential work using psychedelics or techniques developed by humanistic and transpersonal psychology, and by the great spiritual traditions of the world. Identical changes have also been described by Abraham Maslow in his study of individuals who had spontaneous mystical experiences (or "peak experiences") and as a result moved in the direction of what he called "self-actualization" or "self-realization" (Maslow, 1964).

People who move psychologically from the dominance of the negative perinatal matrices (the memory of the survival struggle in the birth canal) to that of positive perinatal matrices (memory of nourishing perinatal and postnatal experiences) and of the transpersonal domains of the psyche tend to be deeply transformed by this experience. The interaction of the fetus with the maternal organism is equivalent to the interaction of the adult with all of humanity, all of nature, and the entire universe. Prenatal and perinatal experiences thus represent a prototype and template for the adult perception and experience of the world. The nature and quality of the perinatal matrix influences will shape a person's attitude to other people, to the world, and to existence in general. Profound transpersonal experiences then move the individual out of the narrow framework of identification with the body-ego and lead to feeling and thinking in terms of cosmic identity and unity with all creation.

An individual who connects experientially with the positive perinatal matrices and with the transpersonal domain feels a great increase of zest and joy in life and develops a capacity to draw satisfaction from many ordinary situations and activities such as simple human interactions, creative work, admiration of nature and art, playing, eating, sleeping, and lovemaking. This is typically associated with deep awareness of the critical importance of the spiritual dimension in the universal scheme of things.

The person involved in such a process usually retains interest in creative activity and enjoys it much more than before. At the same time, there is much less emotional dependence on complicated schemes, fantasies, and future plans as the source of satisfaction. In this state of mind, it becomes obvious that the ultimate measure of the standard of living is the quality of the life experience and not the quantity of material achievements.

At the same time, the level of aggression is drastically reduced and the individual develops tolerance toward others, reverence for life, and appreciation for the adventure of existence. The concept of human life as a life-and-death struggle for survival gives way to a new image of a cosmic dance or divine play. The critical importance of synergy, cooperation, harmony, and ecological concerns is deeply felt and becomes self-evident.

The aggressive and controlling attitude toward nature (Mother Nature) reflected the precarious experience of the fetus with the maternal organism in the process of delivery. The new values and attitudes are based on the experiences of the prenatal or postnatal interaction with the mother ("good womb" and "good breast" if there were no serious interferences during these two periods). They are characterized by a strong emphasis on the mutually nourishing, symbiotic, and complementary nature of all relationships in contrast to the exploitative and competitive nature of the old value system.

It becomes obvious that the universe is a unified web, of which we all are meaningful parts. It is, in principle, impossible to do anything to other people, to other nations, or to nature, without simultaneously doing it to ourselves. Thinking in terms of all of humanity, all of life, and the entire planet clearly has to take priority over interests of individuals, families, religious and social groups, political parties, nations, and races should life on this planet survive. The hopeless "us and them" attitude has to be replaced by a clear realization that we are facing a problem of a collective nature that only a determined cooperative effort can solve.

It seems clear that if large numbers of people in different countries of the world felt, thought, and acted along these lines, our chances of survival would increase. To achieve this, we must complement our efforts in the world of technology that has given us instruments of awesome power by placing an equally strong emphasis on the technology of human transformation. The resulting changes in human consciousness would make it possible for us to use the fruits of modern science constructively and with wisdom.

The broad spectrum of techniques that can increase self-understanding and facilitate consciousness evolution includes a variety of ancient spiritual practices, as well as modern approaches developed by humanistic and transpersonal psychology. Some of them could be integrated into education, others could find their way into mass media, or be communicated in various art forms. However, the ultimate success or failure of this approach will depend on the determined and focused effort of each of us and the willingness to add to our external activities in the world a systematic effort at self-exploration and inner transformation.

Whatever questions or doubts one may have about the feasibility of this strategy as a world-changing force, it could well be our only real chance under the present circumstances. It is difficult to imagine that the crisis in the world can be solved with the same attitudes and strategies that were instrumental in its development in the first place. And since, in the last analysis, the current global crisis is the product and reflection of the stage of consciousness evolution of humanity, a radical and lasting solution is inconceivable without inner transformation and a move toward global awareness.

Presented at the Ninth Conference of the International Transpersonal Association (ITA) entitled *Tradition and Technology in Transition*, April 1985, Kyoto, Japan.

REFERENCES

Bateson, G. (1972). *Steps to an ecology of mind*. New York: Ballantine Books.

Bateson, G. (1979). *Mind and nature*. New York: E. P. Dutton.

Bohm D. (1980). *Wholeness and the implicate order*. London: Routledge & Kegan Paul.

Capra, F. (1975). *The tao of physics*. Berkeley: Shambhala.

Capra, F. (1982). *The turning point*. New York: Simon & Schuster.

Davies, P. (1983). *God and the new physics*. New York: Simon & Schuster.

Fromm, E. (1973). *The anatomy of human destructiveness*. New York: Holt, Rhinehart & Winston.

Grof, S. (1976). *Realms of the human unconscious*. New York: E. P. Dutton.

Grof, S. (1980). *LSD psychotherapy*. Pomona, CA: Hunter House.

Grof, S. (Ed). (1983). *Ancient wisdom and modern science*. Albany, NY: SUNY Press.

Grof, S. (1985). *Beyond the brain: Birth, death, and transcendence in psychotherapy*. Albany, NY: SUNY Press.

Grof, S. (1987). *The adventure of self-discovery*. Albany, NY: SUNY Press.

Grof, S., & Grof, C. (1980). *Beyond death*. London: Thames & Hudson.

Huxley, A. (1944). *Perennial philosophy*. New York: Harper & Row.

Maslow, A. (1964). *Religions, values, and peak-experiences*. Columbus, OH: Ohio State University Press.

Ring. K. (1980). *Life at death: A scientific investigation of the near-death experience*. New York: Coward, McCann & Geoghegan.

Ring, K. (1984). *Heading toward omega: In search of the meaning of the near-death experience*. New York: William Morrow.

Pietsch, H. (1981). *Shufflebrain*. Boston: Houghton Mifflin.

Pribram, K. (1971). *Languages of the brain*. Englewood Cliffs, NJ: Prentice-Hall.

Prigogine, I. (1980). *From being to becoming: Time and complexity in the physical sciences*. San Francisco: W. H. Freeman.

Sheldrake, R. (1981). *A new science of life*. Los Angeles: J. P. Tarcher.

Wilber, K. (1980). *The atman project*. Wheaton, IL: Theosophical Publishing House.
Wilber, K. (1983). *Eye to eye*. Garden City, NY: Anchor Press, Doubleday.
Young, A. (1976). *The reflexive universe: Evolution of consciousness*. New York: Delacorte Press.

CHAPTER SIX

Individuality: A Spiritual Task and Societal Hazard

JOHN WEIR PERRY, M.D.

If we trace the historical evolution of *individuality* through the medium of its psychic representation in myth and ritual, we gain a new perspective on current issues related to the meaning of this term. Today, we define individuality with the simple phrase, "self-determination," implying the accomplishment of one's unique selfhood by fulfilling one's potential abilities using whatever method one chooses, with an ultimate goal of integration and wholeness. In ancient and traditional cultures, however, the individual's role was defined by collective agreement; one fulfilled one's duties according to one's place in the social structure. In this historical approach, it is, of course, precarious to make general assumptions about cultures, yet in myth and ritual the evolution of individuality is clearly represented.

My interest in this approach grew from psychotherapeutical observations of persons in various degrees of turmoil—from the vivid imagery in dreams of ordinary cases in practice to the visionary states or spiritual emergencies of deeply disturbed people. In these latter instances, the imagery arising from the psychic depths is found to have parallels in ancient myths and rituals, and this led me to undertake an extensive study of ancient historical ceremonial practices. Although these disturbed states are regarded in psychiatry as "psychotic," they are not merely disorderly chaotic confusions. On the contrary, they reveal a process with regular features, involving experiences of death and birth, world destruction and creation, and messianic callings that include ideas of cultural reform and sacred marriages.

In both the ancient practices and in the experiences of people today, the imagery of a spiritual center is prominent, a center from which order and organization are produced either in the individual psyche or in the whole society. In these ancient practices, it is impressive to observe the strong emotional investment of honor and reverence toward the representation of this center. It is in the historical development of the representation of this spiritual center that we find the clearest evidence of the step-by-step evolution of individuality. This image of a spiritual center is, of course, what Jung has called the "archetype of the Self," characteristically represented as a quadrated circle or mandala that combines or unites or reconciles the opposites.

The ritual figure of the Great Man or Unique man as ruler initially occurred in the context of the first appearance of the true city cultures of the Urban Revolution, which took place in four great river valleys of the Near and Far East; the Nile, the Tigris-Euphrates, the Indus, and the Yellow River, in the third and second millennium B.C. Here, the term *city* meant a culture organized according to the functions and specialized occupations of its inhabitants, as opposed to the earlier clan structure, in which organization had been framed in family systems.

In these Bronze Age city states, the Unique Man was often ceremonially represented as a sacral king with divine attributes, and his function was placed at the cosmic axis or world center, at the mid-point of the world image. The world was regarded as kingdom, the kingdom as the world. These sacral kings were usually personifications of the center and of the very life of the kingdom, as its soul, so that whatever happened to the king also happened to the entire realm. Thus, the society was usually regarded as a corporate body with the king as its very heart and soul. Examples of the sacral kingship in the ancient Near East afford the clearest parallels to the renewal process seen in the visionary states of today, while those in the Far East present the most vivid imagery of the theme of the center.

The New Year Festivals for rejuvenation of the king and the kingdom in the city kingdoms of Mesopotamia exactly followed the groundplan of the renewal process: taking place at the center, reversing time to the beginning of creation, using the symbolic death and rejuvenation of the king, the ritual combat between order and chaos, the reenthronement of the victorious king and his *hieros gamos* of sacred marriage, and reading the destinies as a reaffirmation of the will of the gods and the society's allegiance to it. The temple's stage tower represented a world mountain and cosmic axis called *Dur Anki*, the Bond of Heaven and Earth. In the early Sumerian years, the king was called *Lugal*, the Great Man, playing the role of the god of the high sky as upholder of order, and that of the storm god as warrior and chief executive.

Egypt's festivals of reenthronement followed roughly the same pattern, but its kingship was noteworthy for ascribing absolute divinity to the Pharaoh: he was Horus, god of the light of the sky, and Horus was the Pharaoh in the early dynasties. As Giver of Life and Giver of Order, his *Ka* (soul) provided the *Kas* for all his subjects, who thereby participated in his life as he did in theirs. As the source of life, order, and soul for the realm, the king's position in the scheme of things was at the center, his throne set upon the Primordial Mound that represented the spot of land from which all creation spread in four directions; his capital city, Memphis, was set at the midpoint of the Egyptian world between the Two Lands, Upper and Lower Egypt. The kingship was also dual in another sense; as Horus, the Pharaoh ruled the realm of the living, while the recently deceased king was transfigured into Osiris, who then reigned over the realm of the dead, the ancestors.

India, too, though in much later centuries, had its sacral kingships in which the monarch's person was regarded as a composite of eight divinities. As *Chakravartin*, Wheel King, his rule was universal. The rites of enthronement and reenthronement emphasized centrality and also rebirth, vividly and explicitly dramatized by his assumption of the cowl of the chorion and of the amnion, and of the waters of the amniotic fluid of the foetal state.

Among the ceremonial expressions of sovereignty in the ancient world, the Chinese ritual is outstandingly satisfying both spiritually and esthetically. Its cosmological setting is a source of delight to modern evolutionists with a systems theory approach, such as Joseph Needham, who said of it that there was no belief in a creator acting from outside, but this cosmos was a self-contained, self-organizing system. In these purely naturalistic terms "the harmonious cooperation of all beings arose, not from the orders of a superior authority external to themselves, but from the fact that they were all parts in a hierarchy of wholes forming a cosmic pattern, and what they obeyed were the internal dictates of their own natures." This was the model upon which the manner of governing in the earliest dynasties was founded. "Heaven" was a barely personified presence presiding over the cosmos, and the "Son of Heaven" was sovereign but did not actively rule this confederacy of principalities.

In the Bronze Age, this Heaven was understood to be made up of the spirits of the departed royal ancestors, the *Ti*, acting as a composite whole; only the sacral kings posessed a soul that would become immortalized as a *Ti*. The ideogram for *Ti* was a vertical phallus, suggesting the generative, life-giving function of such ancestral spirits, not unlike the role of Osiris in Egypt.

The theme of the Great Individual was suffused throughout this ideology of the kingship. Heaven, *T'ien*, was, in its earliest written form represented by the character in Figure 1, obviously signifying the Great man, the conglomerate embodiment of the *Ti*. It is now written as in Figure 2. In the second dynasty (first millennium B.C.), the Chou, the sacral king was represented by the character in Figure 3, the Great Man, now with his feet planted on the ground. He was *T'ien-tse*, the Son of Heaven, and participated in the nature of Heaven itself as spokesman and mediator. This meant that the accumulated experience of the ancestors was embodied in the person of the sacral king. The Son of Heaven alone, as the ruling member of the dynasty, could assume the title of *Wang*, the king, as his special prerogative. According to later philosophers, Figure 4 represented a cosmic axis with Heaven, man, and Earth united through the person of the king, a beautiful rendering of the role of the center.

Among the many indications of the central position of this sacred figure there was consistent emphasis on its being not only a midpoint but also a north-south axis. The name of China was written in characters implying this, as seen in Figure 5: *Chung Kuo*, the "Middle Kingdom," "center" as a rectangle traversed by a vertical line as an axis, "kingdom" as a square enclosure containing lines indicating the kingship.

The capital cities of the Shang and Chou Dynasties (second and first millennium B.C.) were laid out in the manner represented in Figure 6. Each was a quadrated square or rectangular city with avenues

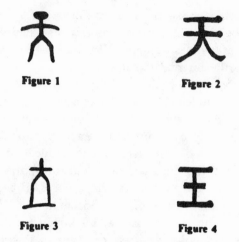

Figure 1   Figure 2

Figure 3   Figure 4

and gates oriented to the cardinal directions, and in the center, the king's palace, facing south on an axis dividing the populace into two moieties or halves, according to lineage. In front of the palace on one side was the Temple of the Ancestors, important to the function of mediator, and on the other side, the Altar of Earth, concerned with the feminine principle of increase and life-giving. Here, then, was a Yang and Yin, Heaven and Earth, division in these two sacred places, temple and altar, on either side of the axis.

A little later on, the realm that is the earth, that is, the whole world, was represented in the bronze cosmic mirrors of the Han Dynasty (the end of the first millennium B.C.) as seen in Figure 7,

Figure 5

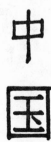

Figure 6

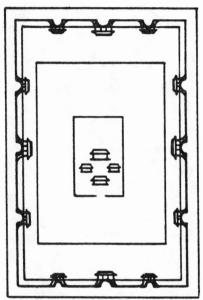

called TLV design. The Middle Kingdom was seen as a square with gates in the cardinal directions (the T's), and marks near the periphery of the design (the V's), indicating that there is an implied cross here with limbs extending out, the L's suggesting a swastika perhaps. These areas, the Four Seas, in the four directions were considered the realms of the barbarians, the chaos that was the king's task to bring into the organization of the ordered world as his cosmocratic function. The Son of Heaven had his position at the center, indicated by a burnished mound.

Also, in the dimension of actuality, the kingdom had roughly the shape of a quadrated circle with the four sacred mountains in the cardinal directions and a fifth at the center, which had a certain ritual significance at that time. The centrality, the quadrating of space, and the strict ordering and balancing of design were thoroughly represented in these symbolic forms. These mandala patterns antedated the Tibetan ones by many centuries.

A very interesting further representation of centrality was the ceremonial building for the functions of the king, which was the

Figure 7

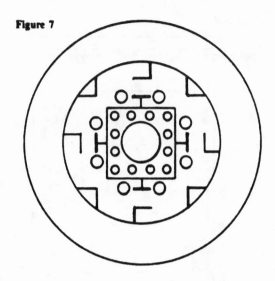

Ming-Tang, the "Hall of Light" or "Hall of Brilliance," where he performed his kingly rituals (Figure 8). It was "square below" representing earth, and "round above" representing the dome of the sky, where he would observe the night heavens and keep track of time and the seasons. It was all surrounded by a *Pi* moat, which signified Heaven again. In the central building was an audience hall where the Son of Heaven would sit on his throne with the Pole Star at his back, facing south. In early times, this was surrounded by four square chapels; later there were eight, and upstairs was the round observatory platform. A king of very early times had the custom of making ceremonial rounds of the entire kingdom by going to the five holy mountains, not to explore, but to confirm his active relation to the four quarters of the realm and "to spread his virtue among them."

It was not too long before the kings considered such a routine wearisome, and instead they travelled only to the four gates of the capital city. Finally, they did all this in the *Ming-Tang* alone, making the rounds of the four quarters and also of the seasons and the months. This was considered a function of the king as "master of time" and "master of space." He faced the south with the Pole Star at his back, toward which the stars of heaven turn and circulate around it. That was the function of the sacral king; like the Pole

Figure 8

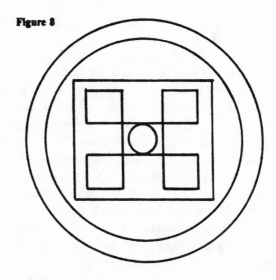

Star, the people would turn their gaze upon him and the life of the realm would circulate about him, so to speak, and thus "remain calm and docile," in harmony.

Scholars have recently discovered that these kings of the Shang and early Chou Dynasties were also considered shamans. They were known as "rain kings" for some while, but that was the least of their functions. They also had the ability to fly like shamans into the heavens, and they could traverse earth, water, and air at will. They had powers of divination and prognostication and they also apparently had healing powers. The Shang bronzes, which have been unearthed during the last century, have animals sculpted around them, facing each other in pairs. Recent studies of these animals have found that they are the helping animals of the shaman, the ones who give him shamanic powers. Therefore, to have big bronze cauldrons, made so exquisitely, with many animals around them, was designated the spiritually effective powers of the sacral king.

The monarch was also a father figure: he had a benevolent role, to care for the people and he carried the responsibility for their well-being. The sage kings of antiquity, of the legendary first dynasty, the Hsia Dynasty of the end of the third millennium B.C., were exemplars of this particular kind of virtue, or responsibility, of caring, and of nonassertion—*wu-wei*—governing without asserting heavy-handed or authoritarian dominance.

There is something about this mythic psychology that is always evanescent; the evolutionary process is relentless. This whole ceremonial system became desanctified very soon. For it to be sacred or sanctified meant that the archetypal conviction or dynamic was in it. At that time, the kingship was filled with potential for the future. It was a psychologically pregnant state about to give birth to many particular attributes of consciousness that would follow in the succeeding centuries, but which were first represented merely in symbolic form or in ritual ceremonial. The myth and ritual were essential to give new meaning for a new lifestyle in that kind of urban society. But the habit throughout history is that myth arises in times of bewilderment among new conditions and gives the necessary guidelines for psychic energies in new culture forms. Then gradually the personifications or representations of those images become desanctified and secular.

The fate of this mode of governing was most clearly represented in the histories of Egypt and of China, where the prerogatives and privileges of royalty were increasingly mimicked by the aristocracy. Petty princes and rulers of the component states comprising the realm took these attributes upon themselves. They governed more and more autonomously, built equally magnificent palaces and tombs for themselves, and gathered large armies to assert their growing power. In this way, the sacred potency and prestige of the status of the "Great Individual" was gradually diffused from the center and became more and more secularized. Ambition and greed for expanding land and mounting wealth led to unceasing wars between these nobles.

The Egyptian experience is noteworthy. In their Feudal Age, the latter part of the third millennium B.C., a kind of prophetism appeared that was to recur in Israel almost two thousand years later on the same model. Wise men such as Ipuwer lamented the lawlessness, marauding, and prevailing poverty, and placed the blame for this chaos squarely on the Pharaoh for not carrying out the duties of his function; this introduced the vision of a messianic hero who would restore the virtues of the ideal of the kingship. Another significant development was the democratization of the role of Osiris in the mortuary cult. In the early dynasties the king alone had the privilege of being transfigured into Osiris; but soon the aristocracy, instead of merely accompanying the monarch on his journey after death, began to assume the right to be similarly transformed, and finally the common man could buy the same funerary procedure to "become an Osiris" at his death. These phenomena graphically portray the diffusion of the attributes of the center downward and outward to the members of the society.

In China, much the same sort of history occurred two thousand years later. During the first half of the first millennium B.C., the Chou dynasty gradually lost its authority in all but name, and a Feudal Age followed in which the parts strove against each other at the expense of the welfare of the whole. Times of dire distress and intense suffering among the people resulted, as crops and manpower were appropriated for the warring armies of the various states in their power struggles against one another. However, in China's "Times of Troubles," in the midst of her most critical years when the very survival of the culture was seriously threatened, a remarkable phenomenon took place. A strong move toward healing was undertaken by the gifted visionaries of the "Hundred Schools" of the philosophers, consisting of efforts at a reexamination of the basic principles of governing and of societal cohesion by spiritual cultivation. Certain of their doctrines were influential in redefining the concept of individuality.

In spite of the public image of Confucius as an advocate of a sort of Victorian propriety, he was one of the great revolutionaries of history, championing a new concept of democracy, a principle that possessed a mystique comparable to that of the *Tao* among the Quietists. This virtue (force) called *Jen*, usually misleadingly translated as "supreme virtue," actually means human-hearted compassion or loving caring. Under its influence, the society would function as one great family in which all men would be brothers; this was the origin of "brotherly love." When asked about perfect knowledge, Confucius said it was "to know all men," and about perfect virtue he said it was "to love all men." He also originated the concept of the Golden Rule, and of the equality of all men, including even the "barbarians," an idea too preposterous to be accepted at the time.

A century later, Mencius, the foremost follower of Confucius, taught that selflessness can lead one to an identification of the self with the universe so that one can realize that the myriad things of the cosmos are all within us. By such spiritual cultivation, all men are capable of becoming sage kings like the great exemplars of the kingship, Yao and Shun. Mencius was a perceptive psychologist who traced the dynamics of societal relationships between rulers and ruled to its origins within the family system, between parents and children. Goodness, he said, was innate.

Mo-tse was an opponent of the Confucian school who proclaimed a doctrine of universal love, *Chien Ai*, a virtue to be developed by cultivating spirituality. He argued that the model of the family was not universal enough, and that all men should hold an equal love for one another. He was a pre-Christian Christian.

The Taoists were also opponents of the Confucian teachings, declaring that those scholars talked too much, and that the more one talks of virtues of love and loyalty and benevolence, the more one betrays the fact that one does not yet have them. Following the Way of Nature, no such admonitions are required. Cultivating the Light in this spirit, the Spiritual Center is found inside; it does not need a representation in the center of government.

These doctrines reveal the insight that societal harmony, once believed to emanate only from the benevolence generated by the Son of Heaven at the center of the world, can be cultivated from within the individuals composing the society. The center of order and integration, once expressed in the myth and ritual of the kingship, can be found inside oneself. Order need not be imposed from above if it is evoked from within. Once more I find a remarkable parallel to the visionary experience called psychotic, which typically starts with imagery of power and dominance and with concerns of inordinate prestige, but ends with equally compelling concerns for the capacities for a loving relationship in the life of the individual and in society.

This level of spiritual sophistication and insight was not reached by the cultures of the ancient Near East, who spent their energies in warring. Sumer disappeared as mysteriously as it had arrived; Akkad overran Sumer, but was in its turn taken over by the Assyrians until both merged into the empire of Cyrus of Iran. None had the chance to reach the full cultural maturity of China; and it was left to Israel to accomplish the task of inward realization and internalization of the kingship. In Israel, many centuries of visionary work by its prophets began with the desire for the restoration of the ideal of the sacral kingship in a strong ruler but evolved into the more subtle concept of a messiah who would be a spiritual shepherd of the people. Jesus brought the various elements of this long tradition into a refined expression of a purely inward and nonpolitical image of his Davidic kingship, characterized by the ethic of *agape*, a love of all the members of this Kingdon of God for one another.

In India, too, Gautama the Buddha had to decide whether to follow the career of a *Chakravartin*, a Universal King, for which he was born and raised, or of an Enlightened One, for which he prepared himself by his meditation under the Bo Tree. He, too, of course, advocated a way of life characterized by compassion and kindliness toward all beings. Both this Buddhahood and this Christ nature represent the perfected form of the inner sacral kingship as a psychic reality.

Thus, through a history of myth and ritual, the evolution of the concept of individuality is seen. At the beginning of the Urban Revolution, the spiritual center was externalized in the figure of the sole Great Individual, the sacral king. As it gradually diffused among the members of the aristocracy, this form of individuality became secularized and desanctified to willful self-seeking. Under the duress of crises, as societies became increasingly chaotic, prophets and visionaries perceived the dynamic of the inward realization of the center and its kingly myth and ritual forms. This internalization marked the beginning of the full democratization of these rituals, and raised the need for a new principle by which order might be preserved in societal structure. For this the visionaries perceived the dynamic of living fellowship and compassion as an absolute prerequisite to make the new individuality work.

This historical account clearly demonstrates that individuality is safe and healthy for society only if it is kept in balance with societal concerns and if the motive of personal power is compensated for by an equally strong motive to care for others.

Needless to say, the problems we face today grow out of a definition of individuality that has come to mean mere self-seeking, and a democracy that has altogether lost its meaning. Especially in America, individuals live in separateness, even isolation. In our competitive system, we seem to think one must be out for oneself. Once again, the parts are functioning without regard for the interests of the whole. Immense numbers of people grow up without any sense of belonging to a community and so they lack feelings of loyalty and caring;

crime, visible and invisible, mounts. One of the principal difficulties is that the mention of love in any but the most personal framework has become sentimentalized, emasculated, relegated to a Sunday school brand of ephemeral idealization. Whole books are written on states of consciousness and their psychology, wherein one finds no mention of love. Yet love remains the most essential dynamic in the healthy functioning of society.

Presented at the Ninth Conference of the International Transpersonal Association (ITA) on Tradition and Technology in Transition, Kyoto, Japan, April 1985.

CHAPTER SEVEN

Thoughts on Mysticism as Frontier of Consciousness Evolution

BROTHER DAVID STEINDL-RAST, PH.D.

I like to think about mysticism as a particular frontier of consciousness evolution. It is under this aspect that I would like to explore the problem of mysticism with you today. In the first part of my talk, I will focus on some general and universal features of the mystical quest. In the second half, I will focus on its Christian version, specifying what makes a certain form of mysticism Christian. But obviously, even in discussing the most general aspects of mysticism, I will already be speaking as somebody standing in the Christian tradition. It will not be a discussion of absolutely pure mysticism, if something like that is at all possible. Rather, I will be looking at mysticism as somebody who discovered it primarily through the Christian tradition. However, I have been very fortunate to be exposed to other mystical traditions, particularly the Buddhist and the Hindu one. This has broadened and deepened my own view of mysticism.

Today's confrontation with mysticism will be a very personal task for you. Of course, if you face the frontiers of consciousness in the right way, you always make it personal, you always apply what you see to your own life. But when Fritjof Capra, for instance, speaks about physics, that is a field of knowledge out there. It is optional to what degree you personalize your insights. When we speak about

---

Presented at the month-long seminar on Frontiers of Consciousness Research coordinated by Christina and Stanislav Grof, Esalen Institute, May 1985.

mysticism as a field of investigation out there somewhere, we have already missed the point. It is your own mysticism that we are talking about—or else it is nothing at all.

The mystics are not a special kind of human being. But every human being is a special kind of mystic. The challenge for you is to discover as soon as possible what particular kind of mystic you are. Find where your own mystical experience lies and explore that. What I am telling you comes out of my own experience and wants to reach your experience. That is the important thing. Allow your own experience to resonate with what I put before you. Ask yourselves here, step by step, "Is this true for me? Does this ring true for me?" If it does not ring true, please speak up. We are cooperating here. Each one of us has to make a contribution so that in the end, we will be able to speak about mysticism in terms that are meaningful for all of us here. It will become clear as we go along that we are speaking about the mental realm in which all of us are one, the point where we all are connected. At the same time, we are speaking about the very experience that shows us what is true, the experience from which we take the standard for what we mean by "real." Our mystic experience is the point where we are all one. And it is at the same time the measure, the standard for what is real. Therefore, it is only on this basis that we can ever agree on what is true or real. Mystic awareness is the deepest anchor for human solidarity. But more of this later.

Our next step must be to remember our own mystical experience. It is necessary that you remember a moment in which you yourself had the kind of experience that we call mystical. We will explore this experience together as we go along, but we need something to work with. So you need to have your own experience clearly in mind. Whatever I say can then be checked out against this experience. Therefore, the first step is that you clearly remember an experience that will qualify. Remember a moment that stands out in your memory as making life meaningful. Something of which you would say, "Well, for that kind of experience it is worth being alive." That would be sort of the lowest common denominator. You ought to be able to say, "At that moment life made sense." Even if you say, "For me, most of the time, life makes no sense whatsoever," there surely was a moment when it seemed to make sense. That is the moment we want to latch onto. For some this is a rare occasion.

Another person may say, "I don't know which one to choose, I'm just showered with this kind of experience. I wallow in it, it comes fifteen times in one day." That does not make any difference. What matters is for you to remember a moment in which life made sense. That will be our starting point.

And in order to prime the pump I will read you a short passage that many of you will be familiar with. It comes from a well-known play, Eugene O'Neill's "A Long Day's Journey into Night." You do not have to know the play or the plot in order to appreciate this passage. Edmund is telling Tyron about this kind of experience. He is slightly drunk at the time, which makes it easier for him to talk about it. See if your own memory associates with what Edmund says.

> You've just told me some high spots in your memories. Want to hear mine? They're all connected with the sea. Here's one. When I was on the Squarehead square rigger, bound for Buenos Aires. Full moon in the Trades. The old hooker driving fourteen knots. I lay on the bowsprit, facing astern, with the water foaming into spume under me, the masts with every sail white in the moonlight, towering high above me. I became drunk with the beauty and singing rhythm of it, and for a moment I lost myself—actually lost my life. I was set free! I dissolved in the sea, became white sails and flying spray, became beauty and rhythm, became moonlight and the ship and the high dim-starred sky! I belonged without past or future, within peace and unity and wild joy, within something greater than my own life, or the life of Man, to Life itself! To God, if you want to put it that way. And several other times in my life, when I was swimming far out, or lying alone on a beach, I have had the same experience. Became the sun, the hot sand, green seaweed anchored to a rock, swaying in the tide. Like a saint's vision of beatitude. Like the veil of things as they seem drawn back by an unseen hand. For a second there is meaning! Then the hand lets the veil fall and you are alone, lost in the fog again, and you stumble on toward nowhere, for no good reason.

Some of this ought to ring a bell within us. That is the great thing about a poetic statement: The key words are all there. "I lost myself."

Maybe this is the only key phrase of which you can say, "I know what he is talking about. In that moment I lost myself." Or, as T. S. Eliot puts it, "Lost in a shaft of sunlight." You see this shaft of sunlight coming out of a cloud, and looking at it you lose yourself. You look into somebody's eyes, and you just drown in them and lose yourself in this vision. "I lost myself." Or, "I was set free," For a moment I was set free. It was like coming out of a cage. Most of the time I am caged, in my own cage. I am my own cage keeper. But for a moment I am out, I am free. For some unknown reason I go right back into the cage. Maybe I feel safer there. But we all have moments when we come out of the cage, "I was set free." Or another key phrase: "I dissolved in the sea. I became white sails." I dissolved in what I saw. I became one with everything that I saw. That is often an aspect of our mystic experience. "I belonged." "I belonged" may be one of the most important key phrases. Most of the time we feel that we are somehow left out. We are standing outside. There is all this wonderful world and life going on, and we are somewhat alienated from it, outsiders, as it were. But for a moment we belong. We are a part of that great dance, everybody welcomes us; everything welcomes us. "I belonged without past or future." That is another aspect of our mystic moments: Time seems to fall away. Time stands still. It is what Eliot calls a "moment in and out of time." It is in time and yet it is out of time. "I belonged within peace and unity and a wild joy, within something greater than my own life or life itself . . . to God if you want to put it that way." We will not bring God in as yet. We are not ready for that. But we will come back to it.

I will now give you a definition for "mystic experience." You may find it in any dictionary. It is nothing very special. But it will be helpful as a working definition. Mysticism in the broadest sense is "the experience of communion with Ultimate Reality." Each of these three points is important. It is an experience. Mysticism is not theory but practical experience—your own. And it is a special kind of experience, namely, an experience of communion. That communion aspect is very important. What stands in the foreground of your particular experience may be communion in a limited sense. You may experience deep communion by sharing with one other person or with an animal, with a pet. You may be focusing, for example, on a moment when you lost your pet and found it again. That may be one of those mystical moments. But this kind of experience always implies a greater communion, it always implies a communion that has no limits. That is why we speak of communion with Ultimate Reality. Now let us go through that definition point by point.

Experience is a helpful word, but it hides its own traps. Experience is a highly inflated term today. When I speak of experience, you may think, "Oh wow, this must be one of those big bangers, but I have never had one of those." But what is important here, when we speak of experience, it not its magnitude. What is important is that you become aware of something. Awareness is what we are after here. This awareness may have come suddenly and overwhelmingly, but it may also have come ever so gradually. My favorite image for this is the coming of spring. Sometimes spring comes suddenly, with a big bang. Yesterday it was still winter, but today spring is in the air. Spring came overnight. In other years it comes so gradually that you can not even say when it came. A long drawn-out battle was going back and forth. But eventually it is spring. You do not know how it came, but all that matters is that spring is here. And so all that matters is that you eventually become aware deep within you of ultimate communion. Whether it came with one sudden explosion or very, very slowly does not make any difference. Remember: Awareness is what counts no matter how it seeps into your consciousness.

You may not notice when you are passing that border of consciousness. Sometimes when you pass into another country you have to check your passport and undergo all sorts of border controls. Then there is no question where you are. But at other times you just pass through on the train. Nobody checked your passport, but there you are. Frontiers are not always the same. You may have passed a frontier of awareness without notice. The important thing is that you have passed it. And the awareness that concerns us here is experiential awareness of communion.

But "communion" is another one of those inflated words today. The perfect community is one of the most alluring mirages in our time. Well, what concerns us here is rather a deep sense of belonging. We may have that sense of belonging without ever finding its external expression in a closely knit community. What matters is our awareness that we belong. We are not aliens, outcasts, orphans in this world. Kabir, the great mystic poet says:

We sense that there is some sort of spirit that loves
Birds and animals and the ants—
Perhaps the same one who gave a radiance to you
In your mother's womb.
Is it logical you would be walking around entirely
orphaned now?

Remember your life in the womb. Something put you together; something fashioned you there; something brought you out; something saw you through. Is it possible that that one would leave you orphaned now? That is the mystical insight of belonging. Before anything else, you belong. Is it imaginable that you should no longer belong? Is it imaginable that you should really be orphaned now? When you ask yourself that question and at least begin to doubt that you should be orphaned now, then you are moving from alienation to belonging.

Belonging and alienation, that is the polarity about which we are talking. That polarity is the pivot of our spiritual life. One pole is alienation. We all know what that is. We know what it feels like: being cut off from everything, from ourselves, from anything that has meaning, from all others. And the opposite pole to alienation is belonging. All that ultimately matters in our life is movement from alienation to belonging, often with many setbacks. This has always been the essential struggle of spiritual life. But we need a vocabulary that makes sense to us today. Alienation is our contemporary word for what has been called sin and, therefore, the contemporary word for salvation is belonging. Sin and salvation have become jargon words, and we may as well declare a moratorium on them. I am only referring to these terms because we do not want to lose the connection with the way people have been speaking about the same realities in the past. For us, "sin" is not a helpful word because our notion of sin has become limited to "do's and don'ts." Originally, the term referred to alienation from self, from others, from the divine reality within and beyond us. For us, today, the word alienation conveys precisely what tradition calls "sin." And if you think of "belonging" in its ultimate, fullest sense, then you also know what "salvation" means. That is what we long for, namely, belonging, wholeness, communion with our own true self, with all others, with the divine.

This reference to communion with the divine leads us to the third element of our definition of mysticism as "experience of communion with Ultimate Reality." If we had problems with the terms "experience" and "communion," these problems are compounded when we come to speak of Ultimate Reality, or the divine, or God. We could avoid misunderstandings by speaking of Ultimate Reality rather than God. All those who feel comforable with the word "God" will certainly agree that God is the Ultimate Reality. But there are many whom the term God makes uneasy, and often for good reasons. Yet, speaking of Christian mysticism, we shall have to face the notion of God sooner or later. Why not do so right now?

We must not start out with what someone else has told us about God. We have to rediscover God from within. And there we discover God as the one to whom we belong. That is all. Before we know anything *about* God, we know God. This is true for every one of us. We know God as the one to whom we belong. Anyone who uses the word "God" correctly uses it in this sense. If it is used in any other sense, you are the judges of how this word is to be used because you know it from experience. Each one of us knows God from experience. The word "God" is a label, we do not need to use it. We could talk about religion forever without using the word God. But it can be a helpful word. It links our own experience with all the theistic traditions. We must start with our experience. But it helps to link that experience with what millions of people have experienced and spoken about in the theistic traditions of the world. Thus, we can profit from what others have experienced. You can compare your own experience with the experience of others if you have this key word. But do not allow anybody to give you this term God loaded already with lots of notions. Discover its content for yourself!

I would like to read you the short description of one of those discoveries of God. It comes from the autobiography of Mary Austin. It is amazing how often you find that kind of experience in the early parts of autiobiographies. And it is important for you to find it in your own autobiography. So Mary Austin says here:

> I must have been between five and six when this experience happened to me. It was a summer morning, and the child I was had walked down through the orchard alone and come out on the brow of a sloping hill where there were grass and

a wind blowing and one tall tree reaching into the infinite immensities of blueness. Quite suddenly, after a moment of quietness there, earth and sky and tree and wind-blown grass and the child in the midst of them came alive together with a pulsing light of consciousness. To this day I can recall the swift inclusive awareness of each for the whole—I in them and they in me and all of us enclosed in a warm lucent bubble of livingness.

Now up to this point there is nothing new. We know it from our own experience. We have heard it in Eugene O'Neill's experience. But now comes the reason why I am reading this particular passage to you. Because Mary Austin describes so wonderfully the discovery of God. "I remember the child looking everywhere for the source of this happy wonder and at last she questioned: 'God?' because that was the only awesome word she knew." So we have two moments here. First, the discovery of God—then putting the word on it. Experience is the real discovery. Then there is this awesome word that does not fit anywhere else, so now you try this word on your experience. You ask yourself—that is the first stage—"God?" Could this experience have anything to do with God? And then, "deep inside, like the murmurous ring of a bell, she heard the answer, 'God, God.' "

That simply means "okay, that will fit." Let us try that word. "How long this ineffable moment lasted I never knew. It broke like a bubble at the sudden singing of a bird. And the wind blew and the world was the same as ever—only never *quite* the same." (From *The Unattended Moment*, by Michael Paffard, London, SCM Press Ltd., 1976.)

That is a discovery, the passing over a frontier of consciousness. From here you cannot go back. You have discovered something that you can explore from here on forever. Mysticism is the "exploration into God." Christopher Fry coined that expression. In his play, "A Sleep of Prisoners," he says, "Affairs are now soul-sized, the enterprise is exploration into God." This is what life is all about: exploration into God. It is like opening your eyes. There it is, the land to which you belong. This is where you are at home. And now you can spend the rest of eternity exploring this territory.

This is where the religious traditions come in. They all start from mystical experience. There is not one religious tradition in the world that starts from anything else. Often it starts historically with the mystical experience of the founder or reformer. Always it starts psychologically with the mystical experience of the believer. This is the starting point. And the end point of every religion in the world is the same. The goal of every religion is to make all experience ultimate belonging and act accordingly. That would be heaven. But if religion is this unifying force, if it starts with our deepest unity and leads supposedly to the point where everything will be an unfolding of this oneness, how come the religions are such divisive factors in the world? In other words, how does one get from the mystic experience that is within to the religions out there? How does one get from religious experience to religious tradition, from Religion to the religions? You know the answer. It is not only a process, something that happens out there. You know from your own experience how mystic experience inevitably turns into doctrine, ethics, and ritual, the key elements of every religious tradition. Let us check this out.

Mysticism is the heart of religion. Admittedly so. The heart of every religion is the religion of the heart. You know the heart of religion from experience. But how does one get from the inner core of religion to its paraphernalia out there? The answer is: inevitably! You inevitably get there somehow or other, even in your own private religion. There are certain things that the human mind inevitably does with any experience. Applied to our mystical experience, the mind turns it inevitably into doctrine, ethics, and ritual. Let us look more closely to see how this happens.

The first thing is that your intellect swoops down on your experience and starts interpreting it. You can not help that. When you were trying to remember your own mystic experience a little while ago, you were already beginning to interpret it. You said something about it to yourself. And by this interpretation, you began to form a religious doctrine. That is where religious doctrine begins. This process is inevitable. Wherever there is experience, there must be interpretation of that experience. We can not help it. Our mind works that way. And that is what doctrine is, interpretation of religious experience.

Every religion contains an element of doctrine. It may be merely rudimentary, or it may be highly elaborate. Even your private religion inevitably contains its own doctrine. If you had a long time to work with it, that doctrine will be more elaborate. In young religion it will be simpler. If a religion has lasted for millennia, you can imagine that a lot of interpretation has happened. At first, doctrine is closely linked with the experience which it interprets. The experience is still very much alive, and you can continue to reinterpret it. The next generation is already a bit removed from that experience. It is interpreting the interpretation of the original experience. And once you have twenty seven generations, each one is interpreting the interpretation of an interpretation of an interpretation. We get further and further removed from the original experience. You cannot help that. But the interpretation, the doctrine, should continuously be linked with your own mystical experience in order to stay alive.

As children, many of us were exposed to all sorts of doctrines about God without anybody ever encouraging us to discover God first-hand within ourselves. This is an injustice, a deprivation. When religion's teaching is no longer linked with your own experience, doctrine turns into *dogmatism*. By dogmatism I mean a hardened doctrine, a doctrine that is no longer alive, that just sits there. Doctrine, as the interpretation of your mystic experience, is necessary. But it always has the tendency to deteriorate into dogmatism. (Please understand that dogmatism and dogma are not necessarily connected. Dogma is simply meant to pin down a doctrine in a form that says, "Well, this one we have settled; now let us go on and continue to explore." Dogma is meant to be a firm sort of stepping stone on the way to further exploration.) Any doctrine can deteriorate into dogmatism. The great task of the intellect is to keep religion healthy by confronting and connecting again and again doctrine and mysticism with one another.

So much for the intellect. But your will (your willingness, not your willfulness) also has its task. Just like your intellect, your will does something with every experience. Whenever you experience something, your will says, "This is nice; let's go after that," or else "I don't want to have anything to do with that!" We are concerned with these two possibilities when we speak of the will. But unfortunately, it is not as simple as that, because our intellect and our will work closely together. After your mystic experience, your will may say, "Wow, this limitless belonging, that's terrific! It's all I ever wanted. Let's go on after that." But your intellect warns you, "Be careful, you're going out on a limb, you don't know what all the implications are. Not so fast!" Your will is willing to commit itself, but you are fearful. Here we are suddenly in the realm of ethics, of morals. The realm where fearfulness struggles against commitment to limitless belonging, that is the arena of morality. That is why morality is another element of every religion.

If I really belong in the way in which I have experienced it in my mystic moments, then I must draw certain consequences. But fear draws a line somewhere. In your wonderful mystical moments you were not drawing lines between educated and uneducated. You were not drawing lines between black and white. You were not drawing lines between male and female, even between human and nonhuman. You are not drawing any lines. And if you belong to all, then you have obligations towards all. At the moment of your mystical experience, you happily accept all these obligations. Ethics, morality, is simply a spelling out of how to live when you take your ultimate belonging seriously.

Inevitably, we begin to formulate our obligations. After all, we do not live in a vacuum, but in society. When morality is first formulated, it is still alive. You can still go back to the experience and understand what you meant by the formulation. But life goes on. Time goes by. The "do"s and "don't"s, once formulated, do not change. But now you have moved to a different spot. You would not express your obligations in the same way today. But there they stand, these "do"s and "don't"s, and they are no longer connected with your deepest sense of belonging. When that happens, morality deteriorates into *moralism.*

Just as we distinguished doctrine from dogmatism, we can distinguish morals from moralism. Morals is the expression of our commitment to belonging. When that commitment is formulated, the formation has a tendency to harden until the expression hardens. Difference sits out there by itself, unconnected with experience. It can even come into contradiction with the living experience of belonging. The more you have had to do with formalized religion, the more you could give examples of morality coming into contrast with what that very religion preaches. To avoid moralism, you have to continuously go back to the experience at the root of religion. Morality has to be judged by your mystic experience.

But that is only one half. The mystic experience, if you really want to keep it pure and healthy, has to be judged by morals. The confrontation works both ways. If you want to have a healthy spiritual life, you have to allow for this interplay. It takes too long to reinvent the wheel. In religion, just as in other areas of human life, certain inventions have been made that can help us a great deal. Explorers check their findings against what other explorers have found. It would be a very impoverished life if you had to do everything yourself. At this point, I would put in a plug for religious traditions. All of them have their real problems, but they also have a great deal of wisdom that has accumulated. I certainly would not advise you to take it all, unchecked; that should be clear by now. But you might benefit by allowing yourself to be formed by tradition, just like artists are formed by a tradition before they set out to make their own discoveries. That is a delicate task.

There is a third area in which religion springs from the mystical experience, namely, ritual. There is no religion in the world that does not have some sort of doctrine. There is no religion in the world that does not have some sort of moral teachings. And there is no religion in the world that does not have some sort of ritual. But how does ritual arise from your mystic experience? Just as the intellect interprets the experience, and the will commits you to it, so your emotions, your feelings, celebrate that experience. And that is where ritual comes in.

Ritual is, first and foremost, a celebration of limitless belonging. Check this out against your own experience. Some of the rituals out there, in the traditional historic religions, may look bizarre. But you may have anniversary celebrations of a deep spiritual experience. Well, there you have a ritual calendar, like most religions have. You may keep going back to the place where that experience overwhelmed you. Well, there you have the ritual of pilgrimage. Let us say it happened at the beach. Every beach in the world is now a sacred place for you because it always brings back that experience. Or a tree becomes in that way a sacred tree for you. Ritual, when it is alive, is the celebration of mystic experience. It is a remembering that makes the experience present again. But ritual can deteriorate into *ritualism*. That happens whenever the ritual action no longer leads you back to the experience, but becomes an end in itself. You know no longer why, you just go through the motions. That is the way it has always been; that is the way it is supposed to be done; and so you go through this ritual; and it does not do anything for you. That is ritualism. But ritual, rightly understood, is meant to lead you continuously back, not only to something that happened in the past, but to your own most intimate mystical experience.

Allow me to summarize briefly what we have seen so far. First, we came to agree on a working definition of mysticism as "experience of communion with Ultimate Reality" (with God, if you can use that term). This definition is based on our own experience. It can be checked out against your own experience, for we are all mystics. The mysticism of which we are speaking here, the religion of the heart, is the heart of every religion. But the question arises, how do we get from the experience of communion with Ultimate Reality to all those religions around us with their specific historical, cultural, and theological peculiarities?

My answer is that different times and different places have provided different conditions for interpreting, applying, and celebrating the mystic experience. This resulted in the variety of religions in the world. All of them, however, spring from the same seed, the mystic experience. And all of them ripen towards the same harvest, the full fruition of the mystic awareness in human society.

The essence of mystic awareness is a sense of ultimate belonging. The various religious doctrines come about as this mystic awareness is variously interpreted by the human intellect. The moral systems of different religions come about when the human will draws more or less radical consequences for human behavior from the mystic awareness of our belonging together. And religious ritual in its many forms comes about when human emotions celebrate the awareness of ultimate belonging, utilizing the different means which different cultural settings offer.

The health and vitality of a given religion depends on the constant interplay between doctrine, ethics, and ritual on the one hand and the mystic awareness of the believer on the other. Where this interplay dries up, doctrine hardens into dogmatism, ethics into legalism, and ritual into ritualism. Only the continuous renewal of a given religious tradition from its mystical core can keep it alive and aware of what religion essentially is, namely, "exploration into God" at the frontier of human consciousness.

An image that I have sometimes used to illustrate the relationship between the mystic experience and religious tradition is that of a volcanic eruption. There is that hot magma gushing forth out of the depth of the earth. And then it flows down on the sides of the mountain. The longer it flows, the more time it has to cool off. And the more it cools, the less it looks like fire. At the bottom of the mountain, you find just layers and layers of rock. No one would think that this was ever bright, hot, fiery. But along comes the mystic. The mystic pokes holes through these layers and layers of rock until the fire gushes forth again, the original fire. Since each one of us is a mystic, this is our task. But as we rise to our responsibility, we will inevitably clash with the institution.

The question is: Do we have the grace and the strength and the courage to take on our prophetic task? You see, the mystic is also the prophet. And the prophetic stance is a double one. It demands a double courage, the courage to speak out and the courage to stay in. It takes a good deal of courage to speak out, not necessarily with words. Often a silent witness is much more of a witness. By word or by silence, the prophet speaks out. It is difficult enough to speak out and then to get out as quickly as you can, to say your thing and run. But the second half of the prophetic stance is to stay in, stay in the community against which you have to speak out. But it will not do to stay in and to blend with the woodwork, to stay in and lie low. That is not prophetic either. The most difficult thing is demanded from us: to stay in *and* to speak out. Nothing less will do.

To stay in would be easy if we could disappear. To speak out would be easy if we could get out. But then you would no longer be a prophet, you would merely be an outside critic; that has happened to many tired prophets. They have become outside critics. As long as they were prophets within, they had leverage; they were able to change things. Now, on the outside, they say the same things, but it does not phase anybody anymore. But to stay in and speak out means crucifixion. The staying in is symbolized by this cross because you stay in; you can not go anywhere else. It is rammed into the ground, and it is the vertical post of the cross. The horizontal post symbolizes the speaking out. It happens to fit in the Christian tradition very nicely. But the cross of the prophet is there in every tradition.

This leads right into the second great question of our topic: What is it that makes mysticism Christian? Mysticism is a phenomenom that we find in all the great religious traditions. It is a basic human phenomenon. Every human being is a mystic, although some may be more talented than others. Some may have developed that capacity further than others; but basically mysticism belongs to every human being. It is universal. Now, among the many different forms of mysticism, we find also Christian mysticism. Why do we call it Christian? What makes it Christian? We could answer that mysticism is Christian when it is related to the person of Jesus Christ in one way or another. That is enough for a starting point.

It seems important to me to start out in this way, because this definition allows for degrees. A particular form of mysticism may be more or less Christian depending on the extent to which it is connected with Jesus Christ. But to the degrees to which it has some relationship to Jesus Christ, we have a right to call a given mysticism Christian. No one has a monopoly on Jesus Christ. Therefore, nobody has a monopoly on Christian mysticism. It is not as if somebody could tell you: "This is Christian mysticism, but now you have crossed the line, and it is no longer Christian mysticism. You have passed out of it, you have fallen." We are not setting up a tidy box, but are establishing a relationship to a radiant center that radiates indefinitely. There may be areas that are just barely touched and dimly lit by this particular light, yet receive the full impact of another light. We can get twilight zones. If we speak about it in this way, we remain closer to actual reality than if we try to impose a more rigid definition.

If mysticism is Christian to the degree to which it is related to Jesus Christ and if our task is to speak about Christian mysticism, then obviously, we have to speak about Jesus Christ. Three aspects under which this topic relates to frontiers of consciousness evolution will be particularly important to us. One is the fact that mysticism as such is a frontier experience, as we have already discussed. The second is that Jesus Christ is a pioneer of consciousness. The third aspect will form the background to our investigations. It consists of the fact that biblical scholarship in the second half of the twentieth century is passing a frontier with far-reaching consequences for Christian counsciousness.

Biblical scholarship today has renounced the ambition to achieve a detailed biography of Jesus. The available data is simply insufficient to do so. But we can achieve something far more important: we can reconstruct quite reliably what kind of person Jesus was. There is considerable interest today in the Jesus before Christianity. The image that emerges shows us Jesus as a pioneer of human consciousness, and this precisely on the frontier of mysticism. The impact of Jesus can be understood as a new phase in the human "exploration into God." Moreover, his life's work and teaching stands and falls with mysticism. It hinges on "the experience of communion with God"— Jesus' own and that of the people to whom his message is addressed.

We can get our teeth into this topic by asking two basic questions about the Jesus before Christianity. *What* did he actually teach? And *how* did he teach? Let me anticipate the answers. (Scholars are practically unanimous on these two points.) The gist of Jesus' message is the proclamation of the Kingdom of God. And his most characteristic teaching method is in parables. But now we will have to unpack the content of these two succinct answers and see what trail Jesus blazed across frontiers of consciousness, allowing others to follow.

Mark, the earliest of our extant Gospels, summarized the teaching of Jesus in Chapter 1:15. He puts it all in a single verse so that you really get the gist. And this is what he says: "Jesus came . . . proclaiming the Good News from God and saying, 'The time is fulfilled, the Kingdom of God is at hand. Be converted and believe the Good News.' " "The time is fulfilled." That means "now." Do not wait for anything else. Now is the moment—"The Kingdom of God is at hand." At hand means right here. Here and now, that is the setting for the proclamation. This is the time, this is the place. do not look for anywhere else; do not wait for any other moment. This is it! (Now you are cornered.) And now comes the message: "Be converted and believe the Good News!"

If you look that up in your King James version, it will say "Repent ye, and believe the gospel." That is a very problematic translation for us today. Repentance means, for most of us, making up for what we have done wrong. And gospel means, for us today, the gospel book. So you get the idea that Jesus told us to make up for our sins and then believe what is written in that book. Unfortunately, that is a widespread misunderstanding. And what a misunderstanding! What would be new about Jesus' message if that were what he meant? And what would be good about it? What Jesus is really saying is this: Here and now God's saving power has been made manifest. Put your trust in it and let it turn your whole life around!

The word Mark uses for conversion means a complete change of heart. It means a turning upside down of our habitual way of thinking and living. What, then, does Kingdom of God mean to warrant such a world-shaking response? The answer to this question leads us right back into the realm of mysticism and helps us understand how Jesus expanded the frontiers of consciousness. Biblical scholarship today is quite unanimous on the meaning of Kingdom of God in the message of Jesus. It does not mean a place, a realm, like the British Empire. Nor does it mean a community—all those who belong to Jesus as king. Nor does it mean God's reign or power in the abstract. On the contrary, it refers to the most concrete, experiential reality. Kingdom of God means for Jesus God's saving power made manifest.

When we understand the term Kingdom in the message of Jesus as "God's saving power made manifest," then we can readily see how relevant it is in our context of Christian mysticism. In our own experience, when do we experience "God's power" and "salvation"? If we understand these terms correctly, the answer will be: in our alive moments, in those mystic moments, about which we spoke already. How, then, do terms like "God's power" and "salvation" link up with our contemporary experience? We might prefer to avoid the term God. Today, it often causes confusion if you introduce this term. But on the other hand, we are talking here in terms of Christian tradition, of Jewish tradition. That is why we must try to understand the terminology of that tradition.

When do we today experience what may be the equivalent to God's saving power? I would suggest that it is in those moments when we are "overpowered," as we say, by an overwhelming inrush of aliveness. Remember the examples I read to you from Eugene O'Neill and Mary Austin. Those were moments in which people were overpowered. And we too, if we remember similar moments, know that we were carried beyond the frontiers of our normal consciousness by a power, a *saving* power. Remember, it is like being let out of a cage. A power beyond ourselves is freeing us, liberating us, pulling us out from drowning.

Normally, we focus narrowly on this life-saver model when we think about being saved. The basic idea is that you are in trouble and somebody pulls you out. Remember how many advertisements play on this particular concept of saving: You are in trouble, and we will save you. First we show you how you are in trouble, and then we will show you how you can be saved by our product. Even the dog faints when you take off your shoes! And then comes the deodorant that will save you. These are the two parts of every advertisement. First they show you *that* you need salvation; then they show you *how* you can be saved.

But that is not the only notion of saving. In fact it is one that we rarely use in everyday language. More often we speak of saving money, saving energy, saving water, or the like. There is a different concept of saving behind this. You are not saving the water from drowning or money from being in trouble! Saving in this context means not wasting. But not wasting is only the negative aspect. The positive aspect is affirming the value—of every penny, of every ounce of energy, every drop of water. And that aspect of saving is most important in our mystic experiences. Suddenly we are saved from alienation. (Remember alienation stands in our terminology today for all that we need to be saved from.) Suddenly we find our value affirmed. That is what saves us. We are at home. We are not orphans. We are not outcasts. We belong. Thus we experience, in our best moments, a saving power, a power that liberates us by affirming us.

We walk taller now that we are affirmed. We are more truly ourselves now that this saving power has been made manifest to us in our experience. That is in itself a conversion, a turning, a thinking upside down. Most of the time we lie as if we were alienated, but now we know that we belong. And this manifestation calls us to further conversion. If we could live out, in every moment of our daily life, what we experience, what we are aware of in our mystical moments, that would be conversion. Life lived in that power would altogether change the world.

On the basis of this experience you can understand Jesus as a person who has experienced profound intimacy with God, a person who experienced communion with God's saving power. How he goes around and tells everybody, "Haven't you experienced that? It's a reality here and now, this Kingdom of God, the manifestation of God's saving power. The time is fulfilled. The kingdom is at hand. Put your trust in that awareness; that is all you need to do. And, above all, live accordingly. That's conversion." But this Good News is too good to be true. That is why we do not live by it. Nor do we live by our own best experiences. We have them and an hour later we almost forget that sense of aliveness. We suppress it again. We doubt it. Maybe it was just an illusion. Our mystic awareness is too good to be true. We repress it. But Jesus says, "Don't forget it. This is reality. Live accordingly!" That message reverberates in so many ways throughout the whole New Testament.

And that is why Jesus teaches in parables. There is no other teacher in the history of religion who taught so predominantly in parables. Jesus taught most typically in parables; not exclusively, but so much so that Mark can say that he taught *only* in parables. That he never taught in any other way except in parables is an exaggeration. But parable was the most typical way. That is why it is so important for us to understand what a parable is. It is a very simple teaching device. It can be a little story, it can be somewhat longer, or it can be just a very short saying like a proverb. The way some proverbs work gives us a good idea how a parable works. Take this one for example: "Early bird catches the worm." That is common sense. You can observe it if you get up early enough. Later on, most of the worms are gone. Late comers do not get any. You may have observed that many times, but it did not mean much to you. But then one day, you find yourself coming late to lunch at Esalen, and you do not get anything. Or maybe you go to a record shop and that new record is sold out. All of a sudden you remember that early bird catching a worm. Your situation has nothing to do with birds, nor with worms, but it has a lot to do with the truth that lies behind the proverb.

That is the way a parable starts out. It reminds you of a common sense observation. Often it starts with, "Who of you does not know that?" Who of you who is a parent does not know how parents feel towards their children? Who of you who has ever baked bread does not know how yeast works? Who of you has ever lost something and does not know to what extent one goes to find it again? The "who of you" appeals to the audience and says, "Don't you all know this anyway?" This is part one of every parable. Who of you does not know that the early bird catches the worm? Something as commonplace as that. Then comes part two. That is the response of the audience. The audience says, "Well, obviously, that's common sense. Isn't it?" And then comes part three, and that is, in the best examples, just silence. But sometimes it is spelled out, and it is the part in which Jesus says, "Ah, so it's common sense, okay. Well then why don't you act accordingly?" Whoops, now you are caught!

Let us look at an example to see how this teaching method of parable works. Most parables deal with the kingdom, but this one is told in answer to a question. The question is this: If I am supposed to love my neighbor as myself, *who* is my neighbor? We call this the parable of the good Samaritan. You have all heard it, I am sure. To call this parable the story of the good Samaritan is like telling a joke and giving it a title that spoils the whole point of the joke. For the Jews at the time of Jesus, there was no such thing as a *good* Samaritan. The only good Samaritan was a *dead* Samaritan, as we would say today. The Samaritans were the absolutely bad ones. And besides, the story is not about the Samaritan. That is another problem. The story is about a man who fell among the robbers. (This is a handy rule of thumb: In parables, as in jokes, you always have to identify with the first person mentioned, otherwise you do not get the point. You may get something else out of it, as in the story of the "good" Samaritan. All sorts of good, interesting teachings have been based on it. But if you want to know what Jesus said, follow the rule for any folk tale, joke, or folksy saying; namely identify with the first person mentioned!)

Well, then, someone asks, "Who is my neighbor?" and Jesus tells this story. There was a man (that's you!), who went from Jerusalem to Jericho, and he fell among robbers. Between Jerusalem and Jericho one can still fall among robbers today. The road leads through a steep canyon, and all sorts of things can happen to you there. So this man falls among robbers, who beat him and strip him. They steal whatever he has, and let him lie there half dead. It is very important that this man is only *half* dead. That means he is still half alive and can see what is going on. Remember, *you* are this man. Parables are not told from the helicopter perspectives, but through the eyes of the first person mentioned.

So you are lying there and somebody comes by. Suddenly you know who is your neighbor. Your heart cries out, "*This* is my neighbor; he ought to help me!" But he walks by on the other side of the road and you lie there. Then somebody else comes by. Again you cry out, "Help me. I'm your neighbor!" But this one, too, walks by. You are still lying there hoping somebody will recognize you as a neighbor and act accordingly. Who comes by next but a Samaritan! Well, do you want this outcast to help you? Yes, of course, aren't we all neighbors? And, lo and behold, this dirty Samaritan does act neighborly. So Jesus asks, "Who showed himself your neighbor?" And the answer is, well, the one who helped me. Can you hear the silence that follows? In that silence Jesus is turning the tables on you. If he is your neighbor when *you* are in trouble, is he still your neighbor when *he* is in trouble?

I came across a wonderful contemporary version of that parable. When I told to a group in New Zealand what I just now shared with you, a Josephite Sister in the audience said: "Wow, this happened to me. I was driving from Auckland to Hamilton not too long ago, and I got terribly tired. All of a sudden I find that my car is on the wrong side of the road. I stopped right there. I pulled over onto the curb (facing the wrong direction), and I said, 'I am going to sleep a little. Driving like this is too dangerous.' " She wakes up, and somebody is knocking on the window. Just waking up, she is totally confused and rolls down the window, contrary to all precautions. There is a man in a leather jacket, and he says, "Are you all right, dear? Move over, you are on the wrong side." In her confusion she moves over. He sits down, pulls her car in the right direction, and says, "You seem to be in pretty bad shape. Where are you going?" "Hamilton," she says. "We'll give you an escort." So this nun in her veil drives into Hamilton escorted by a motorcycle gang in leather.

Jesus proclaims the saving power of God made manifest among us, and he appeals to common sense. This common sense should really be written with capital "C." It is our *common* sense; we have it in common. And it has something to do with *sensing*. These are two very important aspects of Christian mysticism: emphasis on Community and emphasis on the senses. And both are contained in the notion of Common Sense.

It is to this common sense that Jesus always appeals. This fact is important in understanding Jesus and the mystic breakthrough that happened to him and through him. Ask yourself, to what authority did Jesus appeal? The answer is to common sense. When you go to churches and hear sermons, you may get the impression that he appealed to God's authority like the prophets of old. But on closer examination, Jesus never uses the typical prophetic formula, "Thus says the Lord. . . ." He did not simply appeal to God's authority and least of all to his own authority. (People who do that have never much of a following. For that reason alone we can be sure that he did not do it.) He appealed to the divine authority in the hearts of his hearers, to Common Sense.

That is what gets Jesus into trouble; that is how the whole historical crisis in Jesus' life came about. Someone who appeals to common sense necessarily gets in trouble with the authorities. To both religious and political authorities, nobody is more suspect than persons who have learned to stand on their own two feet and empower others to do the same. That is Jesus. And that is the mystics. The mystics continuously get in trouble with religious authorities, but often also with political authorities. By his teaching and by the very way he lives, Jesus drives a wedge between common sense and public opinion. He appeals to common sense and blows the pretense of public opinion to pieces. That is why Mark relates that common people said, "Wow, this man speaks with authority, not like our authorities." You can imagine how the authorities felt about it and how they reacted: "This man has to die!"

This is also the way the Gospels present it to us. Remember, we said that religion starts with mysticism and eventually hardens into doctrine, morals, and ritual. That is why in the gospels, you have Jesus somewhat schematically set over against three groups of the authorities: the scribes (who stand for doctrine), the lawyers (who stand for the law), and the pharisees (who stand for ritual). The gospels in themselves and the rest of the New Testament show— and we would know it even if they did not show it—that there were excellent holy scribes and lawyers and pharisees. But they are turned into types, and these types still exist today. In every church you can meet the scribes, the lawyers, and the pharisees, and we find them within our own heart. They stand for the dead letter over against personal experience, for legalism over against action that springs from a live sense of belonging, for ritualism over against a celebration of life as a whole. But Jesus gets in trouble not only with the religious authorities but also with the political authorities. They make common cause in the end and wipe him out. That is where the cross comes into the story of Jesus.

After the fact, we can interpret the cross in many ways as it has been interpreted by the Christian tradition. But you miss the point if you do not pay attention to how it came about historically. Jesus had to die because he broke through frontiers of consciousness, because he broke through frontiers of what it means to be religious. We better ask ourselves if we have the courage to stand up for common sense against public opinion. You run a frightening risk when you let yourself be caught by the parables. Once I say "yes" to common sense, why do I not live accordingly? Why do I not live with the aliveness of my best moments? Why do I make all these concessions to public opinion? Why do I not stand on the authority of God within me? Why do I bow to the authorities? And there are many hidden authorities. Just think of peer pressure. There are all sorts of authorities to which we bow. And why? If you do not, you end up where Jesus ended up, on your own cross, inevitably.

That is the shattering end of the life of Jesus. This man still comes through so beautifully in some of the earliest writings as one of whom others could say, "Wow, this is what we would like to be if we were really ourselves." He lives out of those mystical moments, and we do not. We just have them once in a while, and then we betray them again. He lives out that reality. Therefore, he is wiped out. Dead. Historically that is the end of his story.

But then comes an event that is not in history and not out of history, an event that marks the edge of history; that event is called the resurrection. You cannot tell the story of Jesus fairly without referring to the resurrection. It is not merely an appendix. Without it, nothing that has happened since and not even the picture that we have of Jesus, makes any sense. But what is that resurrection? How can we reconstruct what really happened?

Let us go back to the earliest report. The earliest report tells us that he dies on the cross. They take him down, they bury him hastily because it is the eve of the great feast, and soon after the feast women find the tomb empty. Women—that was very embarrassing to the earliest church because women had no right to testify. Women had no voice in court. There was no such thing as a female witness. Yet, women were the first witnesses of the resurrection, and their testimony was accepted. That marks a change in the whole status of women. They had (and still have) a long way to go, but from the beginning tradition knew that women were the first to find the tomb empty. And they believed that Jesus, whom they had seen dying and dead, was alive. That went far beyond any account that the tomb was empty. At the time, even those who said that his body had been stolen admitted that the tomb was empty.

Some people look now at this tomb, see it empty and say, "Well, he must have been stolen." Others see the same empty tomb and believe. They say: "Now we understand! Why should we seek the living one among the dead? This man was life personified. He showed us what it means to be alive. It stands to reason that he isn't here among the dead." And then comes the question: "Where is he, if he isn't here?" "He is hidden in God," says an early answer (Col. 3:3). God is also hidden. And yet, we experience the power of God. Jesus is with God, hidden in God, and he continues to empower us with God's power. Thus, the shattered followers of Jesus came to realize that the kind of life he lived is stronger than death. And two thousand years later the world still reverberates from the shock wave of their faith in his resurrection.

What makes all this extremely exciting for us today is that we too are confronted with the empty tomb in an altogether new way. (Again, that is one of those frontiers we have broken through in this century.) How are we confronted with the empty tomb of Jesus? You may have heard about the so-called Shroud of Turin. That is a remarkable piece of historic evidence. It is a linen sheet about fourteen feet long that was used to enfold a corpse. The body was lying on half of the sheet, and the other half was folded over the body. This linen sheet bears some faint marks. With the naked eye you can just barely make out the imprint of a body. But when the shroud was photographed for the first time at the beginning of our century, the negative showed a positive image. In other words, what you have on that sheet is a sort of negative. Its positive shows many details of the face and the body.

After careful study, several pathologists concluded that the image derives from the body of someone crucified in a manner identical to that recorded of Jesus in the Gospels. A few years ago, a team of scientists examined the shroud for several days and nights with the most modern methods. The verdict is that the image was not produced by any method known to us today. Some scientists ventured the hypothesis that the image must have been produced by something like a miniature atomic blast emanating from the dead body before decay set in.

So there was a crucified body wrapped in this shroud, and then before decay set in, there was some sort of miniature atomic blast, and the body was gone. This is *our* version of the empty tomb. It is our confrontation with the question,"Where is he?" Obviously, he is not here. And just as with the empty tomb, two thousand years ago, there are those who say, "It must be a fraud." And there are those who look at the same evidence and believe. The evidence cannot prove his resurrection. At best it can trigger faith that the life this man lived and evoked in others is stronger than death. But that is a lot!

What Jesus proclaimed as the coming of God's Kingdom, the Church throughout the ages proclaims as the Resurrection of Jesus the Christ. Both proclamations have the same content: God's saving power made manifest. There is the mystic core of the Christian religion, the volcanic eruption of a new beginning. And now the whole process begins all over again, inevitably. The encounter with Jesus is interpreted, and experience hardens into doctrine. The implications of Jesus' all-embracing love are formalized and harden into morals. They remember how he celebrated life when he ate with them and drank with them, and they turn this breaking of bread into ritual.

And so you have again and again the Christ-like figures within the church getting into the same troubles that Jesus got into with *his* religious authorities. And yet the Good News is handed on to us through the church, in the church, and in spite of the church. That is where you find all these saints who lived such Christ-like lives throughout the centuries up to our own time. But you also find the pharisees, the lawyers, and the scribes in that same church. When we asked, "What is one who accepts being a mystic to do with religion?" my answer was, "You have the responsibility to make religion religious, because left to itself it will deteriorate into something that is irreligious." Now we ask, "What is a Christian to do who recognizes what Christ is all about?" And the answer is, "Well, spend the rest of your life making the Church Christian." It is called the church of saints and of sinners. It is also the church of the mystics and the church that gives mystics a hard time. That is where we are. Let us be realistic. But at the heart of this church is the mystic element, which is what makes it tick, the very inheritance of Jesus. To penetrate to this mystical core is again and again the ultimate frontier experience of Christian mysticism.

CHAPTER EIGHT

Jesus, Evolution, and the Future of Humanity

JOHN WHITE

The human race is quickly coming to one of history's great divides—perhaps the most critical ever. It will be upon us by the end of the century. If we are to survive it, people must see that the situation is not simply political or sociological or cultural. It is biological.

All life on planet Earth is threatened with extinction from a number of sources. There is the threat of nuclear, biological and chemical warfare. There is the threat from pollution of the air, land and sea. There is the threat from wasting nonrenewable resources. There is the threat from drought and famine due to human interference with the ecosystem. If these are unchecked, even the planet itself could end up as nothing more than another asterioid belt.

All of these threats are man-made. All of them originate in the minds of people. Our behavior is a manifestation of our thinking and emotions, and in turn our thoughts and feelings are dependent upon our state of consciousness. We recognize the threat to life that these forms of behavior contain, yet we persist stubbornly in our ways. Why? It is not that we lack the knowledge of what is threatening our existence. It is simply that the problem goes deeper than intellectual knowledge. Our present world situation is one in which we exhibit life-threatening irrational behavior. That in turn is due to what we might call "a crisis of consciousness."

If this is so, the solution can be stated very simply: *change consciousness*. Survival demands a change of consciousness. Not only survival, but also evolution. As I survey natural and cultural history,

119

I see increasingly complex forms of life coming into being in order
to express more fully the consciousness behind creation itself. The
grand theme of history is evolution, and it is a story of evermore
refined forms of life emerging with ever-increasing degrees of consciousness.

Evolution is always at work. That means now, today. And what
I see today, in addition to the threats to life, are signs that nature
is mobilizing its resources to resist physical extinction in this part of
the universe. It is mobilizing its resources for a quantum leap forward.
The signs that point in this direction are many. Although the media
tend to make them look like confusion, upheaval and strife, I see
in them a deeper significance.

The growing restlessness among people as they search for new
answers and new understanding is bascially taking the form of
exploring their own consciousness—and that, to me, is a very healthy
sign indeed. Of course, these explorations often take a naive or
violent pathway. The strident, angry voices of many so-called liberation groups are to be expected as the disenfranchised come to
mature awareness. The mainstream of exploration, however, is an
increasing interest in psychic and spiritual development. As I see it,
this is an indication of a deep impulse to health which is working
beneath the obvious symptoms of sickness in the body of humanity.
And these approaches are being taken by young and old alike in
the interest of expanding their consciousness. They are signs of a
great awakening going on around the globe.

This great awakening is the way nature will resist man's irrational
behavior. Nature will resist the extinction of life here by evolving
lifeforms that know how to live sanely because their consiciousness
will have changed.

I call this *survivolution*. And I see it happening most dramatically
at the human level. Many of the events in the news today are, from
my perspective, preliminary signs that a higher form of life is emerging, just as the Cro-Magnon people superceded the Neanderthal race.

What is coming to pass today, as you read about it in the news,
is not a generation gap or a communication gap, as some media
commentators say. Rather, it is a *species gap*. A new species is making
its way onto the planet and—in the face of a threatening dominant
species—is asserting its right to live. This inevitably brings it in

conflict with the dominant species. And that dominant species is a dying species.

Paleontologists tell us that during the age of dinosaurs, little tarsier-like creatures lived. They stayed small and under cover because the great lumbering dinosaurs would easily crush them to death otherwise. So in order to survive, they remained small and "on the fringe," so to speak. Then, when the dinosaurs died off, these small creatures emerged from cover into the open and began to grow, to evolve into primates—in fact, into the first manlike creatures.

But evolution did not end there. And so when life reached the level of human development, one of the earlier races, the Neanderthal, was surpassed by the Cro-Magnon. This spelled doom for the Neanderthal. Cro-Magnon people were an evolutionary advance, a higher form of life. Their physique was taller and more massive. They had superior tool-making ability and were the world's first artists, as their cave painting demonstrates. Altogether they showed a superior degree of consciousness.

I see the world scene in terms that parallel this. The chaos and confusion and social unrest around us are signs of what I choose to call "moral evolution." Sri Aurobindo described it as a journey toward perfection; Teilhard de Chardin spoke of noogenesis and a movement toward the Omega point. Whatever the name, there is a rising chorus of voices around the globe demanding widespread social reform—political, educational, nutritional, medical, ecological, judicial, economic, agricultural, religious. It essentially amounts to a call for cultural reformation—indeed, transformation—beyond all racial, national, ethnic, religious, sexual and caste concerns. All this and the greatly accelerated interest and exploration in psychotechnologies, spiritual disciplines and sacred traditions are manifestations of a new, more intelligent species coming into existence and attempting to develop a unified planetary culture.

As such, the emerging species is meeting with resistance from the dominant species. It was ever thus. That is how evolution works. *Homo sapiens*, I think it accurate to say, is in stasis and is rapidly nearing the end of its life cycle. Everywhere we look—in western society, at least—institutions have become overgrown, outmoded and are breaking down. Culture is going into convulsions. Government, education, economics, religion, cities—they are either exploding in

violence or grinding to a halt and becoming moribund, empty shells
that no longer serve a vital purpose suited to the needs of people.

Biologically speaking, a dying species is a dangerous species. It is
prone to go mad and to lash out in blind, massive fury that violently
brings down its edifices upon it and anything else around. The new
species can see this happening and, like the little creatures in the
Age of Dinosaurs, has until lately remained under cover and on the
fringes of a society that is entering its death throes.

But now the new breed is emerging from cover. As an historical
epoch draws to a close, what can be seen around the planet is this:
a mighty leap forward in survivolution is happening, and the result
is a vast sorting-out process among people. Amid the confusion and
upheaval, they are trying to discover what species they belong to.
The larger dimensions of this process are not recognized at present
by most evolutionary forerunners, or else those dimensions are only
dimly intuited by them. The process is still fragmented and lead-
erless—an Aquarian conspiracy. And their numbers are still quite
small in proportion to world population. Nevertheless, higher intelligence is working through them, calling them to self-recognition of
their role in advancing the fabric of life.

Outwardly, of course, these mutant humans resemble the older
form. The difference is inward, in their changed mentality, in their
consciousness. The result, as I said, is a species gap.

Now, it can be terribly painful and anxiety-provoking to stand
with one foot in the old world and one foot in the new. But the
marvelous and hopeful thing is that nature, in its infinite wisdom,
has given us the means to participate consciously in our own evolution. We can become, in a sense, co-creators with the cosmos. We
can systematically work on ourselves in a safe, reliable manner that
can help us to make a quantum leap over the species gap.

That is what meditation and other spiritual disciplines are all about.
The test of their value is whether they are in tune with the biological
imperative to evolve, to advance the refinement and intensity of
consciousness on Earth.

The perennial argument against utopia, against the development
of the New Age, against the coming of the Kingdom, has been:
human nature. We are forever flawed, the argument goes. But my
reply is this: *human nature is changing*. There is an evolutionary
advance taking place in the world today as a new and higher form

of humanity takes control of the planet. "Control," of course, means living in respectful recognition of intimate interdependence. It means living harmoniously with the planet—and therefore surviving the coming global crises while the older species dies out from a massive overdose of irrationalism. Quite simply, the new breed is psychologically adapted to the altered conditions nature is imposing as it restores the balance that the Homo sapiens ignored for so long.

Homo noeticus is the name I give to the emerging form of humanity. Noetics is a term meaning the study of consciousness, and that activity is a primary characteristic of members of the new breed. Because of their deepened awareness and self-understanding, the traditionally imposed forms, controls and institutions of society are barriers to their full development. Their changed psychology is based on expression of feeling, not suppression. Their motivation is cooperative and loving, not competitive and aggressive. Their logic is multilevel/integrated/simultaneous, not linear/sequential/either-or. Their sense of identity is embracing-collective, not isolated-individual. Their psychic abilities are used for benevolent and ethical purposes, not harmful and immoral ones. The conventional ways of society do not satisfy them. The search for new ways of living and new institutions concerns them. They seek a culture founded in higher consciousness, a culture whose institutions are based on love and wisdom, a culture that fulfills the perennial philosophy.

Although *Homo noeticus* is the name I give to the new form of humanity, to the offspring of man, there have been other names proposed, and certainly others before me have suggested the emergency of a higher humanity. Aurobindo, Teilhard de Chardin, Nietzsche and Gopi Krishna are notable among them. Occult traditions such as Theosophy and Anthroposophy also state it explicitly. One of the most memorable statements of this view was given by R. M. Bucke on the last page of his classic *Cosmic Consciousness:*

> . . . just as, long ago, self-consciousness appeared in the best
> specimens of our ancestral race in the prime of life, and
> gradually became more and more universal and appeared in
> the individual at an earlier and earlier age, until, as we see
> now, it has become almost universal and appears at the
> average of about three years—so will Cosmic Consciousness
> become more and more universal earlier in the individual life

until the race at large will possess this faculty. The same race
and not the same; for a Cosmic Conscious race will not be
the race which exists today, any more than the present race of
men is the same race which existed prior to the evolution of
self-counsciousness. The simple truth is, that there has lived
on the earth, "appearing at intervals," for thousands of years
among ordinary men, the first faint beginnings of another
race; walking the earth and breathing the air with us, but at
the same time walking another earth, and breathing another
air of which we know little or nothing, but which is, all the
same, our spiritual life, as its absence would be our spiritual
death. This new race is in act of being born from us, and in
the near future it will occupy and possess the earth.

For the majority of westerners, however, the most familiar term
for this experience was given to it two millennia ago by Jesus of
Nazareth.

When Jesus spoke of himself, why did he principally use the term
"Son of Man?" Others called him the Son of God, but Jesus most
often referred to himself as the Son of Man, the offspring of humanity.
Moreover, he told those around him that they would be higher than
the angels and that those things which he did, they would do also,
and greater (John 14:12).

The reason for this is that Jesus was aware of himself as a finished
specimen of the new humanity which is to come—the new humanity
which is to inherit the earth, establish the Kingdom, usher in the
New Age. His mission and his teaching have at their heart the
development of a new and higher state of consciousness *on a species-
wide basis* rather than the sporadic basis seen earlier in history when
an occasional adept or avatar such as Buddha or Krishna appeared.
His unique place in history is based upon his unprecedented realization of the higher intelligence, the divinity, the Ground of Being
incarnated in him—the ground which is the source of all Becoming.

The Aramaic term for the Greek word "Christ" is *M'skekha*, from
which we get "messiah." It is a title, not a last name, and although
it is conventionally translated as "anointed," it really means "perfected" or "enlightened" or "the ideal form of humanity." Thus,
Jesus was an historical person, a human becoming; but Christ, the
Christos, is an eternal transpersonal condition of being to which we

must all someday come. Jesus did not say that this higher state of consciousness realized in him was his alone for all time. Nor did he call us to worship him. Rather, he called us to *follow* him, to follow in his steps, to learn from him, from his example, to live a God-centered life of selfless compassionate service to the world *as if we were Jesus himself*. He called us to share in the new condition, to enter a new world to be one in the supramental Christ consciousness which alone can dispel the darkness of our minds and renew our lives. He did not call us to be Christians; he called us to be Christed. In short, Jesus aimed at *duplicating* himself by fostering the development of *many* Jesuses. He aimed, as the New Testament declares, to make all one in Christ. And who is Christ? St. Paul tells us that Christ is the Second Adam, the founder of a new race.

The Kingdom is within us. Divinity is our birthright, our inheritance, nearer to us than hand and foot, but the eye will not see and the ear will not hear. Jesus called people to awaken, to change their ways, to repent. The very first words he spoke to humanity in his public ministry were, "The time is fulfilled, and the Kingdom of God is at hand; repent, and believe in the gospel." (Mark 1:14, Matthew 4:17) This is his central teaching and commandment.

But notice that word: repent. Over the centuries it has become misunderstood and mistranslated, so that today people think it merely means feeling sorry for their sins. This is an unfortunate debasement of Jesus' teaching. The Aramaic word that Jesus used is *tob*, meaning "to return," "to flow back into God." The sense of this concept comes through best in the Greek word first used to translate it. That word is *metanoia* and, like *tob*, it means something far greater than merely feeling sorry for misbehavior. Metanoia has two etymological roots. Meta means "to go beyond," "to go higher than." And noia comes from *nous*, meaning "mind." It is the same root from which Teilhard de Chardin developed his term, *noosphere*, and from which the word *noetic* comes. So the original meaning of metanoia is literally "going beyond or higher than the ordinary mental state." In modern terms, it means transcending self-centered ego and becoming God-centered.

This is the central experience Jesus sought for all people. This is the heart of Jesus' life and teaching, although it is now largely absent from the institutional Christian churches. Metanoia indicates a change of mind and behavior based on radical insight into the cause and effect of one's previous actions—insight arising from entry into a condition beyond the realm of time, space and causality. Metanoia is that profound state of consciousness which mystical experience aims at—the state in which we transcend or dissolve all the barriers of ego and selfishness that separate us from God. It is the "summum bonum" of human life. It is the state of *direct knowing, immediate perception* of our total unity with God. St. Paul said it very simply: the renewing of your mind in Christ.

In its best sense, then, metanoia means a radical conversion experience, a transformation of self based on a new state of awareness, a new state of consciousness—higher consciousness. It means repentance in its most fundamental dimension—that of "a turning about in the deepest seat of consciousness," as Lama Govinda phrases it. That turning-about is for the purpose of rebinding or re-tieing ourselves to the divine source of our being—the source we have lost awareness of. That is what religion is all about. *Re ligare:* to tie back, to tie again. That is true repentance—when we "get religion" in the sense of becoming aware of our inescapable ties to God, the creator, preserver and redeemer of the cosmos.

When we are rebound to God, the true meaning of sin becomes apparent. Sin means literally "missing the mark." Sin is not merely misbehavior. It is transgression of divine law or cosmic principle. It is a failure to be centered in God—to be "off target." Religion, then, is in its truest sense *an instrument for awakening us to the evolutionary process of growth to godhood*, which is the aim of all cosmic becoming. When we are guilty of sin, we are fundamentally missing the mark by failing to be God-conscious and all that it means for our behavior and thought.

Thus, the world is indeed in sin, but there is no remedy for it except to change consciousness. For in truth, God does not condemn us for our sins; rather, we condemn ourselves *by* our sins. And thus forgiveness by God is not necessary; it is there always, as unconditional love, the instant we turn in our hearts to God. As *A Course in Miracles* puts it, forgiveness must be offered *from ourselves to the world* for all the offenses, real or imaginary, we have stored in our hearts with rancor, bitterness and longing for revenge. *That* is the turning point; that is when ego transcendence truly begins and the glory of God starts to be revealed. To understand all is to forgive all. God understands all and forgives all and loves all. Love is therefore the greatest "revenge" we can seek against enemies and those who treat us spitefully and wrongly. Is that not precisely what Jesus taught?

There will never be a better world until there are better people in it, and the means for attaining that are democratically available to everyone through the grace and unconditional eternal love of God. If that grace and love were to be withdrawn for even an instant, the entire cosmos would be annihilated. To become aware of that fact is no easy task. But there is no substitute for growth to higher consciousness: recognition that all is God and there is only God. The metanoia process, when completed, results in a state of awareness that Jesus himself had when he said: "I and the Father are one."

That is what Jesus taught and demonstrated—cosmic consciousness, the Christic state of mind, the peace that passeth understanding, the direct experience of divinity dwelling in us and all things, now and forever, creating us, living us, preserving us, urging us on to ever more inclusive states of being so that "he that believeth on me, the works that I do shall he do, and greater than these shall he do." (John 14:12)

The institutional Christian churches tell us that Jesus was the only Son of God, that he incarnated as a human in order to die on the cross as a penalty for our sins, and thereby save the world. But that is a sad caricature, a pale reflection of the true story. It turns Jesus into a magical fairy tale hero and Christianity into a cult of personality. The significance of incarnation and resurrection is not that Jesus was a human like us but rather that *we are gods like him*—or at least have the potential to be. This is the secret of all ages and all spiritual traditions. This is the highest mystery. The Christian tradition, rightly understood, seeks to have us all become Jesuses, one in Christ— beyond all the darkness of mind that results in the evil and suffering so widespread in the world. Jesus himself pointed out this is what the Judaic tradition, which he fulfilled, is all about when he said, "Is it not written in your law, 'I said, you are gods'?" (John 10:34).

Jesus showed us the way. He demonstrated in his life and explained in his teaching that we all have the potential—the God-given right— to enter the Kingdom, to be healed of our sense of separation and alienation, to overcome sin and fear of death—all of which are rooted in the egoic self-sense—and to become whole and holy. We all have this potential, given not by "my" Father but, as the Lord's Prayer says, by *our* Father. Jesus showed in his life, his death and his resurrection that we are eternal celestrial beings whose home is the universe. He showed that heaven is a present reality, not a future reward. He showed that the death of the body is not the destruction of our consciousness, that the Christ consciousness which embodied itself in the man Jesus transcends the known facts of physics and biology, and actually controls conventionally understood physics and biology. He showed that the Christ consciousness was, is and ever shall be present among us, faithfully calling us to reunion, world without end, for it is the source of all creation. So rather than saying that Jesus was the Christ, it is more accurate to say: the Christ was Jesus.

The significance of Jesus, therefore, it not as a vehicle of salvation but as a *model of perfection*, which we must seek to become. This is why the proper attitude toward him is one of reverence, not worship. Jesus showed us the way to a higher state of being and called upon us to realize it, to make it real, actual—individually and as the race. This is the true meaning of being born again—dying to the past and the old sense of self through a change of consciousness. To enter the Kingdom we must die and be born again, we must become as a little child. From the perspective of metanoia, the meaning of Jesus' injunction is clear. To re-enter the state of innocence that infants exhibit, we do not merely regress to an infantile level, forsaking our mature faculties. Instead, we *pro*gress through transcendence of the illusion of ego and all its false values, attitudes and habits. We enter a guileless state of mind without forsaking the better qualities of adulthood. We optimize, rather than maximize, childhood, becoming childlike, not childish. Superficial values and capriciousness are out-grown, so that we function in the service of a transcendent purpose, offering our life's work to God moment-to-moment rather than seek-ing self-glorification and some consoling distant reward in this world or the next. We discover that heaven and hell are not remote places; they are states of consciousness. Heaven is union with God, hell is separation from God, and the difference is not measured in miles but in surrender of ego and self-centeredness.

Jesus showed us the way to the Kingdom, but he will not—indeed, cannot—magically take anyone there. That depends on your own effort. And even then, the timing is unknown. God's grace is still the final factor in crossing the planes of consciousness. Nevertheless, the effort should be made, *must* be made. Like the climber who went up Mt. Everest simply because it was there, sooner or later every human being will feel a call from the cosmos to ascend to godhead. That is our historical love affair with the divine. And as Jesus said, if you ask for bread, you will not be given stones. Knock and it shall be opened unto you.

There is no way to enter the Kingdom except to ascend in consciousness to the Father. That is what the Christian tradition—and, indeed, every true religion—is all about: a system of teachings (both theory and practice) about growth to higher consciousness. That is the key to the Kingdom. But this, by and large, has been lost to the understanding of contemporary Christendom. Instead, Jesus and the Bible are idolized, and heaven is said to be located somewhere in outer space. Awareness of inner space—of consciousness and the need to cultivate it—is sadly lacking.

The original form of baptism, for example, was apparently an initiatory practice in which the person—a convert who would have been an adult prepared through study of spiritual disciplines—was held under water to the point of nearly drowning. This near-death experience was likely to induce an out-of-body projection such as many near-death experiencers report today. The baptized person would thereby directly experience resurrection—the transcendence of death, the reality of metaphysical worlds and the supremacy of Spirit. He would receive a dramatic and unmistakable demonstration of the reality of the spiritual body or celestial body that St. Paul speaks of (apparently referring to his own personal experience with out-of-body projection) in I Corinthians 15:40-44. The degenerate forms of baptism practiced today—even those involving bodily immersion—are tragic debasements of the original purpose and meaning of baptism in the Judeo-Christian tradition. (However, I am not implicitly advocating a return to it because much safer, less riskier methods of inducing out-of-body projection are available today. The present symbolic use of baptism is justifiable if it is supplemented with necessary understanding of its true but esoteric significance.)

Matthew 11:29-30 suggests other spiritual practices which Jesus taught to his disciples and an inner circle: "Take my yoke upon you . . . my yoke is easy." The word "yoke" is conventionally understood to mean "burden" or "work." However, it is better understood in the sense of Sanskrit *yug*, meaning "to yoke or join." It is the root from which "yoga" comes, and yoga is a system of spiritual practices designed to accelerate personal growth and development, physically, mentally and spiritually, so that the yogi attains union with the Divine. That yoking with God was precisely the aim of Jesus' teaching. Thus, esoteric Christianity understands the verses to mean "the practices I prescribe for growth to Christ consciousness."

So long as people believe in an unbridgable gulf between themselves and that which Jesus demonstrated, Christianity will not have accomplished its mission. So long as the focus of attention remains on a naive, romanticized image of the historical person Jesus rather that on his transpersonal Christic demonstration of how to bridge the gulf between God and humanity, Christianity will not have carried out its founder's intent. "Building bridges"—that should be the main thrust of Christianity. Interestingly, this is explicitly acknowledged in the Roman Catholic tradition because its supreme authority, the Pope, is technically termed the Pontifex Maximus, which is Latin for "supreme bridgemaker." Again, however, the keepers of this tradition have not retained understanding of that which they retain.

At present, Christianity tends to demand blind faith, rote words and mechanical behavior. This leaves people empty and unfulfilled. But the cosmic calling we humans have will not be denied forever, despite the ignorance of religious institutions. The Holy Spirit, the life force, will simply move on to new forms, leaving fossils behind.

But if the human potential that Jesus demonstrated is understood to be within us, if the capacity to grow to godlike stature is directly experienced by all Christendom as the key to the Kingdom, then Christianity will fulfill its purpose by encouraging people to evolve, to transform themselves, to rise to a higher state. For we are not simply human beings. We are also human becomings, standing between two worlds, two ages. The marvelous thing about us as nature-becoming-aware-of-itself-as-God is that each of us has the latent ability to take conscious control of our own evolution, to build our own bridge, and thereby become a member of the new age, the new humanity. As St. John recorded the words of Jesus during his visionary experience on Patmos, "Behold, I make all things new." (Rev 21:5)

In the course of this change, there are stages that can be presented in a simple formulation: From orthonoia to metanoia through paranoia. We grow from orthonoia—that is, the common, everyday state of ego-centered mind—to metanoia only by going through paranoia, a state in which the mind is deranged (that is, taken apart) and rearranged through spiritual discipline so that a clear perception of reality might be experienced. Conventional western psychologies regard paranoia as a pathological breakdown. It often is, of course, but seen from this perspective, it is not necessarily always so. Rather, it can be breakthrough—not the final breakthrough, to be sure, but a necessary stage of development on the way to realizing the Kingdom.

Paranoia is a condition well-understood by mystical and sacred traditions. The spiritual disciplines that people practice under the guidance of a guru or master are designed to ease and quicken the passage through paranoia so that the practitioner does not get lost in the labyrinth of inner space and become a casualty.

Because metanoia has by and large not been experienced by the founders of western psychology and psychotherapy, paranoia has not been fully understood in our culture. It is seen as an aberrated dead end rather than a necessary precondition to higher consciousness. It is not understood that the confusion, discomfort and suffering experienced in paranoia are due entirely to the destruction of an illusion, ego. The less we cling to that illusion, the less we suffer.

The world's great spiritual systems, however, understand the psychology of this situation very well, and have developed procedures for curing it by disburdening people of their false self-image, their false identity. It is no accident that society's models of the ideal human being include many saints and holy people. These self-transcendent, God-realized individuals have been revered for many reasons: their compassion, devotion and serenity, their inspirational words of wisdom, their virtuous service to the world. What has been their motivation? Each of them, in his own way arising from his particular culture or tradition, has discovered the secret of the ages, the truth of the saying, "Let go and let God." When the ego-sense is relaxed, when a sense of the infinite and eternal replaces our usual narrow self-centeredness with all its passing, unsatisfying fantasies, there is no longer a mental basis for fear, hatred, anxiety, anger, attachment, desire. Instead, the perfectly harmonious functioning of the cosmos operates through us—and the cosmos is always in balance, always at peace with itself.

The Christian message is essentially a call to be universal—a call to become cosmically conscious. It is a call to place God at the center of ourselves, not through blind faith but through insightful awareness, not through rigid adherence to ritual and dogma but through graceful expression of cosmic principles. It is a call to "be as gods."

Thus, Jesus could speak of what is called "the Second Coming" as the end of the age, the end of history, the end of the world. Waking up from the illusion of ego, from the dream of worldly life, into God-conscious reality does indeed end the world. It ends the world not as global destruction but as transcendence of time, space and causality. Thus also, those Christian preachers who are predicting Armageddon and the end of the world soon may be right—because our culture is indeed critically close to global holocaust—but if they should prove to be right, they will be right for the wrong reasons.

For in the deepest sense, there is no Second Coming at all. The Bible does not speak of "two" comings. Aramaic scholar Dr. Rocco Errico, points out the actual meaning of the phrase is "the coming of Christ." This is confirmed by the passage in Matthew that reports Christ never left humanity: "Lo, I am with you always even unto the end of the world." (Matthew 28:20)

Thus, the final appearance or coming of Christ will be a *worldwide spiritual* appearance, free from all physical limitations. Errico writes, "At that time, the consciousness of mankind will have been raised to a spiritual level so that every eye will see nothing but good. Man will realize the spiritual life and kingdom, and at the coming of the Christ, the whole world will recognize him. His kingdom will be established and the world will be ready to receive him."

Today the world stands critically close to global holocaust. But a problem cannot be solved at the level that generated it. The solution to the problem of history, therefore, will not be found within history— that is, within the state of consciousness which generated history and the nightmare of contemporary world affairs. It is ego which generates time, temptation and trouble.

The answer to this emergency is emergence. The only way out of history into the Kingdom of God, the only way out of our precarious world situation into a New Age is a change of consciousness, a transcendence of the false sense of self from which all destructive human behavior arises. Only metanoia—the emergence of Christ-in-us—can provide the means whereby reality is seen clearly and an enlightened global cuture is possible. And that is precisely what is happening right now.

The Son of Man showed us the way to that higher state of being— the same beckoning evolutionary advance that other enlightened teachers of humanity have shown us at other times and places. I do not mean to present Jesus as the sole path to cosmic consciousness. That would be further debasement of his teaching. We have also been taught by Buddha and Krishna, by Lao Tsu and Moses, Mohammed, Rama, Zoroaster, Quetzalcoatl, Guru Nanak, Mahavira. The human race has been guided by many other evolutionary forerunners who have given us the world's religions, sacred traditions, spiritual paths, metaphysical philosophies and occult mystery schools. They have differed in various emphases and in cultural orientations, but the core truth of them all is the same: *Thou shalt evolve to a higher state of being and ultimately return to the Godhead which is your very self, your ever-present Divine Condition prior to all conditions, names and forms.*

We have the teachings and prophecies from these channels of truth. We have the technical instruction in their holy scriptures. We have information of the most advanced sort from many equally valuable sources, but we have not put it into practice.

This hardness of heart, this resistance to the evolutionary urge, has brought us to what I see as the most critical juncture in our history. The name of the game is survivolution, but no one is guaranteed a place in the Kingdom—within the space of a lifetime, at least. Nature can be pitiless with regard to the individual. Floods, earthquakes, volcanic eruptions, tidal waves, tornadoes, hurricanes, drought, pestilence and famine are no respecters of person or place. It is the species that counts. That is the way evolution works. Many trials and tribulations are ahead for us as we learn to play the cosmic game of evolving in consciousness. There will be many casualties among those who are slow to adapt in these accelerated-learning times. It has always been that way. The species that does not learn to adapt to new conditions goes the way of the dinosaur. But what comes afterward has always been an evolutionary advance.

If Planet Earth should end up as just a blinding flash in the night sky, or as a sterile piece of rock, from the cosmic point of view it will be the loss of just one lifebearing planet circling a minor star in a middle-sized galaxy among the billions of galaxies—just an evolutionary experiment that failed. There are billions of other worlds where evolution of intelligent lifeforms is probably going on. That terminal flash for the earth can happen, but it need not. The source of our being is calling to us through innumerable forms and channels—through nature and through enlightened teachers—calling us to awaken to our true identity and to carry that knowledge forward in the emergence of a higher form of life. Salvation, *liberation or enlightenment* is possible for us at every moment—and that is the key to avoiding species suicide and to transforming, rather than destroying, the earth.

But the choice is always ours. We can listen to nature in its many forms and learn—or we can shut ourselves off from the information and warnings that the cosmos is always giving us. Nature may be pitiless, but it is not unloving. Like a stern but compassionate parent who wants its children to grow up wise and strong, nature gives us hard lessons. But they are always intended for our benefit.

We live in a benevolent universe that nourishes us far better than most realize. But real learning can take place only in a condition of freedom. School is nearly out for *Homo sapiens*. If we survive the coming holocausts, it will surely be a better world, a New Age. And we *can* survive. We are free to survive and evolve. Nature wants us to survive and evolve. But the choice is always ours.

CHAPTER NINE

The Buddhist Path and Social Responsibility

JACK KORNFIELD, PH.D.

One of the most important questions we come to in spiritual practice is how to reconcile service and responsible action in the world with a meditative life based on nonattachment, letting go, and coming to understand the ultimate emptiness of all conditioned things. Do the values that lead us to actively give, serve, and care for one another differ from the values that lead us deep within ourselves on a journey of liberation and awakening? To consider this question, we must first learn to distinguish among four qualities central to spiritual practice—*love, compassion, sympathetic joy,* and *equanimity*— and what might be called their "near enemies." Near enemies may seem to be very close to these qualities and may even be mistaken for them, but they are not fundamentally alike.

The near enemy of love is attachment. Attachment masquerades as love. It says, "I love this person as long as he or she doesn't change. I'll love you if you'll love me back. I'll love that if it will be the way I want it." This isn't love at all—it is attachment—and attachment is very different from love. Love allows, honors, and appreciates; attachment grasps, demands, needs, and aims to possess. Attachment offers love only to certain people; it is exclusive. Love, in the sense that the Buddha used the word *metta* is a universal, nondiscriminating feeling of caring and connectedness, even toward those whom we may not approve of or like. We may not condone their behavior, but we cultivate forgiveness. Love is a powerful tool that transforms any situation. It is not passive acquiescence. As the Buddha said, "Hatred never ceases through hatred. Hatred only ceases through love." Love embraces all beings without exception, and discards ill will.

One near enemy of compassion is pity. Instead of feeling the openness of compassion, pity says, "Oh, that poor person is suffering!" Pity sets up a separation between oneself and others, a sense of distance and remoteness from the suffering of others that is affirming and gratifying to the ego. Compassion, on the other hand, recognizes the suffering of another as a reflection of one's own pain: "I understand that; I suffer in the same way. It's a part of life." Compassion is shared suffering.

Another near enemy of compassion is grief. Compassion is not grief. It is not an immersion in or identification with the suffering of others that leads to an anguished reaction. Compassion is the tender readiness of the heart to respond to one's own or another's pain without grief or resentment or aversion. It is the wish to dissipate suffering. Compassion embraces those experiencing sorrow, and eliminates cruelty from the mind.

The third quality, sympathetic joy, is the ability to feel joy in the happiness of others. The near enemy of this state is comparison—our need to conclude that we are superior to, inferior to, or even equal to someone else. This need to assess ourselves in relation to someone else's experience, or to look for affirmation in relation to someone else's life is a source of pain and delusion in the mind. Sympathetic joy is the source of great personal happiness; it embraces those enjoying happiness and discards dislike and jealousy.

The near enemy of equanimity is unintelligent indifference or callousness. We appear serene if we say, "I'm not attached. I don't care what happens anyway because it's all transitory." We feel a certain peaceful relief because we withdraw from experience and from the energies of life. But true equanimity is not a withdrawal; it is a balanced engagement with all aspects of life. It is opening to the whole of life with composure and with balance of mind, seeing the nature of all things. Equanimity embraces the loved and the unloved, the agreeable and the disagreeable, and pleasure and pain; it eliminates clinging and aversion.

Although everything is empty, we nevertheless honor the reality of form. As Zen Master Dogen says: "Flowers fall with our attachment, and weeds spring up with our aversion." Knowing deeply that all will change—that the world of conditioned phenomena is insubstantial, we are fully present and in harmony with it.

Attachment, pity, comparison, and indifference are all ways of backing away from life out of fear. Spirituality is not a removal or escape from life. It is seeing the world with a deeper vision that is not self-centered, a vision that sees through dualistic views to the underlying interconnectedness of all of life. It is the discovery of freedom in the very midst of our bodies and minds.

In the Eightfold Path the Buddha talks about Right Thought or Right Aspiration, which has three aspects. The first is cultivating thoughts that are free from desire, discarding transitory experience, and developing a sense of inner contentment. The second is cultivating thoughts free from ill will and resentment; this means cultivating thoughts of compassion and gentleness. The third is cultivating thoughts free from cruelty; this means nourishing the forces of kindness and active love within us. With a sense of Right Aspiration we can use all the different situations we face as stepping stones. This is the thread that unites all the moments of our lives. Each moment becomes an opportunity.

While in India, I spoke with Vimala Thaker about the question of meditation and activity in the world. Vimala had worked for many years in rural development and land redistribution projects when, as a result of her longtime interest in Krishnamurti's teachings, she began to teach meditation and devoted many years to this. She has recently returned to development work and to helping the hungry and homeless, teaching much less than she once had. I asked her why she decided to go back to the type of work she had been doing years before. She replied: "Sir, I am a lover of life, and as a lover of life, I cannot keep out of any activity of life. If there are people who are hungry for food, my response is to help feed them. If there are people who are hungry for truth, my response is to help them discover it. I make no distinction."

The Sufis have a saying, "Praise Allah, and tie your camel to the post." Pray, but also make sure you do what is necessary in the world. Meditate, but manifest your understanding of this spiritual experience. Balance your realization of emptiness with a sense of compassion and impeccability to guide your life.

Seeing emptiness means seeing that all of life is like a bubble in a rushing stream, a play of light and shadow, a dream. It means understanding that this tiny planet hangs in the immensity of space amidst millions and billions of stars and galaxies, that all of human history is like one second compared to the billions of years of earth's history, and that it will all be over very soon and no one is really going anywhere. This context helps us to let go amidst the seeming seriousness of our problems, and to enter life with a sense of lightness and ease. Impeccability means that we must realize how precious life is, even though it is transient and ephemeral, and how each of our actions and words affect all beings around us in a most profound way. There is nothing inconsequential in this universe, and we need to respect this fact personally and act reponsibly in accordance with it.

One could make a very convincing case for simply devoting oneself to meditation. Does the world need more medicine and energy and buildings and food? Not really. There are enough resources for all of us. There is starvation and poverty and disease because of ignorance, prejudice, and fear, because we hoard materials and create wars over imaginary geographic boundaries and act as if one group of people is truly different from another group somewhere else on the planet. What the world needs is not more oil, but more love and generosity, more kindness and understanding. The most fundamental thing we can do to help this war-torn and suffering world is to genuinely free ourselves from the greed and fear and divisive views in our own minds, and then help others to do the same. Thus, a spiritual life is not a privilege; it is a basic responsibility.

But there is also a convincing argument for devoting oneself entirely to service in the world. I have only to mention the recent horror of Cambodia, the violence in Central America, the starvation in Africa— situations in which the enormity of suffering is almost beyond comprehension. In India alone, 350 million people live in such poverty that one day's work pays for only one meal. I once met a man in Calcutta who was sixty-four years old and pulled a rickshaw for a living. He had been doing it for forty years and had ten people dependent on him for income. He had gotten sick the year before for ten days; within a week money ran out and they had nothing to eat. How can we possibly let this happen? Forty children per minute die from starvation while twenty five million dollars per minute are spent on arms. We must respond. We cannot hold back or look away. We have painful dilemmas to face. Where should we put our energy? If we decide to meditate, even choosing which type of meditation to practice can be confusing.

The starting point is to look directly at suffering, both the suffering in the world and the suffering in our own hearts and minds. This is the beginning of the teaching of the Buddha, and the beginning of our own understanding of the problem of world peace. At this moment on our planet, there are hundreds of millions of people who are starving or malnourished. Hundreds of millions of people are so impoverished that they have little or no shelter and clothing, or they are sick with diseases that we know how to cure, but they cannot afford the medicine or do not have access to it.

For us to look directly at the situation is not a question of ceremony or of religion. We have a mandate to look in a very deep way at the sorrow and suffering that exists now in our world, and to look at our individual and collective relationship to it, to bear witness to it, to acknowledge it instead of running away. The suffering is so great that we do not want to look. We close our minds. We close our eyes and hearts.

Opening ourselves to all aspects of experience is what is asked of us if we want to do something, if we want to make a change, if we want to make a difference. We must look at the world honestly, unflinchingly, and directly, and then look at ourselves and see that sorrow is not just out there, external, but it is also within ourselves. It is our own fear, prejudice, hatred, desire, neurosis, and anxiety. It is our own sorrow. We have to look at it and not run away from it. In opening ourselves to suffering, we discover that we can connect with and listen to our own hearts.

In the heart of each of us, a great potential exists for realizing truth, for experiencing wholeness, for going beyond the shell of the ego. The problem is that we become so busy and lost in our own thinking that we lose our connection with our own true nature. If we look deeply, we discover that the wholeness of our being comes to know and express itself both through meditation and through sharing ourselves with others, and the course to take is very clear and immediate. Whether it is an *inner* or an *outer* path, it has enormous power to affect the world.

I spend most of my time teaching meditation. A few years ago, when many thousands of Cambodian people were fleeing the violence in their homeland only to face starvation and disease in refugee camps in Thailand, something in me said, "I've got to go there," and so I went. I knew the people and a few of the local languages. After being there for a short time, trying to assist, I returned to this country to guide intensive meditation retreats. I did not deliberate much at the time about whether or not I should go to work in the refugee camps. I felt that it had to be done, and I went and did it. It was immediate and personal.

The spiritual path does not present us with a stylized pat formula for everyone to follow. It is not a matter of imitation. We can not be Mother Theresa or Gandhi or the Buddha. We have to be ourselves. We must discover and connect with our unique expression of the truth. We must learn to listen to and trust ourselves.

There are two great forces in the world. One is the force of killing. People who are not afraid to kill govern nations, make wars, and control much of the activity of our world. There is great strength in not being afraid to kill. The other source of strength in the world— the real strength—is in people who are not afraid to die. These are people who have touched the very source of their being, who have looked into themselves in such a deep way that they understand and acknowledge and accept death, and in a way, have already died. They have seen beyond the separateness of the ego's shell, and they bring to life the fearlessness and the caring born of love and truth. This is a force that can meet the force of someone who is not afraid to kill.

This is the power Gandhi called *satyagraha*, the force of truth, and the force that he demonstrated in his own life. When India was partitioned, millions of people became refugees—Muslims and Hindus moved from one country to another. There was horrible violence and rioting. Tens of thousands of troops were sent to West Pakistan to try to quell the terrible violence, while Gandhi went to what was then East Pakistan. He walked from village to village asking people to stop the bloodshed. Then he fasted. He said he would take no more food until the violence and insanity stopped, even if it meant his own death. And the riots stopped. They stopped because of the power of love, because Gandhi cared about something—call it truth or life or whatever you wish—it was something much greater than Gandhi the person. This is the nature of our spiritual practice, whatever form it may take. Living aligned with truth is more important than either living or dying. This understanding is the source of incredible power and energy, and must be manifested through *love, compassion, sympathetic joy,* and *equanimity.*

One of the exquisite experiences of my travels in India was going to the holy city of Benares by the Ganges River. Along the river bank are ghats where people bathe as a purification, and there are also ghats where people bring corpses to be cremated. I had heard about the burning ghats for years and had always thought that being there would be a heavy experience. I was rowed down river in a little boat, and up to the ghats where there were twelve fires going. Every half-hour or so, a new body would be carried down to the fires as people chanted "Rama Nama Satya hei," the only truth is the name of God. I was surprised. It was not dreadful at all; it was peaceful, quiet, and very sane. There was as a recognition that life and death are part of the same process and therefore death need not be feared.

There is a deep joy that comes when we stop denying the painful aspects of life, and instead allow our hearts to open to and accept the full range of our experience: life and death, pleasure and pain, darkness and light. Even in the face of the tremendous suffering in the world, there can be this joy, which comes not from rejecting pain and seeking pleasure, but rather from our ability to meditate and open ourselves to the truth. Spiritual practice begins by allowing ourselves to face our own sadness, fear, anxiety, desperation—to die to the ego's ideas about how things should be, and to love and accept the truth of things as they are.

With this as our foundation, we can see the source of suffering in our lives and in the world around us. We can see the factors of greed, hatred, and ignorance that produce a sense of separation. If we look directly, we can see the end of suffering because its end is an acknowledgement and a clear understanding of the oneness of light and dark, up and down, sorrow and joy. We can see all these things without attachment and without separation.

We must look at how we have created and enforced separation. How have we made this a world of "I want this; I want to become that; this will make me safe; this will make me powerful?" Race, nationality, age, and religion all enforce separation. Look into yourself and see what is "us" and what is "them" for you. When there is a sense of "us," then there is a sense of "other." When we can give this up, then we can give up the idea that strength comes from having more than others, or from having the power to kill others. When we give this up, we give up the stereotype of love as a weakness.

There is a story from the Zen tradition about an old monk in China who practiced very hard meditation for many years. He had a good mind and became very quiet, but never really touched the end of "I" and "others" in himself. He never came to the source of complete stillness or peace out of which transformation comes. So he went to the Zen Master and said, "May I please have permission to go off and practice in the mountains? I have worked for years as a monk and there is nothing else I want but to understand this: the true nature of myself, of this world." And the master, knowing that he was ripe, gave him permission to leave.

He left the monastery, took his bowl and a few possessions, and walked through various towns toward the mountains. He had left the last village behind and was going up a little trail when there appeared before him, coming down the trail, an old man carrying a great big bundle on his back. This old man was actually the Bodhisattva, Manjusri, who is said to appear to people at the moment that they are ripe for awakening, and is depicted carrying the sword of discriminating wisdom that cuts through all attachment, all illusion, and separateness. The monk looked at the old man, and the old man said, "Say, friend, where are you going?" The monk told his story. "I've practiced for all these years and all I want now is to touch that center point, to know that which is essentially true. Tell me, old man, do you know anything of this enlightenment?" The old man simply let go of the bundle; it dropped to the ground, and the monk was enlightened.

That is our aspiration and our task—to put it all down, to drop all of our clinging, condemning, identifying, our opinions and our sense of *I, me, mine*. The newly enlightened monk looked at the old man again. He said, "So now what?" The old man reached down, picked up the bundle again and walked off to town.

We want to put it all down, which means also to acknowledge where it begins. To see sorrow, to see suffering, to see pain, to see that we are all in it together, to see birth and death. If we are afraid of death and afraid of suffering, and we do not want to look, then we cannot put it down. We will push it away here and will grab it again there. When we have seen the nature of life directly, we can put it down. Once we put it down, then with understanding and compassion we can pick it up again. Then we can act effectively, even dramatically, without bitterness or self-righteousness. We can be motivated by a genuine sense of caring and of forgiveness, and a determination to live our lives well.

A number of years ago I attended a conference at which Mad Bear, an Iroquois medicine man spoke. He said, "For my presentation I'd like us to begin by going outside," and we all went out. He led us to an open field and then asked us to stand silently in a circle. We stood for a while in silence under a wide open sky, surrounded by fields of grain stretching to the horizon. Then Mad Bear began to speak, offering a prayer of gratitude. He began by thanking the earth-worms for aerating the soil so that plants can grow. He thanked the grasses that cover the earth for keeping the dust from blowing, for cushioning our steps, and for showing our eyes the greeness and beauty of their life. He thanked the wind for bringing rain, for cleaning the air, for giving us the life-breath that connects us with all beings. He spoke in this way for nearly an hour, and as we listened we felt the wind on our faces, and the earth beneath our feet, and we saw the grass and clouds, all with a sense of connectedness, gratitude, and love.

This is the spirit of our practice of mindfulness. Love—not the near enemy of attachment, but something much deeper—infuses our awareness, enables us to open to and accept the truth of each moment, to feel our intimate connectedness with all things, and to see the wholeness of life. Whether we are sitting in meditation or sitting somewhere in protest, that is our spiritual practice in every moment.

Presented at the Eighth Conference of the International Transpersonal Association (ITA) on *Individual Transformation and Universal Responsibility*, August 27-September 2, 1983, in Davos, Switzerland.

CHAPTER TEN

Transition to a New Consciousness

KARAN SINGH, PH.D.

The outstanding feature of the last quarter of the twentieth century is likely to be the collapse of the materialistic paradigm that has dominated world thought for many centuries. What may be called the Cartesian-Newtonian-Marxist paradigm has collapsed, and with it, the materialistic philosophies based upon that view, whether Marxist or Capitalist, have also failed. With the impact of post-Einsteinian physics, quantum mechanics, Heisenberg's Uncertainty Principle, Stanislav Grof's extended cartography of the psyche, and many other conceptual revolutions, the old structures have begun to crumble. Solid matter dissolves into waves of probability, and the new physics seems to be approaching the mystic vision of which seers and sages of all traditions have spoken.

At this crucial evolutionary crossroads, mankind is groping for a new model, a new philosophy, a new paradigm, a new consciousness to replace the old. And it is not coincidence that this is happening at a juncture when mankind is in supreme peril—not from another species, not from outer space, but from itself. From deep within the human psyche there has developed a terrible power that threatens not only our own generation but all life on this planet.

Ancient myths often illuminate the human predicament, and there is a powerful Hindu myth of the Churning of the Milky Ocean (the *Samudra-Manthana*), which speaks to us today across the millenia, symbolizing the long and tortuous evolution of consciousness on earth. In this great myth, the *Devas* and the *Asuras*, the dark and the bright powers, combined and cooperated in the churning of the ocean. This went on for aeons, until, at last, the great gifts began to emerge—*Kamadhenu*, the all-giving cow, and *Ucchaishravasa*, the divine horse; *Kalpavriksha*, the wish-fulfilling tree, and *Airavata*, the divine elephant. These and other great gifts appeared, and were happily divided between the two sides. The churning proceeded, as its ultimate objective was the *Amrita Kalasha*, the pot of ambrosia, the Elixir of Immortality for which even the gods crave.

Suddenly, without warning, the ocean started to boil with a deadly poison—the *Garala*—a new, malign dimension of which neither the *Devas* nor the *Asuras* had any knowledge. Rapidly the poison spread through the three worlds—the water, the land, and the skies. The churners fled helter-skelter in terror, striving to escape from the deadly fumes, forgetting all the gifts that they had accumulated. And then *Shiva-Mahadeva* appeared, the great, primal divinity who was aloof from the avarice and materialism of the *Devas* and the *Asuras*. He collected the poison in a cup and drank it, integrating it into his being. His neck turned blue as a result, hence one of his names *Neelkantha*, the blue-throated. Then the danger passed, order was restored. Chanting hymns to the glory of *Shiva*, the participants returned, the churning was resumed until finally the ambrosial pot appeared and the whole process was successfully completed.

This myth vividly illustrates the human predicament today. Prolonged churning has given man the great gifts of science and technology. There have been incredible breakthroughs in medicine, communications, agriculture, electronics, space travel, and cybernetics. We now have enough technology to ensure every human being on earth the necessary physical, intellectual, material, and spiritual resources for a full and healthy life.

And yet the poison is also upon us. Billions of dollars and rubles, pounds and francs, are spent every day on the manufacture of monstrous weapons with unprecedented power of destruction. It is estimated that there are now well over fifty thousand neuclear warheads, each a thousand times more powerful than the bombs that devastated Hiroshima and Nagasaki at the dawn of the nuclear age, each with more explosive force than that used by both sides in the entire World War II.

It is unnecessary to go into the catastrophic impact of a nuclear war, even a so-called limited one, which is a contradiction in terms. *The Day After*, gross understatement that it was, did help to focus our attention, as did Jonathan Schell's admirable book, *The Fate of the Earth*, and the new study by Carl Sagan and others called *The*

Cold and the Dark: The World After Nuclear War. It is now clear that we may commit not suicide but terricide, the destruction of our planet.

There is overwhelming evidence to show that any kind of nuclear war would not only shatter human civilization as we know it, but would poison the air and the oceans and render the planet virtually uninhabitable. When the dinosaurs bowed out after a reign of sixty-five million years they went comparatively gracefully. If and when we go, we will probably leave a charred and ravaged planet, capable of supporting only extremely primitive life. Whether this happens through political foolishness, miscalculation, accident—a flight of geese or a malfunctioning computer chip—matters little.

With all our tremendous knowledge, man has finally come to a single three-letter mantra—MAD—Mutually Assured Destruction. Thousands of years ago, at the dawn of human civilization, the Vedic seers had also discovered a three-letter mantra—AUM—as the symbol of the divinity that pervades the universe. And so in five thousand years we have travelled from AUM to MAD. This is human progress?

It is a sobering thought that we are a privileged generation, not only because we may be the first to see the dawn of the third millennium after Christ but also because we may be the last generation of human beings to inhabit this planet. Can we accept this possibility as passive spectators and drift mindlessly towards disaster? Can we acquiesce in a situation where one quarter of mankind is overfed and three quarters are underfed; where millions suffer from obesity and overeating while hundreds of millions waste slowly away from malnutrition, stunted in body and mind; where millions are overmedicated and hundreds of millions lack access even to elementary medical facilities? Can we close our ears to the cry of the deprived and the oppressed, while the world plunges on toward a rendezvous with the ultimate apocalypse?

If the answer to these questions is negative, as it must be, then we have to move toward global consciousness if we are to survive. We must move toward complementarity instead of competition, convergence instead of conflict, holism instead of hedonism. We must heal the split within the human psyche, gather the fragments of human consciousness and meld them into a glowing whole; we must effect a transition that will replace the present fractured and fragmented consciousness in the human race.

As the caterpiller undergoes the choiceless metamorphosis into a dazzling and irridescent butterfly, we must understand that our transition, too, is choiceless. Transitions are never painless, but we must accept the physical and psychological distress involved in abandoning a comfortable and familiar environment and leaping into a new and hitherto unknown dimension. Though this most crucial of all transitions for mankind will be a painful and protracted affair, the important question is whether it is possible. Can there be a substantial transformation of consciousness on this planet in time to prevent its destruction? Or is this particular adventure in planetary consciousness doomed to failure; is man a creature programmed for self-destruction? No one knows the answer, but the Bhagavad Gita teaches that we must act in the manner we feel to be right, and not be obsessed with the consequences; act not from our inflated or deflated egos but from the deepest recesses of our being. Indeed, at this juncture in planetary history, creative action is a spiritual imperative.

We are then led to inquire as to what exactly can be done to hasten the transition. I suggest a five-point program that could help in the process, provided it is widely publicized and acted upon. This is a program of which many elements are already in operation to some degree, but which needs to be coordinated and accelerated so that we can achieve a creative symbiosis.

The first requirement is to work out the philosophical underpinning of the new global consciousness. For this we must draw on many of mankind's traditions, both in the religious and secular mode, and also upon the latest insights of science. In the Vedas we have ideals that are startling in their contemporary relevance. Such concepts as the spiritual unity of all that exists, the divinity inherent in each human being, mankind as a single family, the harmony of religions, the welfare of all sections of society, for example, provide an ideological framework for the new consciousness; and the writings of great evolutionary thinkers of our century like Sri Aurobindo, Teilhard de Chardin, and Pandit Gopi Krishna can greatly help to refine and illuminate the new philosophy.

Once this is done, the tremendous resources of the modern mass media must be pressed into service so that these concepts become part of the mental structure of mankind. This is a task in which not only national governments and nonofficial agencies need to be involved, but even more importantly, international and multilateral organizations. This year happens to mark the fortieth anniversary of the founding of the United Nations. What better opportunity can there be for the United Nations to take the initiative in working towards creating a global consciousness? Other U.N. agencies, especially UNESCO and the U.N. University in Tokyo, should also be actively involved in this process.

Simultaneously, the third task is to set up a worldwide network linking the hundreds of groups and millions of people who acutely feel this great anxiety about our future. This must cut across all barriers of race or religion, nationality or ideology, sex or sexual preference, economic or social status. It must unite East and West, North and South, rich and poor, white and black, believer and atheist, into a massive, coordinated thrust to save mankind from annihilation. Organizations like the International Transpersonal Association (ITA) can play a pivotal role in helping this worldwide transition to a new mode of thinking relevant to the realities of this nuclear age.

The fourth task is the imperative necessity of halting the suicidal and now essentially meaningless nuclear arms race. With enough fissionable material already available to destroy every human being on this planet a dozen times over, the whole syndrome has become absurd, especially when we realize that an equivalent of ten days of this world's expenditure on armaments could permanently abolish hunger from the globe. While there are a number of nations with nuclear capability, it is really the rulers of the two superpowers (the contemporary *Devas* and *Asuras*) who will have to cooperate in any revival of sanity. We must try to create a tremendous pressure of public opinion and mobilize leaders of religious and philosophical thought so that the conscience of mankind can be heard.

Finally, any movement for the new global consciousness must revert and relate to an individual search for inner peace. In our own lives we must move toward a realization of the truth at the core of our being, and toward the higher consciousness that is the birthright of each of us. In the ultimate analysis, it is in the crucible of our individual selves that the poison around us can be contained and transformed into a new, global consciousness. In this lies the hope for individual salvation as well as the survival of this earth.

The ancient spiritual traditions of both East and West have always known that our planet is not just a ball of earth and stone, lava and water. A most dramatic illustration was provided by the unique first photograph of earth taken from outer space that showed our planet as a tiny speck of life and light against the unending vastness of outer space, pulsating with energy and with a strange, fragile beauty.

In the *Atharva Veda*, one of the world's most ancient scriptures, there is the magnificent *Bhumi Suktam*, Hymn to the Earth (X11.1) Composed over five thousand years ago by the great seer Atharvan, it speaks to us today with a new resonance, a fresh urgency. It has sixty-three verses, from which I have abstracted the twelve that follow (in translation by Abinash Chandra Bose).

Truth, eternal order that is great and stern,
Consecration, Austerity, Prayer and Ritual—
these uphold the Earth.
May she, Queen of what has been and will be,
make a wide world for us.

Earth which has many heights, and slopes
and the unconfined plains that bind men together,
Earth that bears plants of various healing powers,
may she spread wide for us and thrive.

Earth, in which lie the sea, the river and other waters,
in which food and cornfields have come to be,
in which lives all that breathes and that moves,
may she confer on us the finest of her yield.

Earth, which at first was in the water of the ocean,
and which sages sought with wondrous powers,
Earth whose heart was in eternal heaven,
wrapped in Truth, immortal,
may she give us luster and strength
in a most exalted state.

Earth, in which the waters, common to all,
moving on all sides, flow unfailingly, day and night,
may she pour on us milk in many streams,
and endow us with lustre.

Pleasant by thy hills, O Earth,
thy snow-clad mountains and thy woods!
O Earth—brown, black, red and multicolored—
the firm Earth protected by Indra,
on this Earth may I stand—unvanquished, unhurt, unslain.

I call to Earth, the purifier,
the patient Earth, growing strong through spiritual might.
May we recline on thee, O Earth, who bearest power and
    plenty,
and enjoy our share of food and molten butter.

May those that are thy eastern regions, O Earth,
and the northern and the southern and the western,
be pleasant for me to tread upon.
May I not stumble while I live in the world.

Whatever I dig from thee, Earth,
may that have quick growth again.
O purifier, may we not injure thy vitals or thy heart.

May Earth with people who speak various tongues,
and those who have various religious rites
according to their places of abode,
pour for me treasure in a thousand streams
like a constant cow that never fails.

May those born of thee, O Earth,
be, for our welfare, free from sickness and waste.
Wakeful through a long life, we shall become
bearers of tribute to thee.

Earth, my mother, set me securely with bliss
in full accord with heaven.
O wise one,
uphold me in grace and splendor.

This Earth has nurtured consciousness from the slime of the primeval ocean, billions of years ago, and has sustained the human race for countless centuries. Will we repay our debt by converting her into a burnt-out cinder circling the sun into eternity? Or will we so marshall our inner and outer resources so that even at this late hour we may succeed in making the crucial transition to the new consciousness? Time will tell. But if we do not make the transition, no one will be here to record our ending.

Presented at the Ninth Conference of the International Transpersonal Association (ITA) on *Tradition and Technology in Transition*, in Kyoto, Japan, April 1985.

CHAPTER ELEVEN

The Darkness of God: Theology After Hiroshima

JAMES GARRISON, PH.D.

The path to wisdom that Hiroshima and the advent of nuclear weapons challenge us to take is to the good of life itself. We are being summoned to direct our energies upon the creative source of life and values rather than upon specific values as they are expressed through the narrow provincialism of a particular group. This is and has been a primary ethical component of the Judaeo-Christian tradition from its inception. Indeed, it was a fundamental aspect of the mission of Jesus himself to break down the separateness and exclusiveness of the individuals and groups he encountered so that they could be receptive to the kingdom of God and openly responsive to one another. He taught them to love their neighbor as themselves, particularly the neighbor oppressed by the guilt induced by orthodox legalisms and social ostracism. As Henry Weiman puts it, Jesus "split the atom of human egoism."[1] His presence was like a catalyst inducing creative transformations in the persons who believed in him.

Weiman amplifies this observation concerning Jesus with a note that has striking similarity to the concept we shall be dealing with in relation to Hiroshima.

> The creative transformation power was not in the man Jesus, although it could not have occurred apart from him. Rather he was in it. It required many other things besides his own solitary self. It required the Hebrew heritage, the disciples with their particular capacity for this kind of responsiveness, and doubtless much else of which we have little knowledge.

The creative power lay in the interaction taking place between
these individuals. It transformed their minds, their
personalities, their appreciable world, and their community
with one another and with all men.[2]

What occurred in the group surrounding Jesus was the elevation
of a creative event, happening within the bounds of their history,
to a place of dominance and centrality in their lives. They understood
and believed the creative event to be Emmanuel, and they were
willing to open up the walls of their separateness to the transforming
power of Christ and the all-encompassing community of fellow-
believers. Their leap of faith was in their willingness to incorporate
a newly enacted historical event within their confessional heritage
and in allowing their old modes of understanding to be opened up
to the freedom of spirit at work in the new event. They experienced
thereby a new dimension of human possibility and could give witness
to the fact that the Christ event had produced a new order of human
awareness and potentiality.

We are being confronted in our day with the same necessity to
transform our old modes of understanding if the human race is to
survive. We must first of all be willing to recognize that what is
occurring is Emmanuel—God with us. To make this leap in consciousness, however, will be as difficult for us today as it was for
the Pharisees and Sadducees to make concerning Christ two thousand
years ago, steeped and secure as they were in their orthodox legalisms.
Yet, even as the early believers were able to see the handiwork and
overall control of God in the midst of the crucifixion and resurrection
of Christ, so too must we be willing to perceive God at work in the
atom bomb.

Hiroshima confronts us as never before with the imperative to
take the wrath of God seriously. We must be willing at long last to
give up our monopolar prejudice concerning God being merely an
expression of the Summum Bonum and capable of only love and
mercy and "goodness." We must recognize that God is the God of
all possibilities and that God utilizes all the instruments of power.
Ultimately, what we are witnessing in our day is a great attempt on
the part of the Godhead to reveal deeper dimensions of the divine
pleroma, and to compel us to explore even more deeply the mystery
of Christ crucified.

The second point we must recognize in order fully to appreciate the Hiroshima event is that, with the power of mass destruction in our hands, we have taken upon ourselves that last category attributed to God in the traditional view: the belief that God would end the world in apocalyptic judgment and then recreate heaven and earth. But what the apocalyptists believed was fixed by the counsel of God and brought to pass by divine will and action alone is now something within the realm of human decision. This means that we must internalize theologically both the terror and the salvation of the traditional Judaeo-Christian concept of apocalypse as something that will not be done to us by divine fiat alone, but as something that might well be done by us through our own decision, God working divine wrath through human arrogance. Hiroshima has humanized the eschaton.

To assert that Hiroshima represents an era of new dimensions of human power, while at the same time asserting that it points us to the darkness of God at work in Christ crucified, may sound contradictory. But it is not; it is complementary. Both are happening simultaneously and must be kept in a dialectical tension if we are to give any sense at all to the claim I shall be setting forth: that the relational encounter between God and humanity coheres relationally in a single event that draws each according to its degree of freedom and affects each according to its respective vulnerability. Hiroshima is the nexus point in our day when God and humanity meet to reveal deeper dimensions within the reality of both. As such, therefore, Hiroshima is numinous, holding forth to the eyes of faith the ambiguity involved in all creative events.

In order to speak of God in a way in which modern humanity can experience the power of this "unspeakable mystery," it is fundamental that we dispense with classical theism while remaining grounded in the biblical witness. This will be difficult, because for centuries the notions of classical theism were considered to be the biblical witness. However, the God of the Bible is much more alive and versatile than the straitjacket of theism allows for. Dispensing with theism will allow us to return to the Bible and see more profound dimensions of the God that Jews and Christians worship. What I wish to draw attention to before proceeding, therefore, are certain themes enunciated by the Judaeo-Christian confessional witness which will remain constant, for they form part of the distinctive claim of our religious heritage. They can be reworked but not dispensed with.

What emerges as basic to the concept of God that Hebrews developed, and which the Christians later amplified, is that God is at once the Cosmic Creator of heaven and earth and also inseparably linked with human history. For the Hebrews, God was an eminently social God who had made a covenant with humanity. The importance of this is that the historical element gives the cosmic dimension placement in space and time.

A second element in the Judaeo-Christian belief concerning God is in terms of divine creativity. "In the beginning God created . . ." are the opening words of the scriptures, an understanding inherent even in the name "Yahweh." God created the heavens and the earth; God created humankind; and God has been creatively active in human history ever since—redeeming the people of Israel from Egypt, making the convenant with them at Sinai, leading them through the vicissitudes of their history to the promised land, exiling them for their disobedience, forgiving them and bringing them again to Israel, finally becoming incarnate in their midst as Christ Jesus.

The creative activity of God in history is not limited to working salvifically only amongst the chosen people. God works the divine will in all nations, both to lift up and to bring down. This point is brought out most forcefully by Isaiah when he prophesies concerning Yahweh's punishment of Israel. It is clear to the prophet that Assyria is a tool in the hands of God.

> Ah, Assyria, the rod of my anger,
> the staff of my fury!
> Against a godless nation I send him,
> and against the people of my wrath I command him,
> to take spoil and seize plunder,
> and to tread them down like mire of the streets (Isa. 10.5–6).

Isaiah is quick to point out that although Assyria is being used by God, Assyria is unaware of it. The Assyrians think they are defeating Israel by their own power, saying

> By the strength of my hand I have done it,
> and by my wisdom, for I have understanding (13a).

Therefore, prophesies Isaiah, when the Lord has finished using Assyria to punish Israel, the Assyrians will in turn be punished for their "arrogant boasting" and "haughty pride" (12):

> Shall the axe vaunt itself over him who hews it,
>   or the saw magnify itself against him who wields it?
>   As if a rod should wield him who lifts it,
>   or as if a staff should lift him who is not wood (15)!

God is sovereign over history, working the divine will creatively in our midst. It is a creative activity with both light and shadow dimensions before which the believers can only kneel in awe, filled with both reverence and trembling.

These themes will be amplified as we proceed, for they must be understood if we are to perceive the handiwork of God in the atomic bombing of Hiroshima. What is important for our purposes here is to make clear that the assertion that God acts in history is the cornerstone of any Judeao-Christian ontology of God.

The modern hermeneutical challenge is to be concurrently so deeply rooted both "in God" and in the modern world as to create a relevant context of confessional witness. We must discern the hand of God in historical events in a way that touches modern humanity while remaining consistent with the ancient Judeao-Christian credo that history is "in God" and that God acts decisively and centrally in certain historical events which shape the whole.

There are two aspects which must be kept in a creative synthesis in order to grasp the presence of divinity in history: the aspect of historical fact and the aspect of confessional response. That Jesus died on the cross is the historical fact. That "Christ died for our sins in accordance with the scriptures" is the confessional response. Both are necessary components of the actual occurrence. Only when historical facts and confessional discernment interprentrate do we have history "in God": Heilsgeschichte.

The intersection of the historical event with the confessional response yields a dialectic that gives a dynamic quality to the biblical concept of divine action. The confession is not made static within the recitation of cosmogonic myth nor is it solidified into a juridical system of doctrine; instead, divine action is an evolving development made discernible within the continual interpenetration of new events with confessional heritage.

This can be seen in the prophecies of Deutero-Isaiah 40–55. After several centuries of Israelite nationhood, Assyria destroyed the ten northern tribes of Israel. Babylon then conquered the two remaining tribes, ruled by the house of David, and took them captive to Babylon. For seventy years they remained in exile. Then Persia moved against Babylon and Deutero-Isaiah prophesied that the Jews would be allowed to return to Jerusalem. This hope was crystalized by the campaign of King Cyrus of Persia, reflected in Isaiah 41.2–3 and 45.1–3, in which Cyrus defeats King Croesus of Lydia in 546 B.C. and prepares to take Babylon in 539 B.C. This web of circumstances set in motion by Cyrus's campaign was understood in Isaiah 42.13 as typologically a new exodus.

> The Lord goes forth like a mighty man,
> like a man of war he stirs up his fury;
> he cries aloud, he shouts aloud,
> he shows himself mighty against his foes.

Yahweh is seen here as reenacting the exodus from Egypt, only this time it is from Babylon after the years of exile and the initiator is Cyrus rather than Moses. Again in captivity, the chosen people of God are being miraculously delivered by their sovereign and gracious Lord. The "God of our Fathers" is again seen to be leading Israel out of bondage.

Indeed, the prophecy recites the all-inclusive power and understanding of Yahweh, the epistemological function of which is clear; to designate the new exodus event as profoundly universalized but as still entirely within the purposes of the one true God, who proclaims

> I am the Lord, and there is no other,
> besides me there is no God;
> I gird you, though you do not know me,
> that men may know, from the rising of the sun
> and from the west, and there is none besides me;
> I am the Lord, and there is no other (Isa. 45.5–6).

This model implies a "hermeneutic of engagement." It is thus described because through it the believing community engages simultaneously with the two facets of divine activity in human affairs: heritage and event. In this way the believing community brings the confessional heritage, through which the community perceives the purposeful movement of God through the historical process, into a living encounter with contemporary reality. In this engagement the heritage is amplified, and through it the believing community interprets the event as a further illumination of a pattern already witnessed and confessed to as in some sense numinous. In the hermeneutic of engagement, therefore, the meaning and context of contemporary events will be clarified and given their religious depth by interpreting them in the light of the paradigmatic events of the community's past.

Even as the return from exile was a new exodus, so the advent of nuclear weapons is a new apocalypse. This dialectic between Hiroshima and the apocalyptic challenges us to explore the coming together of humanity and God in our new found powers of global destruction and our capacity for planetary renewal. It is important to stress the co-creative character of the apocalyptic possibilities in our day. Hiroshima humanizing the apocalypse means that if the wrath of God must come, it is human hands which will push the button; and if the righteousness of God will replace the old order with a new one, it is human work which will create it. In history, God never works alone, but always in conjunction with human beings. Therefore, it is imperative to find the locus of the divine/ human interface within the human realm, for whatever God is in divine transcendence, God is only concrete to humans when divinity is made manifest in history.

What must be discerned is that locus in which three things occur: first, where the human realities of darkness and light are felt most strongly; second, where these human feelings and drives engage with and are affected by God; and third, where some type of synthesis can occur not only between the forces peculiarly human but also between the human and the divine.

The locus in which all these three dynamics occur is the human psyche, for it is here that the active inner and spiritual life of human beings takes place; where religious experience takes place, meaning our inner encounters with God; and where we can synthesize the contradictions within us to achieve some type of reconciliation. As I said, Hiroshima has made imperative this journey inward; therefore, theology, if it is to internalize adequately the historical event Hiroshima represents, must take seriously the psychic dimensions of human experience. Not only does our psyche influence what we perceive, receive, mediate, and express in terms of our spiritual life, but it is only as we find reconciliation within the psyche that we can deal adequately with the polarities inherent in the external world. A psychotheology has, since Hiroshima, become inescapable in understanding the dilemma we are confronted with. We are all survivors of Hiroshima and Nagasaki because we have all had "engraved" in our psyches the death immersion the atomic bombing of Japan represents. As Robert Lifton points out, this death immersion has caused a "psychic mutation" in us all.

In exploring our psychic reality I have chosen to follow primarily the discoveries of C.G. Jung because he appreciated the psyche as the locus in which the human and the divine meet, mutually affect one another, and co-create. Besides offering a practical and open model of the psyche which must be taken seriously, Jung also delved with profound clarity and perception in the area that concerns us— the advent of nuclear weapons. Particularly in his *Answer to Job*, he struggled with the question of why it is that after several thousand years of religious culture in the West, Western civilization has brought all planetary life to the brink of extinction through thermonuclear war. For Jung, this meant dealing most fundamentally with the problem of evil and with the shadow aspect of reality, not only in humanity but in divinity—areas not amenable to the neat categorizations of rational logic. This led him to an affirmation of the antinomial character of God, a reality in which a "both . . . and . . ." complementarity of opposites is much more constructive than the "either/or" dichotomy of logical reasoning.

In grappling with this complex problem, Jung is also helpful in deepening our understanding of the hermeneutic of engagement discussed earlier. His model of the psyche is based on the interaction of consciousness with unconsciousness and the interaction of the logic of time, space and causality with symbols and mythic images. Consciousness uses the categories of time, space and causality; the unconscious uses symbols and mythic images. The interrelationship between these two aspects of the psyche form a *complexio oppositorum*, a tension of opposties, which can be integrated only by the self—the unifying force in the psyche—if we are to reach the goal of wholeness. To reduce symbol to rational logic or mythic images to the literalism of the categories of time, space and causality on the one hand—or to swallow up the reality of the world of time, space and causality into symbol and myth on the other—is to miss the real profundity and dynamic power of the psyche. The same holds true for scripture: to reduce divine action in history to either literalism or demythologized rationalism on the one hand, or to deny the physical historical truth of Jesus of Nazareth by swallowing it up in symbol or myth on the other, is to emasculate the mystery of the biblical witness. The hermeneutic of engagement holds both historical fact and confessional response in creative tension. Jung's model of the psyche does the same. Consciousness is in tension with the unconscious; and the categories of time, space, and causality are in tension with the expressions of symbol and myth. The resulting complexio oppositorum, while not amenable to rationalist reduction, leads us closer to an appreciation of the mystery of scripture and the antinomial reality of both the human psyche and our experience of God.

The individuation process is in effect a co-creation of consciousness with the unconscious. In asserting God to be an autonomous complex and a symbol whose affects are psychologically measurable, God is bound to become relative; for if God is placed in an intimate relation with the soul, God in effect becomes vulnerable to the soul. In so far as God is to have any communication with us and be psychologically effective, God must be mediated through an image within the psyche; that is, through a symbol.

Symbols, however, arise in the human psyche, evolve to a certain point where their content becomes explicable in some other way, and then fade. Such is the case with the recent demise of the God-image presented by theism—it is an image whose time is past; therefore, "God is dead" says the theologians. However, a new image is in the process of arising. Note that I am not saying arising through our actions, but taking shape of its own accord. I stress the overwhelming role of God and the unconscious in any symbol formation. We can only consciously participate in what is already occurring at its own initiative. This evolving of God-images, while certainly not affecting the absolute dimension of God, certainly establishes that there is a consequent aspect very much subject to human participation.

When a new symbol is brought into the history of a people, it may be adopted owing to the exigencies of the moment and for seemingly short-term parochial reasons, but it has in fact arisen after much preparation in the depths of the collective unconscious of that people. What counts is the demise of the previous unifying symbol and the psychic readiness of the society for a new one.

In attempting to make clear the hermeneutic of engagement, I offered as a prototype the prophecies of Deutero-Isaiah. Once the model was clear structurally, it was easier to proceed with the contemporary components of the model. Here again I feel it necessary to make clear in a structural way what happens when an archetype arises in history to "possess" a people.

I wish to explore this point by examing the experience of Germany under the Nazis. I do so not only because the Nazi situation offers perhaps the classic case of archetypal "possession" but because the archetypal experience in question was one consisting almost in its entirety of its shadow aspect.

In a lecture delivered in Cologne and Essen in February 1933, Jung stated that "just as for the individual a time of dissociation is a time for sickness, so it is in the life of nations. We can hardly deny that ours is a time of dissociation and sickness."[3] He then went on to term this sickness a "crisis," meaning the time when "the sickness has reached a dangerous climax."

As time went on, Jung became increasingly disturbed by the state of affairs in Germany. He saw the Nazi phenomenon as a "possession," one that clearly indicated to him as a psychologist that Germany was being possessed by archetypal forces from its collective unconscious. In March 1936, he published an article entitled "Wotan" in which he stated that a "curious" phenomenon was occurring; namely, that

> an ancient god of storm and frenzy, the long quiescent Wotan, should awake, like an extinct volcano, to new activity, in a civilized country that had long been supposed to have outgrown the Middle Ages.[4]

According to Jung, "Wotan is a Germanic datum of the first importance, the truest expression and unsurpassed personification of a fundamental that is particularly characteristic of Germans."[5] As an autonomous psychic factor, Wotan produced effects on the collective life of Germany, revealing both Germany's inner nature and his own. Because of this enormous impact upon the German psyche, we can speak of Wotan as an archetypal image, for Wotan has a peculiar biology of his own, quite apart from the nature of human beings. Moreover, it is only from time to time that Wotan surfaces to overpower individuals and societies with his irresistible influence. Germany under National Socialism was one such time.

Jung points out that with the "conversion" of the teutonic tribes to Christianity, Wotan was changed into a devil and forced to live on only in fading local traditions as a ghostly hunter wandering through the sky on stormy nights. Wotan the god did not die, Jung argues, but was only repressed back into the teutonic collective unconscious.

> He simply disappeared when the times turned against him,
> and remained invisible for more than a thousand years,
> working anonymously and indirectly. Archetypes are like
> riverbeds which dry up when the water deserts them, but
> which it can find at any time. An archetype is like an old
> watercourse along which the water of life has flowed for
> centuries, digging a deep channel for itself. The longer it has
> flowed in this channel the more likely it is that sooner or
> later the water will return to its old bed.[6]

Since Wotan was the principal god of the pre-Christian Teutons, with a cult prevailing over all others, his power was firmly entrenched and not to be wiped away.

As a psychic force, therefore, Wotan remained alive even if latent. Remaining subterranean, he formed the shadow of the superficial layer of Christianity the German consciousness embraced, biding his time until Germany had become so "civilized" that it lost all contact with its roots. Then, as the laws of compensation and enantiodromia came into effect, Wotan surfaced as Wotan recidivous with the fantasies of Nietzsche, becoming historicized in the person of Hitler.

What occurred in Germany was that "fate" confronted the Germans with their own "God-almightiness." Faust was put face to face with Mephistopheles and could no longer say, "So that was the essence of the demonic." Rather, Faust must confess instead, "Mephistopheles is my other side, my alter ego, my own inner shadow, which, because I did not see it, has possessed me."[7] But what fate brought upon the Germans is in store for all those nations for whom "God is dead," for the same psychological laws apply. The loss of our God-image, the loss of the centrality of Christianity in our lives, is an event whose awesome consequences are still to come.

> Christianity was accepted as a means to escape from the brutality and unconsciousness of the ancient world. As soon as we discard it, the old brutality returns in force, as has been made overwhelmingly clear by contemporary events. This is not a step forwards but a long step backwards into the past. . . . Who throws Christianity overboard and with it the whole basis of morality, is bound to be confronted with age-old problem of brutality. We have had bitter experience of what happens when a whole nation finds the moral mask too stupid to keep up. The beast breaks loose, and a frenzy of demoralization sweeps over the civilized world.[8]

What happens is that, like Faust, each one of us, because we do not acknowledge the existence of the unconscious nor how much it controls us, projects our unconscious contents, including the shadow, upon our neighboring countries, races, and religions. Once this projection is complete, and both sides are doing it, it then becomes the sacred duty of both to have the biggest guns and the most destructive weapons systems in order to defend themselves against the evil they see on the other side. While in the grip of the problem, therefore, each group, by projecting its shadow upon the enemy, psychologically absolves itself of any guilt and can continue to build up destructive weapons systems under the illusion that it is in fact the solution. Therefore, German companies could calmly discuss improved models of gas chambers within the meetings of their boards of directors, even competing amongst themselves for the government contracts to build them; and German soap companies could go so far as to argue for more Jewish children to be gassed because they had discovered that making soap from the bodies of young Jews was cheaper than making it by normal means.

The great tragedy of post-war Europe is that the willingness to own up to one's own guilt and recognize the inner existence of the shadow has not happened. We are forever forgetting this truth, says Jung,

> because our eyes are fascinated by the conditions around us and riveted on them instead of examining our own heart and conscience. Every demagogue exploits this human weakness when he points with the greatest possible outcry to all the things that are wrong in the outside world. But the principal and indeed the only thing that is wrong with the world is man.[9]

The fanaticism of the Germans against the Jews had been replaced by the anticommunism of the West in general, the Americans in particular, only now the weapons are not gas chambers but nuclear weapons and the other side is not meekly going to the slaughter but is equally armed and dangerous, caught up in its anti-imperialism. The conflagration that broke out in Germany was the outcome of the psychic conditions which are universal; but while the Germans threatened a single people with genocide, the nuclear arms race threatens the entire human race with extinction.

In the face of this, in the face of nuclear annihilation, the time has come to turn our minds to fundamental things and stop projecting our shadow selves onto others. And yet, because we are refusing to come to grips with our collective guilt, because we are refusing to acknowledge the power of the unconscious over us, we have produced a world in which the question has at last become one of existence or nonexistence—for all of us. It is an issue that demands to be addressed, for as Jung points out, "the danger that threatens us now is of such dimensions as to make this last European catastrophe seem like a curtain-raiser."[10]

First we must appreciate the gravity of our situation. Jung saw more deeply than any that "God is dead"; but he also saw what others did not see, that given the inexorable law of enantiodromia, Christ's spirit was being replaced by that of the Antichrist, symbolized by the atomic bomb. To understand this necessitates a deeper appreciation of the realities of evil. Jung asserts that

> there are things which from a certain point of view are extremely evil, that is to say dangerous. There are also things in human nature which are very dangerous and which

> therefore seem proportionately evil to anyone standing in their line of fire. It is pointless to gloss over these evil things, because that only lulls one into a sense of false security. Human nature is capable of an infinite amount of evil, and the evil deeds are as real as the good ones so far as human experience and so far as the psyche judges and differentiates them. . . . Today as never before it is important that humans beings should not overlook the danger of evil lurking within them.[11]

The net result of two thousand years of teaching the Summum Bonum and the *privatio boni* has been a too optimistic conception of the evil in human nature and a too pessimistic view of the human soul. Indeed, Jung argues that it has been the steadfast refusal to acknowledge the reality of evil that has blinded the Christian religion and paralyzed it in a day when the reality of evil has become so great that the light of Christ has all but been snuffed out. In commenting on this, Eleanor Bertine makes the point quite clearly.

> Of the great religions, Christianity has gone farthest in splitting the original unity of good and evil and cleaving exclusively to the good. This extreme emphasis on spirit as over against instinct was probably necessary to compensate the previous one-sided bondage to physical nature, which dominated paganism; but certainly it has in its turn constituted an act of violence against the psyche's shadow side, and the price has been nothing less than the possibility of wholeness. This imbalance has led to a sense of incompleteness and guilt and, finally, to an inevitable swing of the pendulum to the opposite extreme. Thus we are now experiencing, in the wake of Christian civilization, a mass evil, perhaps greater than ever known before.[12]

Bertine's point is helpful in providing a proper context within which the doctrines of the Summum Bonum and privatio boni should be understood. They served a purpose in helping the church to focus on the light side of God in Christ. However, now, like theism, these doctrines must be transcended and balanced, for their continued presence has become negative rather than positive.

According to Jung,

if we see the traditional figure of Christ as a parallel to the psychic manifestation of the Self, then the Antichrist would correspond to the shadow of the Self, namely the dark half of the human totality. . . . The archetype of the Self must include both dimensions and cannot omit the shadow that belongs to the light figure, for without it this figure lacks body and humanity.[13]

It is interesting to note here that the ancient Gnostics taught that Christ "cast-off his shadow from himself."[14] It was precisely this cut-off counterpart, says Jung, that the Christian writers, specifically St. John the Divine, recognized as the Antichrist who would appear at the "end of time." He would be the true "imitating spirit of evil," says Jung, "who inversely parallels Christ's presence like a shadow following a body."[15]

With the coming of Christ, the archetype of Antichrist is activated. Christ is without blemish; but right at the beginning of his career he encounters Satan—the adversary who represents the counterpart of that tremendous tension in the human psyche which the Christ even signified. We thus hear of the millennial reign of Christ and of the coming of the Antichrist, almost as if there were an arbitrary division of the world between two royal brothers.

Indeed, this polarity led very early to the doctrine of the two sons of God, the elder of whom was called Satanael. In the hermeneutic writings of the Church Fathers, Christ has a number of symbols and allegories in common with Satan: the lion, the snake, the bird, the raven, the eagle, and the fish. It is also worth mentioning that Lucifer, Morning Star, means Christ as well as Satan.

What emerges from an examination of these symbols is that Christ corresponds to only one-half of the archetype of the Self. The Antichrist or Satan symbolizes the other half. "Both are Christian symbols," says Jung,

> and they have the same meaning as the image of the Savior crucified between two thieves. This great symbol tells us that the progressive development and differentiation of consciousness leads to an ever more menacing awareness of the conflict and involves nothing less than a crucifixion of the ego, its agonizing suspension between irreconcilable opposites.[16]

When John spoke in the Book of Revelation about a final outpouring of the vials of the wrath of God and the coming of the Antichrist, therefore, he was not just articulating a prophetic prediction of the future; he was also prophesying an inexorable psychological law. The incarnation of the light side of God in Christ gave rise in his mind to the archetypal image of the Antichrist, an archetypal image he foresaw would one day be historicized with an intensity equal to the incarnation of Christ. He thus outlined the program for the whole of the Christian age, says Jung, "with its dramatic enantiodromia, and its dark end which we have still to experience, and before whose—without exaggeration—truly apocalyptic possibilities mankind shudders."[17]

Although Jung argues that what the appearance of the atomic bomb implies is a veritable incarnation of God's shadow side, even as Christ is an incarnation of God's light side, I do not agree. Rather, I will use the term "revelation" to describe the present outpouring of divine wrath. There are two reasons for my disagreement with Jung on this point. First, nuclear weapons are objects while Christ is a person. Incarnation has no meaning in terms of nonmoral agents. Much more to the point is that there is a prevailing spirit of evil which indicates the presence of the collective archetype of Antichrist similar to the archetype of Wotan which possessed the Nazis. Yet while Wotan became personified by Hitler, no such parallel phenomenon has occurred with the archetype of the Antichrist; rather, it has remained diffuse, permeating the decisions and activities of many nations, not just one.

Second, I believe that the primary focus of Hiroshima is not on itself, as an incarnation would suggest. Rather, the focus of Hiroshima seems to be to direct Christian attention back to the Christ event, only this time not upon the person of Christ so much as upon the act of God in Christ crucified. We are being given in our day the experience of the wrath and evil of God, comingling, to be sure, with our own depravity and sinfulness.

While the light side of God was incarnated in Christ, God's antinomial character was made manifest in the crucifixion of Christ. Through Hiroshima, God is calling us again to witness the antinomial character of the Divine and to assimilate Antichrist into the power of Christ. Only a solid basis in the light (God's incarnation in Christ) is sufficient to integrate God's antinomy. Hiroshima, therefore, points back to Christ crucified in order to inform our present challenge more deeply.

The last two thousand years have been an indispensable preparation for this hour. The moral impact of salvation through Christ is the indispensable element needed to enable humanity to begin to grapple with the darkness of God in Hiroshima, a darkness to which the antinomial character of the cross bears silent terrible witness and in which Christians discern in fear and trembling the nature of the vocation to which we are now called.

In Christ, humanity discovered God. Today, with the advent of the spirit of Antichrist, humanity is discovering God anew in the inexhaustible depth of our being from which emerge all the archetypal images which govern our conscious lives: images of the light, images of the dark.

The closer one comes to God, the greater the danger of being scorched by the divine flame and burned away. The Christ event dramatically changed history; the Hiroshima event is doing the same. One cannot be touched by the numinous without being transformed. In Christ it is our salvation that is at stake; in Hiroshima it is our very existence on earth. The former one is invisible to all but those with the eyes of fate and so humanity can and does pass it by; with the latter, the threat is visibly upon us all. Hitler was essentially a prophetic phenomenon: his damage was cruel but local; Hiroshima is essentially an apocalyptic phenomenon, for the damage now possible is global: all live under the threat of a radioactive Final Solution. As Jung puts it, "The four sinister horsemen, the threatening tumult of trumpets, and the brimming vials of wrath are . . . waiting . . . the atom bomb hangs over us like the sword of Damocles. . . ."[18]

Hiroshima and Christ form a neat oppositional parallelism. Christ is the symbol of the salvation of the world; Hiroshima symbolizes the destruction of the world. Hiroshima is the negation of Christ and is therefore to be understood as Antichrist, for it potentially marks the final death knell of human history.

The Christian era began with what I have already described as the equation of the perfection of the person of the Christ with the wholeness of the God-image, an assertion that was given philosophical justification with the doctrines of the Summum Bonum and the privato boni. The power of the church, of Christ on earth, reached its highest point in the Middle Ages, when Catholic dogma was

undisputed and the pope, the vicar of Christ, claimed supremacy in
both heavenly matters and earthly power. The architecture of this
period, with its Gothic spires lifting upwards to the sky, represents
the heights to which Christ as the symbol of God had climbed. With
the Renaissance, however, the vertical orientation of human consciousness began to become increasingly horizontal. The planet, humanity, and the past were rediscovered; and voyages of discovery,
experiments in natural science, and the secular power of the state
began to replace the church, Christ, and God as the focus of human
attention. Anthropocentricity replaced theocentricity. The Enlightenment took this reorientation one step further by replacing objective
"revealed truth" as given by the Bible and the church with the
subjectivity of the human mind itself. Finally, Nietzsche prophesied
the death of God, and the theistic God-image considered synonymous
with Christianity itself began its final descent from being an object
of attack to being a concept considered irrelevant.

Even as the human mind reached the point of rejecting Christianity
and the theistic notion of God, human hands constructed a weapon
that represented total nihilism, complete anti-God, complete anti-
Christ. Human beings were now confronted, for the first time in
history, with not only the prospect of personal death but the distinct
possibility of the death of the species. What had been started by
Christ as the light of the world, the salvation of humanity, had now
turned into its polar opposite: Christ had engendered Antichrist, and
one royal brother replaced the other. Humanity is now confronted
with the prospect of annihilation, even as two thousand years before
it was offered the possibility of salvation.

Herein lies another oppositional parallelism. We were challenged
to accept Christ. We did not, choosing rather to reject him. The
result: crucifixion—the death of one human being. Out of death came
the risen Christ, however, and salvation for all humanity. We are
today being challenged to integrate Antichrist within a Christ-oriented
consciousness. We are not doing so, choosing rather to accept him
in place of Christ. The result: potential planetary annihilation—the
death of the species. Out of this annihilation may come a few
survivors. Christ came to save; Antichrist comes to destroy. The
tragedy of our time is that we are rejecting the savior to embrace
the destroyer, using our life's energies to build the weapons of our
death.

Hiroshima, the possibility of planetary devastation and human annihilation, has become our new God-image. All nations seek for it, they lust for it, depriving themselves of simple human needs in order to build more weapons of mass destruction to offer on the altar of the new God. When God became incarnate as Christ, the Magi came offering gifts of gold, frankincense and myrrh. Today a new God-image appears as a result of our Faustian ego-inflation since the decline of theism, and we offer vials of plutonium which we have named for him—Pluto, the god of hell. We even ignited the first atomic bomb on the day commemorating the transfiguration of Christ, thus unconsciously signalling that we intended likewise to transform the world, only not after the light but after darkness— with a blast that burned several times hotter than the surface of the sun.

Yet, we do not recognize Antichrist for what he is any more than we recognize Christ for what he was; for, many who are looking at all continue to look beyond the world to a fatherly God to break through nature to save them. Yet God is already here, living amongst us, coming from within us, acting in our midst incognito save to those who discern the mysteries of incarnation and revelation.

The question then was: How could God be appearing in a suffering servant? He had no form nor comeliness, and when people saw him there was no beauty that they should desire him (Isa. 53). He was despised and rejected by humanity, a man of sorrows, acquainted with grief, whom people esteemed not and finally crucified, bruised not only by them but by the will of the Lord (Isa. 53.10).

The question now is: How can God be appearing in plutonium? It causes cancer and genetic damage and is the essential ingredient in fast breeders and nuclear bombs. It must be stored for tens of thousands of years, Yet, it is attracting the wealth of Babylon to its service and the minds and hearts of the people who are constructing the military-industrial complexes around the world. Can what the whore of Babylon is worshipping truly be called God? Can the weapons of mass destruction we are building each day come from the same source as the suffering servant of God?

The book of Revelation depicts such a situation; it describes such a God. The Lamb of God who was at first in conflict with death and the forces of Satan, now commands the angel of the bottomless pit. The Lamb of God who came first to give his blood as a ransom for many, now rides forth and treads the winepress of the wrath of God, spilling the blood of millions. And the God of the Summum Bonum pours out vial after vial of wrath, destruction, and torment upon a defenseless humanity, seeking now to destroy the very world this same God sought to save through Christ. God is in Christ, God is in Antichrist, "The Lord gave and the Lord has taken away; blessed be the name of the Lord" (Job 1.21).

Indeed, the Antichrist is the feeling of God-forsakenness, even as Christ is the feeling of God-acceptedness; it is the symbol of hell even as Christ symbolizes heaven, the negative God-image even as Christ is the positive God-image. To quote Moltmann's description of the rejection of Jesus by God, I would say to the Antichrist

> The experience of abandonment by God is in the knowledge that God is not distant but close; does not judge, but shows grace. And this, in full consciousness that God is close at hand in his grace, to be abandoned and delivered up to death as one rejected, is the torment of hell.[19]

The final point that needs to be made is that God and humanity co-creating the apocalypse in our day brings about the interweaving of the wrath of God with the Faustian ego-inflation that arises after the death of a God-image. Their intermingling is complex and their result empirically one. As the crucifixion of Christ served to demonstrate the implacable demands of an antinomial God. ("I will strike the shepherd"), as well as to bring into focus the worst human sin, so Hiroshima is demonstrating the absolute perversity of the human personality following the "death of God", while simultaneously revealing the wrath of a living God as never before. Thus the paradox of co-creation: on the one hand, Hiroshima humanizing the apocalyptic possibilities previously ascribed only to God; on the other hand, at that point where humanity believes it has totally secularized the world and gained full autonomy and mastery of its fate, even of the end of historical time, God appears, deep within our psychic depths, working in and through our sin, indeed, creating evil through the manifestation of the archetype of the Antichrist, and challenging us once again to recognize that all of history is "in God."

The interface between the abandonment of God and the acceptance of God, between God becoming incarnate in Christ and God as revealed in Antichrist, is a difficult one; for it means that we must see "the mighty acts of God" as spanning the pleroma of reality from the heights of heaven to the depths of hell. It is an understanding that lifts God beyond the confines of our morality, leaving us with the question of what is good and what is evil, where is God and where is God not. It is an understanding that can easily lead to cynicism and despair, for it is one that must be intuitively grasped, not logically constructed.

A symbol which I believe to be helpful in understanding the Christ/Antichrist complex is that of baptism. The crucifixion and resurrection of Christ are symbolized by this sacrament, as are the events of our day, laden as they are with the revelation of Antichrist.

It is generally agreed that to be baptized "into Christ" not only symbolized public acceptance of Christ and admission into his body (the church) but means to be "baptized into his death" (Rom. 6.3), to be "circumcised with Christ" (Col. 2.11). It signifies the death of the believer to his or her natural self and the resurrection into the spirit of truth.

If we are truly to appreciate the hand of God in Hiroshima, then it is imperative that we see a baptism in what is happening; otherwise we will have no choice but to give up hope and to despair. The left hand of God can only be understood within the context of the right hand of God.

John Robinson, in his study of baptism in *Twelve New Testament Studies*, is helpful in discerning the baptism motif in the Apocalypse itself.

The final conflagration in which the vials of the wrath of God consume the world and the armies of the one riding forth with a garment dipped in blood vanquish the Satanic host, he says, is

> the great universal Baptism in which Christ the whole world
> has been plunged—a baptism of blood, in fire of judgment,
> yet a baptism nevertheless from which the nations may finally
> find healing, through the "river of the water of life, bright as
> crystal, proceeding out of the throne of God and of the
> Lamb" (22.1f).[20]

Citing the Psalmist, that the enemies of God have poured out the blood of the saints "like water round about Jerusalem" (Ps. 79.2), Robinson offers the further insight that in the apocalypse it is not the enemies of God spilling the blood but the Divine itself. The pouring out of the seven vials of the wrath of God in Revelation 16

> is given them by God—poured out in the Cross like water
> round about Jerusalem. So . . . once more the bath of blood
> and the bath of baptism are one; and in the work of
> redemption so understood we have a category of interpretation
> among the most profound and universal in the New
> Testament.[21]

In baptism one can see the left and right hands of God working as closely as in Christ crucified and Christ resurrected. It is clear that they form a complementary whole in which both death and life, crucifixion and resurrection play a part. Therefore, our trust and hope in God is not shattered when God appears in Antichrist, for we know that it is in death and through death that life comes.

However, the Apocalypse, even when seen within the symbol of baptism, presents us with a paradoxical concept of God, one which orthodox Christian theology evaded so long as it asserted the notion of God as the Summum Bonum and of evil as the privatio boni.

These concepts are adequate for prophetic times when consciousness can afford to be one-sided. We are in apocalyptic times, however, when it is not only the enemies of God that are making the blood "flow round the city" but God as well. We are experiencing a side of God peculiar to the time just prior to a radical transformation of history, a side that is dark, brooding, destructive, merciless; the polar opposite of all that was manifested by God's incarnation in Christ. We are in a universal religious nightmare where all our old concepts and notions, made almost indelible by the heavy weight of a long tradition, have been shattered. Our old skins have been filled with the new wine of Hiroshima and have been burst asunder. We have been placed in the position of Job, where what we have heard with our ears about God is being contradicted by what we are seeing with our eyes of God.

What must be recognized is that the integration of the opposites must take place in the human psyche, for Hiroshima has humanized the eschaton and therefore it is our own psyches in which the cosmic battle is being fought.

What Jung emphasizes is that

everything now depends on man: immense power of destruction is given into his hand, and the question is whether he can resist the will to use it, and can temper his will with the spirit of love and wisdom. He will hardly be capable of doing so on his own unaided resources. He needs the help of an "advocate" in heaven, that is, of the child who was caught up to God and who brings the "healing" and making whole of the hitherto fragmentary man.[22]

The child referred to is the child of Revelation born of the woman pursued by the dragon. Most commentators assert that the child represents Christ. Without his aid, without his spirit of love and wisdom, we are lost in dealing with the Antichrist. Put more concretely, we shall only be able to integrate the Hiroshima event into our understanding of God's action in history by first truly integrating the Christ event into our own psychic depths. This comes through the presence of the spirit.

The work of the Spirit is a low and complex process. It requires first that we recognize that the light side of God was incarnate in Christ; second, that we genuinely be transformed by the salvific power of God in Christ and at the same time gain in consciousness and moral power sufficient resilience and strength to enable us to deal with the polarities of ordinary life; and third, that we be thus in some way prepared to grapple with the ultimate polarities in human experience: the antinomial character God at work in the cross and in Hiroshima.

With the challenge of Antichrist comes the spirit of wisdom which can lead us into a deeper understanding of Christ crucified. The cross, therefore, is an event in which God has taken the deepest polarities possible and woven them together for a higher good. With the sending of the Holy Spirit, there is at work in us that which brings to our remembrance the whole paradoxical reality of God's action in Christ. It is a spirit of wisdom which comes to our aid through the depths of our unconscious nature, and it is the task of consciousness to respond to this work of the Spirit. Only then will we survive and continue our slow, painful advance towards wholeness, which means activating those resources within us that the ancient apocalypticists attributed to God after the great destruction. They believed God would renew the universe. This we must do, although before giving in to our darker impulses. This can only come about if we discover our own feminine.

It is historically important that at the height of the apocalyptic visions of the ancient Jews, the wisdom tradition, called Sophia by the Greeks, flourished. She was the great feminine force in ancient Judaism and was conceptualized as the "ordering principle of creation." The ancient Jews never saw God appearing in the sky and destroying the world. Rather the interaction of apocalyptic despair and the renewing impulses of Sophia gave rise to an even more radical transformation. God in fact appeared, but not from *outside* history. Jesus of Nazareth came from *within* history.

It is synchronistic for us today that the advent of a technology of mass destruction came co-terminous with the liberation of women. If the pattern of crisis and renewal experienced by ancient Jewry holds forth any illumination over the millennia, we can at least rest assured that it is the feminine that holds the key to the renewal needed to ensure human survival.

Athanasius spoke long ago about God becoming human in order that humanity might become divine. St. Paul before him spoke of redeemed humanity being hidden with Christ in God and also that God and Christ to be sin who knew no sin that in him we might become the righteousness of God. This "ingoddedness" is a critical dimension to be understood if we are to appreciate the process panentheistic claim that all of human history is indeed "in God." It can also provide us with a clue to a contemporary meaning of Jesus' words to those who were blind to his signs and deaf to his teaching: "Is it not written in your law, 'I said, you are gods' " (John 10.23)?

If we can appreciate the numinosity of Hiroshima and take seriously its demand that we grapple anew not only with the light of Christ but with the antinomial character of God—that is to say, with the darkness of God as well as the Goddess in God—we shall be empowered to "transcend and divinize our humanity using it as an instrument of the divine within."[23]

This is the work of the Holy Spirit in the present age, for the Holy Spirit is the "mute, eternal, unfathomable One in whom God's love and God's terribleness come together in wordless union."

T.S. Eliot gives yet deeper insight into this unfathomable mystery.

The dove descending breaks the air
With flame of incandescent terror
Of which the tongues declare
The one discharge from sin and error.
The only hope, or else despair
Lies in the choice of pyre or pyre-
To be redeemed from fire by fire.
Who then devised the torment? Love.
Love is the unfamiliar Name
Behind the hands that wove
The intolerable shirt of flame
Which human power cannot remove.
We only live, only suspire
Consumed by either fire or fire.[24]

It is this shattering paradox out of the depths of Judaeo-Christianity that Eliot is addressing: Love bringing torment, forcing humanity to wear "the intolerable shirt of flame"; Christ the giver of life confronted by Antichrist the taker of life, masculine crisis activating feminine renewal. This is a paradox that can only be resolved within the movement of the human psyche. We must integrate the antinomial polarity within our experience of the Godhead we worship; we must choose between "pyre and pyre." Only if we do this, only if we meet the darkness of God and the Goddess in God, will we be able to say within Eliot that

All shall be well and
All manner of thing shall be well
When the tongues of flame are in-folded
Into the crowned knot of fire
And the fire and the rose are one.

NOTES

1. Henry Weiman, *The Source of Human Good*, London, 1946, p. 40.
2. Ibid., 41.
3. Jung, *Collected Works*, London, 1953-79, Vol. X, paragraph 290. (Hereafter, only volume and paragraph numbers to be noted.)
4. Ibid., 373.
5. Ibid., 389.
6. Ibid., 395.

7. Ibid., 439.
8. Ibid., 341.
9. Ibid., 441.
10. Ibid., 487.
11. Ibid., IX, ii, 97–98.
12. Ibid., X, 290.
13. Ibid., IX, ii, 76.
14. Irenaeus, *Adversus Haereses*, II, 5, 1, in Jung, ibid., 75.
15. Jung, *Collected Works*.
16. Ibid., 79.
17. Ibid., XI, 733.
18. Ibid.
19. Jurgen Moltmann, *The Crucified God*, London, 1974, p. 272.
20. John Robinson, *Twelve New Testament Studies*, London, 1962, p. 174.
21. Ibid., 175.
22. Jung, XI, 745.
23. Athanasius, *Orat*, iii, 53.
24. T.S. Eliot, *Four Quartets*, London, 1944, ii, 200–213, 255–259.

CHAPTER TWELVE

The Incomplete Myth: Reflections on the "Star Wars" Dimension of the Arms Race

MICHAEL E. ZIMMERMAN

INTRODUCTION

The human imagination is marvelous, but double-edged. On the one hand, it enables us to envision new possibilities for the human spirit—new ways of building, making, thinking, and doing. But on the other hand, imagination also creates frightful scenarios, particularly regarding people who are unknown, strange, or foreign. If foreigners turn out to be the enemy, we project onto them an evil and darkness that is frequently in excess of the whatever crimes they may have in fact committed. Moreover, onto ourselves we project only goodness and light. By splitting up good and evil so that the enemy alone carries evil and we alone carry good, we engage in an imaginative act rooted in a ditorted or partial interpretation of basic human mythology. In this essay, I shall argue that incomplete, distorted mythology is partly responsible for the current nuclear arms race, of which the so-called "Star Wars" Strategic Defense Initiative (SDI) is a recent development.

By "myth," I mean a symbol that serves to integrate and to provide meaning for human life. Such symbols are at work in religious traditions, legends, sagas, fairy tales, and lore of all ages. Myths do not serve their symbolic function unless they are internalized by someone; only then can they provide guidance and unification. Although sometimes defined dismissively as merely fictitious narratives of supernatural characters, myths cannot be understood adequately as false tales.[1] They play a basic role in human existence, often even for people who claim to live life wholly "rationally." Indeed, the myth for such people is that it is both good and possible to be an unemotional intellect that controls everything.

One of the most universal and multifarious myths is the myth of the hero. This myth is particularly important in world religions. Both Jesus Christ and Gautama Buddha were incarnations of the hero. Following their heroic examples gives people both guidance and encouragement in seeking to become individuated. As Ernest Becker has pointed out, without the symbol of the hero we would have difficulty not only with personal and cultural crises, but also with the demands of everyday life.[2] The myth of the hero usually tells the story of an individual who is called away from the monotony of everyday life in order to begin the quest for the Self, which is often represented by an extraordinary object (Holy Grail) or person (beautiful Prince or Virgin). Along the way, the hero must confront evil, darkness, and mortality, often portrayed in the form of dragons and other terrible forces.

Although heroes may be described as slaying the obstacles standing between them and redemption, their slayings are best understood as tamings or integrations of those obstacles. The whole heroic world—including hero, dragon, and treasure—represent psychological aspects of each individual, aspects that are often divided by conflict and fear. Understood psychologically, the myth of the hero describes the struggle involved in the process of individuation. In explaining this process, I follow Carl Jung in distinguishing among ego, shadow, and Self.[3]

Ego is the "island" of rational consciousness floating atop the great sea of the unconscious aspects of the psyche. Shadow refers to aspects of psychic reality which the ego regards as unacceptable: mortality, finitude, limitation, evil, darkness, pain, and so on. Self means the supra- or trans-personal power that originates and sustains the ego, and with which the ego must establish the appropriate relationship. Jung maintains that each individual undergoes at least part of the process of individuation. The first stage of this process, which takes up most of the first half of life, involves attaining ego-consciousness. This is accomplished by separating oneself from one's parents and from the collective cousciousness of one's tribe. Mythic symbols celebrating the escape of the hero from captivity, and re-counting the hero's triumph over the dragon, help the young person in the process of establishing an identity over against parents and authority figures. The young hero seeks to escape from the concrete, relational, cyclical, personalized domain of the mother and so turns to the more abstract, separate, linear, de-personalized realm of the father. This struggle for separate existence is both very demanding and guilt-producing. Hence, ego-identity is frequently a tenuous stage of human development. Moreover, people often inflate the ego and identify it with the transpersonal Self. Such inflation leads to gran-diosity, *hubris*, and denial of death.

In the second half of life, the process of individuation can continue, but only if the proper mythic symbols are available. These symbols puncture the inflated ego and disclose that *genuine* individuation involves going beyond the state of separateness and toward the state of being an individual-in-relationship. The inflated ego portrays itself as wholly independent, immortal, purely spiritual, and limitless. In the second half of life, however, a person discovers and affirms limitation, mortality, dependence, and relationship. The once-solitary ego surrenders to its relationships not only to other people, but also to the transpersonal and collective realms that the ego once denied and repressed. Contemporary feminists argue that the stage of isolated ego-consciousness is characteristic of people (primarily men) within patriarchal society.[4] While acknowledging the importance of this critique, we do not have time to pursue it here. Suffice it to say that the move to a non-isolated, non-hubristic level of existence involves in part integrating the repressed "feminine" aspect of humanity, the aspect that emphasizes relationship, mortality, dependency, finitude, natural cycles, concreteness, and a sense of the Divine as immanent, not utterly transcendent. Jung would call this "feminization" of the abstract, isolated ego *the integration of the anima*. Such integration manifests itself as the ego's surrender to its incarnation as a limited, finite center of consciousness existing in direct relationship with other such centers in the material world. Only through this "going-under" of the formerly self-centered, isolated ego, a process which amounts to a death-experience, does the person achieve proper integration with the transpersonal Self. In Jungian terms, this is the meaning of Christ's crucifixion, descent, and resurrection.

Thus, successful integration and individuation amount to redemption from the suffering and isolation produced by ego-centrism. The integrated person, then, does not regress to the pre-egoic state of unconscious, collective identification with all things, nor does such a person remain at the stage of isolated ego-consciousness. Instead, the integrated person becomes an individual-in-relationship. Individuation means being in relationship with or integrating not only one's own mortality, passions, emotions, desires, body, dark side, weakness, and so on, but also the collective, transpersonal, and divine aspects of reality.

The process of individuation is an integrative event guided by mythic symbols. The very word "symbol," in fact, connotes integration. In *Ego and Archetype*, Edward Edinger explains that "symbol" comes from the Greek *sym* ("together, with") and *bolon* ("that which has been thrown"). A symbol, then, is that which has been thrown together.

> In original Greek usage, symbols referred to the two halves of an object such as a stick or a coin which two parties broke between them as a pledge and to prove later the identity of the presenter of one part to the holder of the other. . . . A symbol was thus originally a tally referring to the missing piece of an object which when restored to, or thrown together with, its partner recreated the original whole object. This corresponds to our understanding of the psychological function of a symbol. The symbol leads us to the missing part of the whole man. It refers to our original totality. It heals our split, our alienation from life. And since the whole man is a great deal more than the ego, it relates us to the suprapersonal forces which are the source of our being and our meaning.[5]

If myths are symbols designed to guide and integrate the psyche, an incomplete or distorted myth can either be of no use for this end, or—worse still—it can serve to fragment further a dis-integrated psyche. All too often, however, heroic myths are distorted because they are interpreted either literally or incompletely. Taken literally, the myth of the hero suggests that there is someone else "out there" who has already fought with evil, death, and darkness; the struggle is therefore finished. Such an interpretation, however, lacks psychic power, because the person hearing the myth has not *identified* with the hero. Yet, even when such identification does occur, a person may still continue to take the myth too literally. The hearer may identify himself with the hero, but may interpret the dragon (mortality, evil, darkness) as being embodied in the stranger, the foreigner, the enemy.

Primitive peoples, who do not effectively distinguish between the "inner" psychological world and the "outer" natural world, often project evil and darkness onto enemy tribesmen, animals, and denizens of the spirit-world. Such people operate in terms of a dualism between tribe and non-tribe. People living in modern countries have attained a level of consciousness that operates in terms of the dualism of ego and non-ego. Despite the development of separate ego-consciousness, however, modern people are often like primitives in failing to distinguish between genuine characteristics of other people and characteristics that are in fact projections of the unconscious. For modern people to be able to make such distinctions, integrative symbols and myths are required. Yet Western symbols have become attenuated and belittled because ego-consciousness identifies itself one-sidedly with reason and science, and thus has no room for "myths." By splitting-off and repressing the shadowy, irrational, unconscious aspects of the psyche, ego-consciousness places itself in danger of being overwhelmed by the "return of the repressed." Where the symbol is lacking, as it is in most modern cultures, the radically separate ego is terrified by death-anxiety and simultaneously deluded by fantasies about being able to control everything by rational-technical means. According to Erich Neumann, modern mass movements occur when the separate ego is overwhelmed by long-repressed, unconscious collective contents that force the ego to surrender its separateness and return to a semi-tribal condition, such as occurred in Nazi Germany.[6] There, horrendous crimes were committed when modern technology was mobilized to destroy the "enemies" of the tribal nation-state. Such enemies were carriers of the projected German shadow. In Neumann's view, the German people were so readily re-collectivized because they lacked a symbol capable of maintaining ego-consciousness in the face of shadowy, collective forces, and because they lacked a symbol capable of helping them to integrate those collective forces to begin with.

Marxism, as Robert Tucker has argued, can also be interpreted as a distorted mythic symbol in which the struggle of good and evil within the individual is projected onto social classes: the blood-sucking capitalist class fights (vainly) to dominate the creative-productive working class.[7] When the capitalist class is destroyed by the proletariat, alienation will supposedly be destroyed as well, since it is "carried" and "produced" by the capitalist class. If Marxist revolutionaries can bring down the center of capitalism, the United States, world-history will supposedly begin its Golden Age. This myth is so attractive to many people because it portrays in social-class terms the problems that each individual must face. So long as a person is committed to the revolutionary cause, he or she can regress to a semi-collective state and postpone the painful process of individuation that requires integrating the shadowy, dark side that is being projected onto the ruling class. It goes without saying, of course, that capitalism is in fact responsible for social ills, but neither the capitalist class nor its individual constituents are the embodiment and source of evil. The dark side is an aspect of every human being; it cannot be eliminated by a social revolution.

Many Americans also share a a distorted heroic myth, the roots of which are grounded partly in religious sources.[8] Early American settlers depicted themselves as leaving the corrupt, sinful European countries for the pristine shores of the New World, in order to found "a city on a hill" which would be a sign of goodness for all nations. For these early settlers, the Christ-symbol was sufficiently distorted that it could not play its integrative role. Hence, the settlers had a love-hate relationship both with the American wilderness and with its native people. Wilderness was a projection screen for the settlers: on the one hand, they cast upon it their yearning for the virginal and unspoiled; on the other hand, they saw it in terms of what they regarded as unacceptable: sensuality, passion, irrationality, and death. The settlers tended to deal similarly with native peoples. They detected in the Indians the "naturalness" and "freedom" that contrasted sharply with the artifice and corruptness of the Old World. But the settlers, unable to integrate their own shadowy side, projected this onto the Indians as well. By killing Indians, the settlers convinced themselves that they were killing evil, death, sensuality, and beastiality. Such splitting-off and projecting have continued for many people throughout American history. Today, it would appear that we are projecting our dark side onto the Soviet people, the new Indians: bloodthirsty, insidious, cruel, and rapacious.

In addition to the myth which describes Americans as the embodiment of goodness, many Americans have also adopted the heroic myth of the "self-made man." The self-made man is the wholly independent individual who, by dint of effort and intelligence, conquers the obstacles standing in the way of fame and fortune. Since Marxist communism allegedly denies the value of the individual and seeks to bar the way to his self-actualization, the communist Soviet Union appears to be the threat to individuality, selfhood, freedom, and all the values associated therewith. By destroying the Soviet Union, a distorted mythology suggests, human individualism, freedom, and self-actualization will flourish as never before.

There is no denying the importance of values such as individual liberty and the right to self-development. Indeed, the mythic symbol of the self-made man, even if distorted and incomplete, can give ego-consciousness sufficient support for it to resist recollectivization. On the other hand, however, the myth of the self-made man can enhance the ego's false identification with the transpersonal Self, thereby leading to arrogance and grandiosity. The self-made man, then, is a symbol that over-estimates the value of ego-consciousness, with its rationality and separateness. Such a symbol elicits behavior that falls under the title "eternal child" (*puer aeternus* or *puella aeterna*).[9] The self-made ego avoids being "pinned down" by decisions calling for permanent limitations; he (or she) is always ready to "light out for the territories"; he leads a provisional life and is always waiting for the "real thing," which never comes along. Anything standing in his path toward "success," is viewed as a deadly threat. The self-made ego projects all evil, darkness, and mortality onto merely "mortal" types who are satisfied to lead less adventurous, less restless lives than that preferred by the self-made ego. Terrible deeds can be justified because they are done out of the "good" motives of the ego seeking to become God incarnate! If a country is populated by such self-made egos, it too is ripe for regression to a semi-collective state of consciousness, especially where the integrative symbols are lacking. The reader can judge the extent to which American claims to "individualism" are belied by the collective, mass behavior of people governed by the symbol of the self-made ego.

Since the topic inspiring this essay is the Strategic Defense Initiative (SDI) involving space-based ballistic missile defense, it is appropriate to examine the mythological aspects of the film series whose name—

Star Wars—has been applied by the media to SDI. George Lucas' famous *Star Wars* trilogy is so popular because it is based on structural elements drawn from universal myths of the hero. A few years ago, Lucas acknowledged that he had been reading Joseph Campbell's book, *The Hero with a Thousand Faces*, before he began producing the first *Star Wars* episode.[10] Although Lucas' films are set in a distant era and in another galaxy, they portray the archetypal human struggle to deal with evil, mortality, and limitation. Fortunately, the mythological element in these films is relatively complete and undistorted. The films do not pretend that evil is something wholly outside of and separable from the hero, who represents each of us. There is a dark side to the hero himself, the handsome, blond Luke Skywalker. His great challenge is not simply to destroy the evil force outside of him, Darth Vader and the cruel Emperor, but also to come to terms with and to integrate his own "dark side." Hence, *Star Wars* exhibits important aspects of a genuine mythic symbol.

Lucas' extraordinarily popular trilogy depicts the adventures of a hero who has been called away from his humdrum existence on a drab planet in order to fulfill his dream of being a heroic star-fighter pilot.[11] At this stage in his life, he is under the sway of an incomplete myth, which suggests that evil is "out there" to be conquered. Through many fantastic struggles, and through meetings with extraordinary beings, he discovers that he must acknowledge and integrate his own dark side if he is to become a Jedi knight—symbolic of genuine heroic status. So long as Luke denies and resists his own darkness, he risks falling victim to it, as did the mighty Darth Vader, strong-arm of the evil Empire and (as we learn in the second film) Luke's own father. Luke is also encouraged to move beyond his one-sidedly rational ego-consciousness. His mentor, an aging Jedi knight, urges him to get in touch with his feelings if he hopes to become accessible to the mythical life energy know as "the Force." In the second film, Luke encounters another Jedi knight, a strange, dwarflike creature who has integrated dark and light, reason and intuition, thought and feeling, good and evil, yin and yang in such a way that he is endowed with extraordinary powers. From his teachers, Luke learns that he must cease dividing himself and reality according to dualistic schemes, which block the Force. He must move beyond the stage of ego-consciousness toward genuine individuation.

In the final film of the trilogy, Luke, Darth Vader, and the evil Emperor are together at the command center of the Empire's home base. The Emperor tries to entice Luke to come over to the "dark side." Having sufficiently integrated his own dark side, Luke manages to avoid being seduced by the wily Emperor, but ends up in a titantic battle with his father, Darth Vader. Understood psychologically, this battle signifies the son's continuing resistance to and rejection of the father, who is seen as the incarnation of darkness. Luke mortally wounds his father, at which point the Emperor intervenes and begins to kill Luke in a torturous process. Darth Vader cannot endure this cruelty against his own son; we see him struggling to overcome his long-standing identification with his dark side. Finally, in his moment of redemption, Darth Vader realizes that he had gone over to the dark side because he had denied and resisted it in his zeal to be a perfect Jedi knight. A victim of dualistic thinking, he had been overwhelmed by the polarity (darkness, mortality, evil) that he had so long repressed in his zeal to become a perfectly "good" Jedi knight. Now dying, Darth Vader finally surrenders to his incarnate, finite, limited, mortal status, instead of striving to be "all good" or "all evil." Now an integrated individual, he intervenes to halt his son's torment and hurls the Emperor into an abyss. Before dying of the wounds received in fighting with Luke, Darth Vader allows his son to remove the black helmet and face-mask that were a trademark of Vader's allegiance to the dark side. Beneath the helmet is a human face, wounded by time and age, but softened by suffering and insight. At this moment, Luke realizes that the dark side he has feared is not located in other people, such as his father, but is in himself. Reconciliation with his father enables Luke to integrate his own dark side without wholly identifying with it. In addition to becoming individuated through the process of integration and to becoming reconciled with each other, Luke and his father have also managed to destroy the dreaded Empire. The Empire itself is a manifestation of the awful consequences that follow when the ego-consciousnes of millions of people is overwhelmed by repressed and projected aspects of their own psyches. The film's message is clear: winning the battle against the evil embodied in others cannot substitute for dealing with the evil and darkness within oneself. And unless those shadowy, evil aspects are integrated, every person risks "going over" to the dark side.

Back in our own galaxy and era, the President of the United States has described America's chief opponent, the Soviet Union, as "the evil empire." And the leading Soviet newspaper has compared American behavior to that of Hitler. While there is no doubt that both countries have reasons for criticizing each other, the nature of the rhetoric often seems to be guided by an incomplete mythology which projects evil onto the other side. Neither side is willing to acknowledge what is good and life-giving about the other side; and both sides are eager to spot the signs of decay and corruption in the other. Guided missiles and hydrogen bombs are not the cause of the arms race, but symptoms of fear produced by incomplete, distorted myths. The latest round in the arms race, "Star Wars" or SDI, provides a good example of how incomplete mythology leads two countries to attribute the worst possible motives to each other's behavior. In the first part of this essay, I shall provide a discussion of SDI both as a symptom of incomplete mythology, and as a politically and technically infeasible way of handling the threat of nuclear war. In the second part, I shall present the view that only a complete mythology can lead us out of the current arms race. The widespread adoption of such a mythology would be tantamount to a new stage in human evolution, a stage necessary for the survival of the species.

TECHNICAL AND POLITICAL OBSTACLES TO A SPACE-BASED BALLISTIC MISSILE DEFENSE

On March 23, 1983, in a nationally televised address, President Ronald Reagan declared: "I call upon the scientific community who gave us nuclear weapons to turn their great talents to the cause of mankind and world peace; to give us the means of rendering these nuclear weapons impotent and obsolete." The President summoned American scientists to develop a space-based ballistic missile defense that would protect the United States from attack by Soviet ICBMs. No doubt, the President was inspired in part by the noble motive that guides the warrior: to protect and defend one's people against the aggression of the enemy. But he may have been guided by other motives as well, motives based upon an incomplete myth that portrays the Soviet Union as the evil empire that must be destroyed. While President Reagan seems to view the "Star Wars" proposal as a revolutionary step that will end the threat of nuclear war, critics argue that "Star Wars" is merely another technological "fix" that will bring forth a "counter-fix" by the Soviet Union, thereby continuing the spiral of the arms race.

The search for a technological fix is understandable. Even if it were true that the threat of nuclear war can only be ended by a shift in human self-understanding, that shift may be a while in coming. In the meantime, it is appropriate to be open to the possibility that technological innovations can help to ease tensions while we await the hoped-for change in human consciousness. Unfortunately, in addition to being burdened with apparently insuperable technical obstacles, the "Star Wars" fix seems to fuel the fires of suspicion rooted in incomplete mythology. Supporters of SDI regard it as a defensive weapon wielded by the forces of good against the war-loving evil empire: Soviet critics regard SDI as a part of an American plan to execute a successful "first-strike." My discussion of the technical and political problems of "Star Wars" will be limited, since my major aim is to show that this newest twist in the arms race is a manifestation of an incomplete myth.

President Reagan's call for a SDI was immediately criticized for a variety of reasons. There appear to be three major criticisms:

1) SDI is too complicated to work and can never be tested until needed for battle; hence, it should not become the basis for national defense.

2) SDI can be easily destroyed, overwhelmed, or evaded by relatively simple means.

3) This objection has two parts, both of which are based upon the following critical interpretation of SDI. SDI can never succeed in protecting American cities from Soviet warheads, but it might be developed sufficiently to be used as part of a first-strike strategy. With SDI in place, the United States could launch a surprise against Soviet missiles in their silos; against the weakened, disorganized Soviet response, SDI might provide a significant measure of protection. The two objections based on this interpretation are:

3A) SDI, which the Soviets regard as a first-strike plan that meshes with President Reagan's call for American nuclear "superiority," undermines President Reagan's own "build down" plan for arms control, for the USSR will vastly increase its highly accurate, land-based ICBM force as a way of overwhelming the American SP-BMD;

3B) SDI might lead the Soviets to "strike first as a last resort" if they thought the U.S. could attack the Soviet Union without fear of successful retaliation;

In addition, there are three other objections which are not as important for our purposes;

4) SDI continues the militarization of space;

5) SDI would have an uncertain, possibly detrimental, effect, on our relationship with our allies in NATO;

6) SDI appears to abrogate the ABM treaty signed in 1972.

Let us now discuss the three major objections briefly in turn.

1. The Problem of Complexity and Testing. SDI is too complex to trust without extensive testing, and it could never be tested until it is first used in a real situation. According to many scientists and technicians, space-based BMD poses apparently insurmountable technical problems. Richard De Lauer, Undersecretary of Defense, says that there would be eight components to the SP-BMD system, "every single one . . . equivalent to or greater than the Manhattan Project [that led to the production of the first atomic bomb during World War II]".[12] Another critical report concludes that

> For laser weapons to be effective against ICBMs, they would require targeting capabilities far beyond anything ever accomplished. The lasers would have to maintain near-perfect accuracy long enough to inflict damage upon targets traveling at more than 10,000 miles per hour, up to 3,500 miles away. A senior Pentagon weapons designer compared this targeting challenge to that of 'being on top of the Washington Monument, shooting a rifle, and hitting a baseball on top of the Empire State Building.'[13]

The technical problems have become so widely acknowledged that even proponents of SDI are now saying that it will be used primarily as a defense of American missile silos against Soviet ICBMs. It would be impossible fully to protect American society from a Soviet missile attack, because even if only 5 per cent of 8,000 warheads got through, the remaining 400 warheads would mortally wound the United States.

2. The Problem of a Soviet Anti-"Star Wars" Defense. Critics claim that a SP-BMD could easily be destroyed, overwhelmed, or evaded by means currently available to the Soviet Union. The Soviets could develop warheads that confuse radar tracking; release decoys that behave like warheads and thus saturate the defense; produce warheads that do not travel in straight lines toward the target; build warheads that are hardened and have deflectors that blunt the effect of lasers. Moreover, the space stations that would be needed to house the defensive missiles themselves would make fat targets for enemy attack, possibly coming from Soviet satellites. The Soviets could also reach American targets by Cruise and submarine missiles that would evade the system. Further, if the Soviets managed to produce an effective anti-satellite weapon (ASAT), they could use it to knock out the satellites that are necessary to guide the workings of an American SP-BMD. Many experts argue, in other words, that the proposed SDI has too many holes in it.

3. **Problems Resulting from Soviet Perceptions of SDI as a First-Strike Initiative.** Since the Soviets tend to interpret SDI as part of an American plan to attain first-strike capability, they would probably respond to SDI in a way that undermines President Reagan's own arms control strategy, which calls for both sides to "build down" their ICBMs. When the current administration came into power, there was much talk of a "window of vulnerability" opened up by the fact that large, highly accurate, land-based Soviet ICBMs could allegedly destroy American Minutemen missiles in their silos before launching. The loss of our land-based missiles in such a first strike would leave the U.S. President with an unacceptable set of options: 1) to attack Soviet cities with submarine-based missiles that are too inaccurate to hit hardened military targets, thereby inviting the Soviets to destroy our cities in turn; or 2) to surrender after the first strike. The Reagan-sponsored "build down" calls on the Soviets greatly to decrease their accurate land-based missiles so that American fears of a first-strike would be alleviated. But the Soviet response to any American SDI would be to vastly increase these accurate, land-based ICBMs in order to be able to overwhelm the defensive system. Hence, there is a basic incoherence to the present American administration's strategic arms policy.

The fact is that while 75 per cent of Soviet ICBMs are land based, only about 25 per cent of U.S. ICBMs are land based. This Soviet disadvantage in terms of vulnerability of forces leads the Soviets to suspect that the Reagan administration's SP-BMD plan is not defensive in nature, but offensive—part of a first-strike strategy that is reflected in the American drive deployment of highly-accurate MX,

Trident II, Cruise, and Pershing II missiles. Even if our intentions were wholly defensive in nature. the important thing is that the Soviet Union operates according to an incomplete mythology, in light of which our behavior appears to have the most evil possible intentions.[14]

Fears induced by highly accurate missiles are greatly aggravated by the possibility that one side will develop a successful SP-BMD. Secretary of Defense Weinberger is quoted as saying that a Soviet SB-BMD would be "one of the most frightening prospects imaginable."[15] Weinberger sees the Soviets in terms of an incomplete mythology according to which their intentions can *only* be evil, just as the Soviets regard our actions as necessarily evil in intent. We are mirror images of each other. Every move we make "defensively" appears to the other side as an aggressive move that calls for stronger defense; and we see this defensive reaction as a sign of aggression that calls for more defense.

American officials seem oblivious to the extent to which the Soviets are dominated by fear of being attacked once again by what they regard as the "imperialist" West. Having been invaded many times in their history, most recently by Hitler's army during World War II, the Soviets are resolved never again to be taken by surprise, just as the American people have sworn that they will never again be victimized by a "sneak attack" such as the one on Pearl Harbor. Although Soviet citizens may be somewhat cynical about communist ideology, they remain devout patriots. As Hedrick Smith notes in his excellent book. *The Russians,*

> In an age grown skeptical of undiluted patriotism, Russians are perhaps the world's most passionate patriots. Without question, a deep and tenacious love of country is the most powerful unifying force in the Soviet Union. . . . For Russians, *rodina* [motherland] stirs the gut patriotism that freedom and democracy used to for Americans. . . . It captures the profound spiritual meaning that the nation has for the Russian psyche.[16]

While Americans may have legitimate reasons to be suspicious of Soviet motives, we must learn to see the "enemy" not as a faceless monster, but instead as a society composed of human beings with their own struggles with good and evil. It is one thing to maintain a defense that can deter a Soviet attack, but it is another thing to design a system that would enable us to destroy the Soviet Union while remaining relatively unharmed ourselves. The drive to develop such a system strikes fear into the heart of a people who are operating in light of their own version of the incomplete mythology that leads us to seek to annihilate them in the first place. In turn, the Soviet Union must retract its shadow and acknowledge that its own behavior can appear as menacing to the United States. Given the distorted nature of the mythologies guiding each superpower, however, it will be difficult for either side to integrate its own darkness.

The second half of the third objection to SDI is that the Soviets might become so fearful about its development that they would "strike first as a last resort" if SDI were about to become operational. Reporting on his trip to the Soviet Union, Thomas Powers notes that

> I heard many Russians say they felt it would come to war in the end. I have *never* heard an American say this. I heard many Russians cite Chekhov's famous principle of dramaturgy: If there is a gun on the wall in the first act, it will fire in the third. I have *never* heard an American official or professional defense analyst speak in such fatalistic tones. One man even told me that the American nuclear buildup might force the Russians to launch a pre-emptive attack on the United States.[17]

This pessimistic Russian view contrasts sharply with the optimistic American view. It is a mistake to assume that our behavior will be interpreted by others in the same way that we ourselves interpret it. Morever, it is important to see that Soviet perceptions and behavior are determined to a large extent by a national inferiority complex. The Soviets (and here I am thinking primarily of the Russians) have long felt that they are regarded as backward. They yearn to be respected and accepted by the world, especially the West, and they are unwilling to be "pushed around" by anyone, as is often the case with people who feel inferior. Hedrick Smith claims that

> It is almost impossible to exaggerate the importance of this gnawing inferiority complex as a clue to Soviet motivation in relations with the West today. The Russians are determined

not to be backward, not to be second best, but to be *seen* as the *equals* of their chief rival on the world arena today—the Americans. By today's standards the greatness of a state is measured by its might as a nuclear power and its prowess in space. Hence, the Russians will make the sacrifices necessary to attain equality with America, or at least to project the image of equality, especially in those fields.[18]

In summary, the initial claim that SDI would bring about an end to the threat of nuclear war appears to be false. At best, SDI would simply raise the arms race to a new, more intensified level. "Hair-trigger" computer commands would probably have to be established in light of the speeds at which SP-BMD would operate. Control of nuclear forces would be turned over to machines. Moreover, SDI aggravates the fears and reinforces the stereotypical projections of the Soviet Union, just as Soviet-sponsored research for their own SB-BMD frightens us and reinforces our convictions about their evil intentions.

Is there *any* justification for SDI? In giving a very cautious "yes," I agree with Freeman Dyson, who maintains that defensive shields against enemy missiles make sense only if both sides possess such shields and only if both sides first drastically reduce their offensive weaponry.[19] If such a reduction were to occur, however, the need for the shield itself would be called into question. And for a reduction in offensive missiles to take place, a dramatic shift would have to occur in relations between the United States and the Soviet Union. In the second half of this essay, I shall consider the extent to which a new, complete mythology would contribute significantly to such a shift.

TOWARD THE DEVELOPMENT OF A COMPLETE MYTHOLOGY

In the history of warfare, many defensive shields have been invented, and just as many offensive weapons have been devised to penetrate them.[20] The cannon rendered useless the fort, and the crossbow made obsolete the armor worn by knights. Just so, new offensive weaponry will be devised to penetrate SB-BMD. The arms race cannot go on indefinitely; eventually, the weapons will be used. The situation is desperate. What is to be done?

The first step would be to *experience this despair.*[21] At present, however, people deny that they are desperate. They do so because of an incomplete mythology which enables them to project death and evil onto the enemy, and to imagine that by building more weapons they can protect themselves against death and evil. Real despair, as Kierkegaard once remarked, is not knowing that you are desperate. The desperate pace of the arms race is a sign of the profound despair being denied by the leaders and citizens of both superpowers. Denial of despair leads to the condition that Robert Jay Lifton has called "psychic numbing."[22] Such numbing leads us either to deny the threat of nuclear war, or to continue thinking in the dualistic way that spurs on the arms race. To experience despair means to discover the illusory quality of one's dream of being able to control everything and to make things turn out alright. To experience despair means to encounter both one's impotence in the face of death and one's complicity in evil. Surrendering to despair, then, is a crucial step in retracting the projections of the shadow and in integrating the psyche. Such integration frees us from numbness and dualism. It enables us to become involved in the process of finding an alternative to the suicidal arms race, without succumbing to the temptation that "the generals" or "the politicans" are the "bad guys" responsible for our situation. Psychic integration and individuation elicit compassion for people in power who are doing what they think is best in terms of their own understanding of things. Those who persist in blaming President Reagan, or his Soviet counterpart, for the current situation are still projecting their shadow and thinking dualistically. A "peace movement" that engages in polarization is engaging in warfare. Military officers and politicians are not the enemy; they are only reflections of who we ourselves are.

The nuclear arms race, then, can be viewed not merely as a threat to be defended against, but also as an opportunity to begin integrating the projected shadow that gave rise to such weapons. Through such a process of integration, humanity would evolve into a higher form of life. The opportunity is to evolve as a species; to move beyond the dualistic, we vs. them, good vs. evil thinking that is the root cause of warfare. Only such a change in human awareness will provide the context necessary for ending the arms race. Humanity's current dualistic mode of self-understanding is the product of thousands of years of evolution, a crucial stage of which occurred when human beings became aware of their separateness both from their tribes and from Nature. The separate self experienced its differentiation from the world. The original dualism of self vs. other became the categorial matrix for describing all of reality. There arose the dualities of black vs. white, good vs. evil, life vs. death, male vs. female, culture vs. nature, light vs. dark, right vs. left, even vs. odd. Accompanying this dualism, moreover, was fear of annihilation, or death-anxiety.

Ken Wilber has argued that dualism and death-anxiety are responsible for the origin of murder and warfare.[23] People developed heroic myths which, primarily in their distorted interpretations, suggested that by killing the enemy, death and evil would be destroyed. Hence, the historical popularity of warfare. Wilber uses the term "Atman project" the effort by the separate, finite ego to make itself immortal.[24] The God project may be a manifestation of patriarchal culture, according to which nature, body, sex, limitation, and death are female, while culture, mind, soul, language, power, and immortality are male. To gain security, the anxiety-ridden ego must control everything. This drive for control is tempered to some extent for as long as traditional religious formations retain some influence. Such traditions guarantee eternal life only for those who obey the Divine proscriptions against murder, theft, adultery, idolatry, and so on. But the idea of eternal life is easily mis-interpreted to mean the immortality of the ego, i.e., the everlastingness of a finite creature. In the middle ages, spiritual "techniques" were developed to guarantee the certainty of salvation for their practitioners. This quest for certainty was translated into the quest for secular security, as traditional religion waned during early modern times. The application of modern science through machine technology is the modern version of the quest for security. Modern humanity views nature merely as an object, a commodity, or raw material whose value lies in its usefulness for humanity.[25] Everything, including human beings (the most important "raw material"), must be monitored, disciplined, utilized, and ordered about in accordance with the imperative of survival. People construct missiles with nuclear warheads for the sake of saving life, even though using such missiles will destroy life, because people are still operating from within an incomplete, dualistic mythology.

As the danger mounts, there are some signs that a shift in human self-understanding may be occurring. The encounter between East and West is playing an important role here. Whereas it was previously thought that West was transforming East via science, technology, and industry, it now appears that East is also transforming West via the introduction of nondualistic thinking. Eastern mythology is essentially nondualistic, despite the fact that Eastern peoples have often distorted their own myths and have therefore murdered and plundered just as their Western counterparts have. Nevertheless, the increasing influx into the West of relatively undistorted, nondualistic Eastern mythology can help Westerners rediscover the nondualistic aspect of their own myths. For example, exoteric Judaeo-Christian tradition is usually interpreted in dualistic terms. God is radically distinguished from Creation, humans from nonhumans, good from evil. However, an increasing number of Christians and Jews maintain that such distinctions are not absolute and ought not to be taken literally. The Divine both transcends Creation and is present within it.[26]

Nondualistic thinking involves integrating opposites. The Taoistic teaching of yin and yang, for example, holds that vitality depends on the creative interplay of apparent polarities. In our own Western tradition, Heraclitus tells us that "the way up and the way down are the same." Dualistic thinking, by way of contrast, denies any relation between opposites. The anxiety-ridden, dualistic-thinking ego, for example, identifies solely with rational, abstract, linear, atomistic, and hierarchical categories, while repressing or belittling intuitive, relational, circular, mutuality-enhancing categories. Rational, linear thinking offers the ego the illusion of control. At work in both Washington, D.C., and Moscow, the rational ego keeps coming up with a new device, technique, or plan that will throw the enemy off balance once and for all. The ego, under the illusion that it is actually capable of forestalling death and evil, is highly suspicious of alternative approaches to human relationships—approaches based on acknowledging limitations, mortality, and complicity in evil, but also based on recognition of mutual need, relationship, and shared vision.

For skeptics who wonder how doing something so "trivial" as retracting the shadow can have any impact in the complex realm of international relations, I offer the following example from recent history. Prior to Richard Nixon's historic visit to the People's Republic of China in 1972, the United States had regarded the communist

Chinese as the very incarnation of evil: yellow devils who deserved to be "nuked" before their rot infected other countries. Naturally, so long as the United States berated China and insisted that it conform to American expectations, the Chinese persisted in their allegiance to a rigid communist orthodoxy (later upset by Mao's tragic "cultural revolution"). The United States projected almost limitless evil onto the Chinese. However, when Henry Kissinger and Nixon decided that friendship with the Chinese was important both in and of itself and strategically, they created a new context for relationship between the United States and China. This creative move involved two steps. First, it was declared that China and the United States would henceforth be in a relationship that, despite disagreements, would endure. Second, both the United States and China retracted much of the evil and darkness that they had been projecting onto each other. The facts about both countries remained unchanged. Suddenly, however, China appeared very differently to people in the United States. Americans began seeing the Chinese once again as exotic, enchanting, mysterious. Moreover, the Chinese, no longer reacting against the evil being projected upon them, began experimenting with their social and economic system. Communist orthodoxy gave way to a pragmatic willingness to try out free-market practices to improve the economy. So long as they felt that the Americans were forcing them to change, the Chinese resisted; they had to "save face." When the context was created in which China could be itself *and* also be in relationship with the United States, there were set into motion enormous social changes that were wholly unpredictable so long as China was viewed from within a context colored by projected evil.

It is possible that our relationship with the Soviet Union could be significantly altered if we were to withdraw the projections we cast upon them. Withdrawing projections does not mean unilateral disarmament; it does mean, however, devising one's foreign policy and military planning in terms of perceptions that are not distorted by projected evil. We insist that the Soviet Union stop being a "bully" and enter into the "civilized" community. How well do any of us, however, change in the face of people who are projecting their own shadows onto us and insisting that we change? Even if we recognize that there is some truth to their criticism, we resist giving in to their demands.

The present world-situation is portrayed in the following image: A lifeboat floats on a shark-infested, stormy sea. Two groups of people, clearly afraid of each other, are huddled at either end of the boat. Each group has a heroic individual armed with a cannon pointed at the people at the other end of the lifeboat. The heroes tell each other: "If you make a false move, I'll blow up your end of the lifeboat." While the people at both ends of the lifeboat want to be saved from the cannon of the enemy, they are becoming aware that if *either* cannon is used, everyone will die. Dualistic thinking, incomplete mythology, and projection of their shadow prevents them from finding a way to live together on the lifeboat.

The lifeboat of the superpowers is the planet Earth. The extraordinary satellite photographs of our brilliant, blue-green planet reveal no political boundaries. Such boundaries are human constructs which we tend to absolutize. Today, however, faced with the existence of nuclear weapons that could destroy lifeboat Earth, we must learn not to absolutize political boundaries and nation-states. Just as tribes halted their intertribal warfare and banded together into larger communities, and later into nations, humanity as a whole must learn to bond together into a human community in which nuclear warfare is simply unacceptable. We must extend our sense of identification to include the whole Earth and all its people. For this to happen successfully, however, we require a nondistorted mythology that supports people both in achieving ego-consciousness and in moving beyond it toward nondualistic consciousness.

Currently, however, many people misinterpret nondualistic thought as the opposite of dualistic thought. Hence, if dualistic thought is aggressive and controlling, nondualistic thought must be timid and passive. Thus, a genuinely individuated person would be some kind of wimp. Nondualism, however, is *not* the opposite of dualism, but operates at a different level altogether. Nondualism integrates the psyche in such a way that energy once used to repress or project now becomes available for more creative, interesting activity. An individuated person is more "active" than any person driven into incessant business by false hopes of evading death. Moreover, the individuated person is more "calm" than any person driven into depression or lassitude by unintegrated unconscious forces. The nondualistic, integrated person recognizes differences among things, but does not absolutize them. Moreover, such a person manifests the creative interplay of forces that Heraclitus called *polemos*. Nondualism does not mean the end of conflict, but the end of that polarizing thinking that absolutely divides the participants in conflicts. Nondualistic thinking means that even in one's enemy, one continues to see oneself.

Moreover, nondualistic thinking enables one to see that one's "enemy," far from being radically other and alien, is in fact necessary for one's own personal development. Nietzsche wrote in a penetrating way about the importance of the "friendly enemy." More recently, Robert Fuller has spoken of the need to develop a "better game than war."[27] Hitherto, the war game has provided the opportunity for heroism, self-sacrifice, nobility, and devotion to duty. The murderous character of war, however, was enhanced by an incomplete mythology that portrayed the enemy as the very instrument of death and evil. In an age of nuclear weapons, the bloody version of war is no longer viable. What we require is a new game, one that can still inspire people to great heights, but in a way that is more complete and less destructive than war. This game would be a manifestation of a new myth that would take the place of the old myth that heralded victory and conquest. The new myth would herald the achievement of completion. The game arising from this myth would provide opportunities for people to find ways of completing themselves, of integrating their shadows, of becoming whole, through the process of competition with the "enemy." An enemy is useful, according to Fuller, to motivate a person to discover and integrate those areas which one represses, denies, or projects. A great enemy challenges one to work toward completion, either of oneself or of one's society.

Currently, both superpowers regard each other merely as obstacles to the achievement of their respective purposes. In light of the new myth and its corresponding game of completion, however, the superpowers would regard each other as ideal enemies that help each side to confront and integrate its own darkness, mortality, limitation, and possibility. Competition would not be aimed at eliminating the enemy, but instead at cultivating and appreciating the enemy so that the enemy could become more effective in bringing out the best in one's own side. I do not wish to appear naive. There are people in high places in both Moscow and Washington, D.C., who want nothing more than to obliterate the enemy, and for whom all talk of cooperative enmity is ridiculous. We live in an age, however, that does not permit us the luxury of continuing to think in "sensible" ways. While those pushing the current arms race might find that it is perfectly coherent from the inside, the same arms race reveals itself as insane when viewed from without. As Einstein once noted, it is not possible to use old ways of thinking to solve the problems created by those same ways of thinking.

Another factor that might help to promote the emergence of nondualistic mythology is the re-emergence of interest on the part of scientists, philosophers, and theologians in cosmology. Contemporary cosmologists now portray humanity as matter-energy in the process of becoming aware of itself.[28] Much previous cosmology was governed by the view that the universe is nothing but a great machine. Morever, the dualistic view of scientific thought described the human subject as essentially distinct from the natural object being studied. Nature was allegedly "value-free" and purpose-less, while humanity was the source of value and purpose. During the nineteenth century, Western humanity increasingly arrogated to itself characteristics that once belonged to the Biblical God. We came to portray ourselves as the measure and even the origin of all truth, reality, and value. Nature became raw material to be dominated for human ends. But many people, including scientists, are now saying that humanity itself is an organ by which the cosmos studies itself. We have not created ourselves, but have been brought forth by the open-ended, value-creating, novelty-producing processes of cosmic evolution. Our purpose on Earth, then, is not merely to survive through domination, but instead to play an as-yet-undefined role is cosmic evolution. We are, as it were, the eyes and ears of the cosmos. We did not ask for this role, but instead were born to it. The new mythology will make clear that modern science can be shown to be consistent with the accounts of Creation provided by many major religious traditions. The Divine, some theologians have speculated, empties or surrenders Itself to matter-energy and is confident that eventually matter-energy will bring forth self-conscious forms of life through which the Divine can know Itself once again.[29] Other theologians are taking a cue from feminists and are re-discovering the "Goddess" who has been subordinated so long to the male God.[30] It would require another essay, however, to discuss the importance of the re-emergence of the feminine principle in our dark time. Suffice it to say that the mythic symbol now developing will be one that integrates male and female.

Although I believe that only a renewed mythology can bring an end to the nuclear arms race, and make all talk of "Star Wars" obsolete, I am also aware that mythology cannot be renewed or invented at will. All individuals can do is to work on themselves such that they can become accessible to the possibility of a shift toward non-dualistic thinking. A new heroic myth for our times is that each of us is responsible for helping to initiate that shift in consciousness. The time may be ripe for the evolution of a new stage of human awareness and history. If the Divine is in fact at work in the world, we may have faith that the shift will occur in time to avert the total destruction of the Earth. It is important to recall, however, that the Divine is not "out there," but present within each of us. In surrendering to mortality, paradoxically, we enter into relation with the Divine. When our projections are withdrawn, and when our egos are integrated with the unconscious and with the Self, then we are capable of seeing our own humanity in the eyes of the enemy. This, in turn, encourages them to see themselves in us. At this point, something other than war occurs.

NOTES

1. The first definition of "myth" in *The Oxford English Dictionary* is "A purely fictitious narrative usually involving supernatural persons, actions, or events, and embodying some popular idea concerning natural or historical phenomena."

2. Ernest Becker, *The Denial of Death* (New York: The Free Press, 1973).

3. Jung's *Collected Works* are voluminous. A selection of his writings include: *Symbols of Transformation*, trans. R.F.C. Hull (Princeton: Princeton University Press/Bollingen, 1976); *Analytical Psychology: Its Theory and Practice* (New York: Vintage, 1968); *Two Essays on Analytical Psychology*, trans. R.F.C. Hull (Princeton: Princeton University Press/Bollingen, 1966); *Modern Man in Search of a Soul*, trans. W.S. Dell and Cary F. Baynes (New York: Harcourt, Brace & World, Inc., 1933); *The Spirit in Man, Art, and Literature*, trans. R.F. C. Hull (Princeton: Princeton University Press/Bollingen, 1971); *The Portable Jung*, ed. by Joseph Campbell (New York: Viking Press, 1971).

4. Cf. for example, Rosemary Radford Ruether, *New Woman New Earth: Sexist Ideologies and Human Liberation* (New York: The Seabury Press, 1975). For an interesting defense of Jung's views of the development of the self, cf. M. Esther Harding, *The I and the Not I* (Princeton: Princeton University Press/Bollingen, 1973).

5. Edward F. Edinger, *Ego and Archetype: Individuation and the Religious Function of the Psyche* (New York: Penguin Books, 1972), p. 120.

6. Erich Neumann, *The Origins and History of Consciousness*, trans., R.F.C. Hull (Princeton: Princeton University Press/Bollingen, 1970). Ruether, *New Woman New Earth*, offers an insightful feminist critique of Jung and Neumann's views on individuation.

7. Robert Tucker, *Philosophy and Myth in Karl Marx* (Cambridge: Cambridge University Press, 1972).

8. For a very insightful, mythological treatment of early American attitudes toward Indians and the land, cf. Richard Slotkin, *Regeneration through Violence: The Mythology of the American Frontier, 1600-1860* (Middletown: Wesleyan University Press, 1973).

9. Cf. Marie-Louise von Franz, *Puer Aeternus: A Psychological Study of the Adult Struggle with the Paradise of Childhood* (Santa Monica, California: SIGO Press, 1981).

10. Joseph Campbell, *The Hero With a Thousand Faces* (Princeton: Princeton University Press/Bollingen, 1968).

11. For a very helpful analysis of the first film from the series, cf. *"Star Wars*: The Modern Developmental Fairy Tale," by John F. McDermott, Jr., M.D. and K.Y. Lum, M.D., *Bulletin of the Menninger Clinic*, 49 (No. 4), 1980, pp. 381-390.

12. Richard De Lauer, as cited in *Space-Based Missile Defense*, ed. by The Union of Concerned Science (Cambridge, Mass.: 1984); an abridged version of this report appeared in *The New York Review of Books*, XXXI, No. 7, April, 1984. Since 1983, a vast critical literature has been produced about SDI. A sampling includes: *Journal of the Federation of American Scientists*, "Special Issue on Anti-Satellite Weapons," 36 (November, 1983); Richard L. Garwin, Kurt Gottfried and Donald L. Hafner, "Antisatellite Weapons," *Scientific American*, 250 (June, 1984), 45-55; Hans A. Bethe, Richard L. Garwin, Kurt Gottfried, and Henry W. Kendall, "Space-based Ballistic-Missile Defense," *Scientific American*, 251 (October, 1984), 39-49; George W. Ball, "The Way for Star Wars," *The New York Review of Books*, XXXII (April 11, 1985), 39-44; Herbert Lin, "The Development of Software for Ballistic-Missile Defense," *Scientific American*, 253 (December, 1985), 46-53; Charles L. Glaser, "Star Wars Bad Even if it Works," *Bulletin of the Atomic Scientists*, 42 (March, 1985), 13-16; Frank von Hippel, "Attacks on Star Wars Critics a Diversion," *Bulletin of the Atomic Scientists*, 41 (April, 1985), 8-10; Gerald E. Marsh, "SDI: The Stability Question," 41 (October, 1985), 23-25; Wayland Kennet, "Star Wars: Europe's Polite Waffle" *Bulletin of the Atomic Scientists*, 41 (September, 1985), 7-11. An interesting defense of SDI is found in Thomas H. Krebs, "Tsar Wars: The Soviet Space Challenge," unpublished MS.

13. The Union of Concerned Scientists, "The New Arms Race: Star Wars Weapons," Briefing Paper No. 5, 1983.

14. Talk of an American first-strike may be confusing to those who continue to believe that American defense policy is one of deterrence based on the doctrine of mutually assured destruction (MAD). MAD worked on the

premise that if the Soviets attacked us with nuclear weapons, they would be committing suicide, for we would reply with a devastating counterattack. American military leaders have never been particularly happy with the MAD approach, not only because suicide is not an acceptable military outcome, but also because MAD works on an immoral basis: each side holds as hostages the civilians on the other side. MAD was maintained, however, because of the inaccuracy of ICBMs until the mid-1960s. Inaccurate missiles could not be certain of destroying enemy missiles in their protected silos. Increasingly accurate missiles, however, *can* destroy enemy missile silos. A fact that has led the United States away from MAD toward a "counterforce" strategy, i.e., one aimed at destroying the enemy's military targets, and away from a "countervalue" strategy, i.e., one aimed at civilian targets. Both superpowers now possess these highly accurate missiles. Hence, tensions have increased, since both sides suspect that the other side may be planning to use the new missiles in a "sneak attack."

15. As cited in *Space-Based Missile Defense*, op. cit.

16. Hedrick Smith, *The Russians* (New York: Quadrangle / The New York Times Book Co., 1976), p. 303.

17. Thomas Powers, "What Is It About?," *The Atlantic Monthly*, 253, No. 1 (January, 1984), p. 48.

18. Hedrick Smith, *The Russians*, pp. 234-235.

19. Freeman Dyson, in *Weapons and Hope*, as it originally appeared in *The New Yorker*, February 6, 13, 20, 27, 1984.

20. On the history of military technology, cf. William H. McNeill, *The Pursuit of Power: Technology, Armed Force, and Society since A.D. 1000* (Chicago: The University of Chicago Press, 1982).

21. On this topic, cf. Joanna R. Macy, *Despair and Personal Power in the Nuclear Age* (Philadelphia: Society Publishers, 1982).

22. Robert Jay Lifton, *The Broken Connection: On Death and the Continuity of Life* (New York: Simon and Schuster, 1979); cf. also Jerome D. Frank, *Sanity and Survival in the Nuclear Age: Psychological Aspects of War and Peace* (New York: Random House, 1982); Jonathan Schell, *The Fate of the Earth* (New York: Alfred A. Knopf, 1982).

23. Ken Wilber, *Up from Eden: A Transpersonal View of Human Evolution* (Boulder: Shambhala, 1981).

24. Ken Wilber, *The Atman Project* (Weaton, Illinois: Quest Books, 1980).

25. Martin Heidegger wrote extensively on the human objectification and domination of nature. For a treatment of his thought,cf. Michael E. Zimmerman, "Toward a Heideggerean *Ethos* for Radical Environmentalism," *Environmental Ethics*, V (Summer, 1983), 99-131. For an analysis of the role played by anthropocentric humanism in the nuclear arms race, cf. Zimmerman, "Humanism, Ontology, and the Nuclear Arms Race," *Research in Philosophy and Technology*, ed. Paul T. Durbin and Carl Mitcham, V (1983), 157-172; and Zimmerman, "Anthropocentric Humanism and Nuclear Weapons," in *Nuclear War: Philosophical Perspectives*, ed. Michael Fox and Leo Groarke (New York/Bern: Peter Lang Publishers, Inc., 1985).

26. On the non-dualistic basis of the Christian tradition, cf. Alan Watts, *The Supreme Identity* (New York: Vintage, 1972).

27. Robert Fuller, "A Better Game than War: Interview with Robert Fuller," *Evolutionary Blues*, Vol. II (Arcata, California), 1983.

28. Recently, a great deal has been published about how new trends in science are leading to a reassessment of humanity's place in the universe. Cf. for example, John Barrow and Frank Tipler, *The Cosmological Anthropic Principle* (New York: Oxford University Press, 1986); John P. Briggs and F. David Peat, *The Looking-Glass Universe: The Emerging Science of Wholeness* (New York: Simon and Schuster, 1984); Paul Davies, *Other Worlds* (New York: Simon and Schuster, 1982); John Briggin, *In Search of Schroedinger's Cat: Quantum Physics and Reality* (New York: Bantam Books, 1984); Fritjof Capra, *The Tao of Physics* (New York: Bantam Books, 1982); Fritjof Capra, *The Turning Point* (New York: Bantam Books, 1983); David Bohm, *Wholeness and the Implicate Order* (Longon, Routledge & Kegan Paul, 1983).

29. Cf. A.R. Peacocke, *Creation and the World of Science* (Oxford: Oxford Universe Press, 1979).

30. Cf. Carol P. Christ and Judith Plaskow, editors, *Womanspirit Rising: A Feminist Reader in Religion* (New York: Harper & Row, 1979); Charlene Spretnak, editor, *The Politics of Women's Spirituality* (Garden City, New York: Anchor Books, 1982); Edward C. Whitmont, *Return of the Goddess* (New York: The Crossroad Publishing Company, 1982); Elaine Storkey, *What's Right with Feminism* (Grand Rapids, Michigan: William B. Eerdmans Publishing Company, 1985).

31. Thanks to Randolf Howell for his helpful critical reading of an earlier version of this essay, and to Teresa Toulouse for her encouragement and editorial assistance.

CHAPTER THIRTEEN

Laying Down a Path in Walking: A Biologist's Look at a New Biology and Its Ethics

FRANCISCO J. VARELA, PH.D.

The great sea
Has sent me adrift,
It moves me as the weed in a great river.
Earth and the great weather move me.
Have carried me away.
And move my inward parts with joy.[1]

Like a fugue we hear from afar, the transition from where we are to where we shall be is ruled by a few chords that play over and over again, everywhere.

What moves me in the poem I have chosen as an epigraph is the swift somersault between the so-called inner and outer. Between mind and nature, between rocks and bowels. Where do we find here the proud distance between us and it? There is no distance, not even the distance between an it and its picture, which makes it possible to ask how accurate a representation the picture is. The theme of the fugue I am hearing, then, moves past a split Cartesianism to give flesh to a world of no-distance by mutual interdefinition.

In these pages I intend to spell out this theme as it plays in biology, and the way in which it shapes some fundamental problems. This is what I understand to be the "new biology." It is a ferment of the current dynamics of biological research. I shall speak here as a research biologist, not as a cultural historian.

Let me make a confession before I plunge into the subject. I am a bigot in epistemology. To me, the chance of surviving with dignity on this planet hinges on the acquisition of a new mind. This new mind must be wrought, among other things, from a radically different epistemology which will inform relevant actions. Thus, over and above their intrinsic beauty, I take these epistemological meanderings as vital. Literally. Therefore, in the discussion that follows, I would like you to direct your mind to the same place you would if the discussion were about, say, animistic cosmology. Our current notions about evolution and brain will be as distant to our grandchildren as this animistic cosmology is to us today.

My strategy for leading you in the direction I am looking will be as follows. First, I shall present a rough sketch of the main issues involved through the use of a metaphor disguised as a thought experiment. Second, I shall show how these issues take flesh in the current notions of evolution and its alterations. Third, I shall examine the brain sciences from a similar perspective. The choice of both of these areas of biology is, of course, no accident, for evolution and cognition are really flip sides of the same conceptual coin (as Gregory Bateson was fond of reminding us). In the fourth section of the paper, you will have, I trust, new conceptual goggles, so that when we come back to the main issues again, they will be virtually redundant to you. You will be able to state them in your own language, for your own concerns.

A First Glimpse into Autonomous Unity

A simple, yet quite accurate way to state what I see as the pivot of the transition from the old biology (half a century) into a new one is as follows. Instead of being mainly concerned with heteronomous units which relate to their world by the logic of correspondence, the new biology is concerned with the autonomous units which operate by the logic of coherence. Thus, the contrast I am proposing is

Current biology: Heteronomous units operating by a logic of correspondence.

New biology: Autonomous units operating by a logic of coherence.

Now, I might as well have written that in Martian, for those two aphoristic remarks are too densely packed. Let us move on to unfold the remarks by the aid of a thought experiment.

Imagine in your mind's eye and ear a mobile, with thin pieces of glass dangling like leaves off branches, which dangle from other branches, and so on. Any gust of wind will cause the mobile to tinkle, the whole structure changing its position, speed, torsion of the branches, and so on.

Clearly, how the mobile sounds is not determined or instructed by the wind or the gentle push we may give it. The way it sounds has more to do with (is easier to understand in terms of) the kinds of structural configurations it has when it receives a perturbation or imbalance. Every mobile will have a typical melody and tone proper to its constitution. In other words, it is obvious in this example that in order to understand the sound patterns we hear, we turn to the nature of the chimes and not to the wind that hits them.

But let's carry this *Gedanken* experiment just one step further and imagine now that the intricate structure of leaves and branches full of tinklers has the unusual capacity of moving the entire thing over the ceiling where it hangs. This could be accomplished, say, through detachable air-sucking devices which are alternately pressurized and depressurized. Thus, in this improved mobile-mobile, any gust of wind will produce not only a tinkling sound, but also a motion in some direction.

Would not it be a surprise if we find that the whole mobile-mobile is moving with some sensible (to us) behavior? For instance, each time a wind blows, the mobile moves around until it finds a place with less wind, or, conversely, it searches for the origin of the air current and thus delights us with almost perpetual melodies.

If this mobile-mobile wind chime were to show such behavior, we would conclude that someone has designed it with cunning imagination so that it can do what it does. It seems utterly inconceivable that a mobile could come up with such smart motions by random arrangement of leaves, branches, and air-sucking devices.

The point of this example is to suggest the relative ease with which a degree of self-involvedness immediately gives the system a desire for autonomy vis-à-vis its medium. That is to say, the fact that it handles its medium according to its internal structure becomes the predominant phenomenon. If you think of the mobile-mobile as having a perception of the world, then clearly perception is not a matter of what gets into it, like, for example, an instruction for a man-made device. Perception has to do, rather, with how the the system is put together, and, moreover, with how it perceives itself, in the sense that its own entanglement is the key to understanding what will happen to it.

A second point of the example is to realize that should an apparently sensible behavior arise, the temptation is to say that is has been engineered in some way. Let us examine this point more closely by introducing the last complication into our thought experiment, as follows. I now assure you that in the case of this mobile-mobile which exhibits such an interesting behavior there has been no design whatsoever; indeed, the structural configuration exhibiting such interesting behavior patterns was arrived at by pure trial and error, a sort of tinkering with the shapes of the branches and the interconnections with the air-sucking devices. What are we then to say?

The traditional explanation (or description) of the situation would be that the system has some degree of internal representation of the physical environment, so that it knows how to respond to the wind. It has a correspondence to the world through a simple mirroring of some of its qualities. The mobile-mobile has become a representational system, that is to say, an active, self-updating collection of structures capable of "mirroring" the world as it changes. Now, if there had been an engineer who had actually figured out how to put the branches together so as to produce this behavior, such a description would seem appropriate. But, *ex hypothesi*, the system came into being by mere tinkering, not design. How then are we to approach this situation?

We need a subtle but powerful twist: we emphasize the system's coherence, instead of taking the perspective of a supposed design. In other words, we understand the system as an autonomous cognitive system: an active, self-updating collection of structures capable of informing (or shaping) its surrounding medium into a world through a history of structural coupling with it.

These, then, are two alternative modes of description. One supposes mirroring and representation of features which are relevant and visible to us as observers, and requires, in some form or another, an agent which designs, because it requires a perspective from which this correspondence of world to the innards of the system is established *ex-professo*. The second perspective is more parsimonious. It states that out of the many possible paths of tinkering, the particular one we observe allows us to see what is a world for the system, that is, the particular way in which it has maintained a continuous history of coupling with its medium without disintegration. There is no mirroring, but in-forming. The first description hinges on a logic of correspondence; the other on a logic by coherence.

There is more than meets the eye in this *Gedanken* experiment. It really underscores a change in attitude and framework that has ramified implications, as we shall presently see. The reasons for this are simple; we have changed our point of view from an externally instructed unit with an independent environment linked to a privileged observer, to an autonomous unit with an environment whose features are inseparable from the history of coupling with that unit, and thus with no privileged perspective. In so doing, we are also on our way to spelling out a mechanism by which cognitive processes can be understood and built, a mechanism by which unities can endow a world with a sense through their structure and history of interactions.

A description by correspondence is essential for relating to units such as computers and washing machines (until they break down), but it turns out to be a rather limiting framework to use when it comes to life and mind (that is, for almost everything). Let us now turn to what this framework does for our understanding of evolution and the brain.

A WALK THROUGH THE ADAPTATIONIST PROGRAM AND BACK AGAIN

Think for a moment of the bar scene in *Star Wars*; picture the beings present there, and let us look at them through the eyes of a zoologist. The most obvious observation is that they are essentially of one kind: vertebrate-like. There are wild varieties in dermatological appearance—type of skin, shape of eyes—but they stand up straight, and most of them even look warm-blooded. How a culture conceives of imaginary beings is a clear indication of its conception of life, because it sets off the limits of what is imaginable. In seventeenth-century zoology texts, next to eagles and chickens, we can find beings with human bodies bearing birds' heads. It was all conceivable, part of the same nature. In the twentieth-century showcase of imaginary zoology in *Star Wars*, we see nothing of the sort; uniformity is the essential guiding principle.

The point of this digression is to introduce the idea that in our culture at large—including science—we see ourselves as the best and only possible way of being intelligent. We have come up from modest beginnings through a direct path of optimization in an evolution guided by natural selection. What are the biological roots of this commonsensical understanding? The answer to that question lies in the main characteristics of evolutionary thinking over the last half century, which is in fact not difficult to state: the search for optimal mechanisms of adaptation to the world. Let me explain.

Stated bluntly, this approach assumes that species and communities have become, through their history, optimally adapted to their niche. The job of the evolutionist is to find the precise ways in which this process has occurred. It is not a matter of if, but how. Natural selection is seen as an ingenious engineer or smart gambler in the game of life versus environment (without assuming an external purpose, of course). The search for this optimization most commonly takes the form of isolating a specific trait from the organism's morphology, physiology, or behavior, and finding what it is optimum for and how. For example, one shows that the shape of cilia in protozoans are such that they are at their hydrodynamic optimum. (This sometimes gives rise to puzzles, when there is no evident feature of the world to deal with: What are the big plaques on *Stegosaurus* for?)

There is another stream of research in evolutionary biology which starts from an entirely different point of view, but ends up at exactly the same place. This is the study of population genetics. The idea here is to produce a description of the genetic endowment of communities on the basis of reproductive patterns and geographical distribution. The goal is to predict the rate and direction of change of genetic pools. The underlying view is still the same: the equations governing the genetic dynamics must have an optimal solution which maximizes fitness.

There has been much discussion, both within science and in popular scientific publications, about how this "classical" view of evolution has recently come under much criticism. I believe, however, that most of these discussions miss how deeply revisions have undercut the evolutionary thinking of contemporary biology.

At the very core of the matter is the question of optimality. In fact, whether at the genotypic or the phenotypic level, the classical approach is to consider separate traits which supposedly undergo progressive betterment in their fitness. But every biologist also knows that genes (or cistrons) are as intricately interrelated as are body organs, and cannot be dealt with separately. Further, the genotype and phenotype are mutually interdependent: one specifies molecular species, the other specifies which of the molecular species gets expressed. (In this sense, to speak of a genetic "program" for a species is at best misleading.) To search for paths of optimization in separate traits, given this degree of mutual specification, is to say that one tries to clamp down this interrelatedness as much as possible and hope for the best. The best is usually expressed as some sort of trade-off or compromise between traits. But even this is too feeble. The search for trait optimization has, in fact, failed to produce basic mechanisms capable of explaining major evolutionary phenomena, either at the genetic level or in morphological change. This failure has been documented in various critical discussions.[2]

The reliance on optimal adaptation is not the only way to understand organic evolution, and its alternatives are quite natural. But we need to move out from the classical framework to see that natural selection was never intended as a trait-by-trait optimization. Rather, it states minimal conditions which will be satisfied under the conditions of differential reproduction among the members of a population. This amounts to setting broad boundaries within which many pathways may be taken, as in a proscriptive rule (what is not forbidden is allowed). But this is a far cry from a prescriptive rule (what is not allowed is forbidden). Here are two concrete illustrations of what this means.

First, natural selection does not necessarily lead to steady betterment in some trait. At the genetic level, this is also true: genetic interactions do not lead to multiple combinations with other genes, all of which are phenotypically equivalent for natural selection. For example, among salamanders it is possible to find remarkable morphological constancy, which nevertheless is mediated through very different genetic pools.[3]

Second, the manifestation of genetic change in a population is to a very significant degree a manifestation of the internal coherence of the organisms themselves, much more so than through a selection process. In fact, genetic changes will inevitably disrupt the well-established paths of embryological development. But this is such a delicate and intricate process that single-step disruption is much less possible than radical alterations resulting in radically different phenotypes. This is, among other things, what underlies the apparent "punctuated equilibrium" which best describes the fossil record of, for example, marine invertebrates. Species mostly stay in evolutionary stasis, and when they change, they do so not in a gradualistic fashion but by sudden jumps.[4]

These two dimensions of evolutionary change, neither of them minor, should suffice for now to illustrate that evolution is poorly described as a process whereby organisms get better and better at adapting. Rather, they allow us to see that there are many paths of change, all of which are viable if there is an uninterrupted lineage of organisms. It is not a matter of the survival of the fittest; it is a matter of the survival of the fit. It is not the optimization of adaptation but the conservation of adaptation that is central: a path of structural change of a lineage congruent with its environmental changes. This view of evolution, centered on the conservation of adaptation as a minimal condition, we call natural drift.[5]

In moving from an adaptationist view to an understanding of evolution as natural drift, we have also moved from a logic of correspondence to a logic of coherence. We have left behind the view of mirroring nature in adaptive terms, for a situation of tinkering with whatever is at hand.

A WALK THROUGH THE REPRESENTATIONIST PROGRAM AND BACK AGAIN

By now, I hope, the ideas I am trying to convey are beginning to take shape in your mind, so that we may quicken the pace in this promenade through a similar conceptual landscape for the brain sciences. Briefly stated: what adaptationism is for evolutionary biology, representationism is for neuroscience.

Imagine for a moment a black and white television set, sitting in your living room, and try to see the color of the screen. It is gray.

Now, imagine that you turn the device on, so that you see images. They will not only be gray, but also black and white. The textbooks say that we see black in the absence of light, white with an intense light, and gray for the cases in between. But when the television is off, it has no way to produce a brightness on the screen through its electron beam, so we should see the screen at its blackest. In contrast, when the television set is on, however dimly, there should not be less illumination than when the device is off. Yet we all clearly agree that we see black when it is on.

In this simple example we have a capsule statement of the predominant way of thinking in neuroscience for the last fifty years. The idea is that the world has some specific features (such as light) which have a corresponding image inside, through some "mirroring" device (such as the eye), so as to produce a perception (brightness, in this case). A feature of the world corresponds to a representation in the system, and this is the key for adaptive actions in the world.

The roots of this mode of thinking in neurobiology are far less clear than in the case of evolutionary biology. On the one hand, there seem to have been a tremendous influence of the newly formed engineering disciplines in the early 1940s. The increasingly sophisticated man-made devices were designed to handle specific forms of specifiable information, and they were successful at that. So there was nothing to prevent the brain from being a fleshy information picker. With the advent of computers, the engineering metaphor was solidly entrenched and became common sense. On the other hand, neurobiology itself began to describe sense organs as true filters detecting specific configurations in the organism's environment. In an extreme form, this became the single-cell doctrine of sensory perception, which, though extreme, is not far from the sensibilities of most contemporary researchers. For this doctrine, not only perceptual items but also cognitive and motor abilities are encoded in particular kinds of neurons which stand for these performances.

The brain-as-computer metaphor, which we tend to take for granted, is, like adaptationism, nothing but one possible approach, and one plagued with problems at that. To illustrate my proposed alternative, let me return to the television set example.

It is evident in this case that black is not simply "represented" inside to correspond to a certain amount of light intensity. What then? One interesting answer is that the perception of black has to do with the relative activities in the overall retina. When we have images on the television screen, there are changes in the ratios of these relative activities, which is not the case with the uniform screen when the set is off. In other words, the perception of black cannot be studied in terms of the light falling on the retina (since we will see black at any level of illumination), but rather depends on the way this component of the nervous system is constructed so that some specific comparisons between light receptors are performed (out of the many conceivable ones). These comparisons establish levels of relative activity which are closely connected to the way brightness appears to us.[6]

Now, the retina is nothing but one tiny portion of this nervous system which throughout has the same characteristic of having multiple interconnections in a network, so that every state of neural activity only results in other states of neural activity, and every one of these states depends ultimately on the overall pattern of the entire brain. To make this a bit more concrete, we may contemplate the fate of the fibers reaching the brain from the retina.

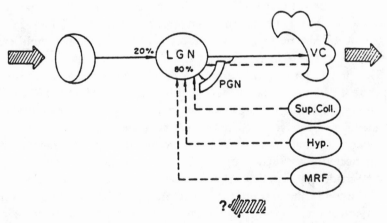

Figure 1. The retina projects to the brain at several places, including the thalamus at a nucleus called the lateral geniculate (LGN). The LGN is usually described as a "relay" station to the cortex. However, at closer examination most of what the neurons in the LGN receive comes not from the retina (less than 20%), but from other centers inside the brain including the visual cortex (VC), superior colliculus, hypothalamus, and the reticular formation (MRF).

What reaches the brain from the retina is only a gentle perturbation on an ongoing buzzing of internal activity, which can be modulated, in this case at the level of the thalamus, but not instructed. This is the key. To understand the neural processes from a nonrepresentationist point of view, it is enough just to notice that whatever perturbation reaches from the medium, will be in-formed according to the *internal coherences* of the system. Such perturbation cannot act as "information" to be processed. In contrast, we say that the nervous system has *operational closure*, because it relies essentially on internal coherences capable of specifying a relevant world.

The differences between adaptationism and operational closure are not mere philosophical curiosities; they entail differences in research strategies. Over the last decades, the preference has been for detectors which embody particular adaptive features. The alternative is to search for cooperative mechanisms which can shape neural coherences. We cannot go further into details here.[7]

AUTONOMOUS UNITY AND NATURAL DRIFT

Let us stand back now from these two quick glances to evolutionary thought and brain science, and see them as matching pieces of a common pattern against which a new conceptual framework emerges. I can now formulate the common ground of a "new" biology in terms of the key notions presented above. This common ground can be stated in terms of two crucial changes of emphasis.

The first is putting the emphasis on the way autonomous units operated. Autonomy means here that the unit described (be it a cell, a nervous system, an organism, or a dangling mobile) is studied from the perspective of (that is, uses as a guiding thread) the way in which it stands out from a background through its internal interconnectedness. Such cooperation of self-organizing mechanisms can be made quite explicit in some cases; the research has just begun.

The second change is putting the emphasis on the way autonomous units transform. Transformation means that natural drift becomes possible due to the plasticity of the unit's structure. In its drift, adaptation is an invariant. Many paths of change are potentially possible, and which one is selected is an expression of the particular kind of structural coherence the unit has, in a continuous tinkering. Natural drift applies to phylogenetic evolution as well as to learning, depending on the unit being considered (a brain in one case; a population in the other).

I have presented a few thoughts about these ideas in the realm of the brain and evolution; clearly they can also be put to work in other realms, such as immunobiology and artificial intelligence.

Autonomy and natural drift, although I have described them separately, are complementary. They are the two basic chords of the fugue I hear in the background. Let me depict them more graphically in relation to the pairs of opposites in which the classical view is rooted.

My proposal is that in this change of conceptual goggles we need to take the middle way between these logical opposites. This is not a compromise, but rather a going beyond the conflict by jumping to a metalevel.

I firmly believe that this growing framework in biology is important, as I said in the beginning, not only because it is an interesting scientific debate. It is also important because biology is the source of most metaphors in current thinking, and within biology it expresses the possibility of a world view beyond the split between us and it, where knowledge and its world are as inseparable as the inseparability between perception and action. In this middle-way view, what we do is what we know, and ours is but one of many possible worlds. It is not a mirroring of the world, but the *laying down* of a world, with no warfare between self and other.

This view of knowledge and action has an obvious *ethics* associated with it. This ethics is based on permanently giving up certainty.

middle-way : meta-level

	dominant view	its logical opposite
Epistemology	eternalism	nihilism
	objectivism	subjectivism
Evolution	adaptationism	creationism
Neuroscience	representationism	solipsism

autonomous units and natural drift:
co-emergence of units and their world

More precisely, it is based on giving up the tendency we living creatures have to bring forth a world (as we discussed before), to forget we have done so, and then to fixate on it as certainty. This temptation of certainty is the solidification of self against other, of delimitation of national boundaries in opposition to other human societies; in brief, the source of suffering. It is also the pivot point that many traditional teachings have cultivated for centuries. It does not seem to have made a great deal of difference on this planet, excepting a few fortunate ones. My hope is that if modern science can rediscover *in its own way* this profound truth, then the ears of our contemporaries will be more open and receptive because of the authority that science carries in our Western world. The learning of the inevitable letting go of certainty, letting go of solid fixation on self and national boundaries, is, in my eyes, the most needed antidote for our times, and the quickest path to survival altogether. I am also aware that to know and understand this is not enough; then comes the slow and patient learning and internalizing that each one of us has to undergo. But understanding is at least a first step.

Actually, this poem by Antonio Machado says it more clearly than I could:

Caminante, son tus huellas
el camino, nada mas;
caminante, no hay camino,
se hace camino al andar.
Al andar se hace camino

y al volver la vista atrás
se ve la senda a que nunca
se ha volver a pisar.
Caminante, no hay camino.
sino estelas en la mar.[8]

(Wanderer, the road is your
footsteps, nothing else;
wanderer, there is no path;
you lay down a path in walking.
In walking you lay down a path

and when turning around
you see the road you'll
never step on again.
Wanderer, path there is none.
only tracks on the ocean foam.)

NOTES

1. Poem by an Eskimo woman, reproduced by R. Bly (Ed.), *News of the Universe: Poems of two-found consciousness*, Sierra Books, California, 1981.

2. A particularly precise discussion is: G. Oster and S.M. Rocklin, "Optimization models in evolutionary theory," in *Lectures on Mathematics in the Life Science*, Vol. 11, Rhode Island, American Mathematical Society, 1979.

3. Z. D. Wake, G. Roth, and M. Wake, "Organismal stasis and evolution," *J.theor.Biol.* 54:123-134, 1964.

4. S. Stanley, *Macroevolution*, Freeman, San Francisco, 1979.

5. See chapters 3–5 of H. Maturana and F. Varela, *The Tree of Knowledge: A new look at the biological roots of human understanding*, New Science Library, Boston, 1986.

6. For details on this experiment see E. Land and J.J. McCann, "Lightness and retinex theory," *J.Opt.Soc. Amer.* 61:1-11, 1971.

7. The notion of closure is introduced and extensively discussed in F. Varela, *Principles of Biological Autonomy*, North-Holland, New York, 1979. For an introductory account, see H. Maturana and F. Varela (1986) *op. cit.*

8. A. Machado, *Soledades*, 1936.

ACKNOWLEDGMENTS

It is a pleasure to acknowledge here my gratitude to the Lindisfarne Association and its Fellows—and to its director, William I. Thompson, in particular—for providing over many years a creative mileu where these ideas and concerns have been shaped.

Financial support from the W. Woods-Prince Trust Fund is gratefully acknowledged.

CHAPTER FOURTEEN

Pacific Shift: The Philosophical and Political Movement from the Atlantic to the Pacific

WILLIAM IRWIN THOMPSON, PH.D.

It is an honor to be here in Kyoto, the place of origin of the Kyoto School of Philosophy. To honor this spirit of place, I would like to begin my talk with the concluding words of Keiji Nishitani's *Religion and Nothingness*. It is especially appropriate for a Westerner to begin with the work of Nishitani-Sensei, for Nishitani has digested Western philosophy and raised it up to a higher level of Buddhist contemplation. Nishitani has gone to Germany and returned to Japan, and so now, like the astronaut Rusty Schweickart, whose talk has preceded mine, I would like to complete the circuit and come round the earth from Europe over America and back to Japan. In coming around from the other side of the earth, I am seeking to bring Nishitani-Sensei's words back to him in a sense of gratitude.

> True equality is not simply a matter of an equality of human rights and the ownership of property. Such equality concerns man as the subject of desires and rights and comes down, in the final analysis, to the self-centered mode of being of man himself. It has yet to depart fundamentally from the principle of self-love. And therein the roots of discord and strife lie

Based on the presentation at the Ninth Conference of the International Transpersonal Association (ITA) entitled *Tradition and Technology in Transition*, April 1985, Kyoto, Japan.

ever concealed. True equality, on the contrary, comes about in what we might call the reciprocal interchange of absolute inequality, such that the self and the other stand simultaneously in the position of absolute master and absolute servant with regard to one another. It is an equality in love.

Only on the field of emptiness does all this become possible. Unless the thoughts and deeds of man one and all be located on such a field, the sorts of problems that beset humanity have no chance of ever really being solved.[1]

What Nishitani has done in his work is to show how all of Western materialism ends in Nihilism: not in the nothingness of Buddhist emptiness, but in the bitterness of void and annihilation. Aesthetically, we Westerners do not really need to look into a Japanese mirror to see this. We have only to look at the history of our own Western art. Think back in your memory to the beginnings of Renaissance painting. Think back on Giotto's *Flight into Egypt*, with the image of the Holy Family of Jesus, Mary, and Joseph set against the gold radiance of space in an iconic epiphany in which there is no ground and, there is no "matter." There is only an epiphany of the sacred. This is the end and the beginning, for then in the Renaissance the modern world takes off. It discovers *matter*, not as a stage for a religious event but as something very *thingish*, something very solid, very human. Think of Breughel's *Conversion of St. Paul*. We cannot see the religious event of the saint falling off his horse. On his journey Saul was struck from his horse to become Paul; he was converted to another mode of consciousness, just as Rusty Schweickart also was on his journey in space, when his camera failed and he let go of his function to see the meaning of what was happening to him.[2] The world was no longer an object to be photographed; it became a *presence*. But we cannot find the religious event in Breughel's painting. We look for the saint, but there is only a long line, a crowd of people. The largest thing in the canvas is the horse's behind. *Presence* has been replaced by *object*. And the momentum of modern art continues until the religious event drops out of the picture completely. Then we have the art of landscape, the landscapes of Ruysdael and Rembrandt. Brilliant as these studies of clouds and lights are, they are landscapes and not icons of an event of sacred history. Then the very *thingishness* of matter begins to take over.

We have not simply landscapes, but still lifes and studies of objects in all their intense materiality, as if the object itself were more *real* than the subject. The "I" as well as the sacred event begin to be displaced to the margins of reality. And so it goes on into the Cartesian geometry of Poussin where all is the solidness of temples and architecture. The buildings are all so structurally real that one begins to wonder where the mind went. But one does not have to wait for long. Psychology begins to dawn and the light over the temples of Claude Lorraine begins to be more important than the temples themselves. The solid temples begin to melt, and then there is no stopping, until Claude's temples melt into Monet's cathedrals. There is no stopping this movement from materialism to nihilism, and Monet's melting cathedrals end in the landscapes of the Rothko Chapel. Rothko's abstract landscapes started with a ground, with a horizon where ground and groudlessness met, but soon all faint traces of ground are lost and we end in the completeness of Nihilism.

So, as you can see, our own history speaks to us of the contradiction, of the inherent void hiding in materialism. The artists told us first, then came the philosophers like Nietzsche. But Nietzsche was a response to the engorged materialism of nineteenth-century Europe. His medicinal nihilism was an enema administered to a sick Europe. But you cannot take in the food of the spirit with enemas, and so the intellectuals like Sartre and Derrida who turn Nietzsche into the messiah of nothingness become sick and cannot take us anywhere. And this is why Nishitani is food for thought and feeling; his Buddhist emptiness delivers us from the annihilations of materialist technologies. Just as materialism camouflaged nihilism, so Buddhist emptiness turns into its opposite as we come out the other side to know mind and matter for the first time.

The culture of the West is now split between the nihilism of the punks of London and the nihilism of the yuppies of New York. One says: "We're all going to get nuked, so nothing matters." The other says: "Before it all ends, I'm going to get mine. I'm going to make money, and to hell with the rest of the world." I had the intellectual misfortune to have to teach at a university this year, and the students told me that the reason they were not reading or studying anything that I was talking about was because there was no point in my idealism, that everything was going to get trashed and nuked anyway. Part of all this, of course, is simply the strategy of the spoiled children of the upper-middle-class who know how to make their parents feel guilty so that they can be free to smoke and snort as they please; but part of it is also the sense of a generation that is profoundly dislocated.

You can *see* this sense of dislocation if you continue on down the line of Western painting and end up watching music video. In music video you see some of the visions of interpenetrating spaces that were first intuited in the canvases of Magritte: the kind of interpenetrating spaces where an eye opens up to become a sky. If you look at videos like The Car's *"You Might Think I'm Crazy,"* you see the flat plane become a door to another space. It is an experience of interpenetrating spaces, much like the experience of an astronaut such as Rusty Schweickart. But, again, notice that the artists are first: that Magritte's canvases anticipate video synthesizers. And notice also that technology is a democratization of the prophetic genius of the artist. In music video an object is a fabrication: strictly speaking, there is no such thing as *res*, as *re*ality. An object becomes open, a plane becomes a door, an object becomes a presence. Thingishness in video, as opposed to still lifes, turns into emptiness.

Video as a form of vision has its way of dislocating us. Sit in front of a program of music videos and you will notice that all human emotions are really in quotation marks. The song, whether it is sweetly sung by Boy George or screamed by Van Halen, is not about love or war, *eros* or *thanatos*, it is about "love," about "war." Ultimately, it is about "civilization," for the cumulative effect of music video is to put traditional civilization into quotation marks. The old literate culture is now simply a *content* within the new electronic *structure* of envelopment.

So we are all being knocked off our horses on the road to Damascus. We are all astronauts momentarily losing our sense of definition and function to participate in *presences*. The cumulative effect of electronics and aerospace technologies is a dislocation, a deconstruction of civilization. The kids and the philosophers understand this better than the technicians and the managers, for those in the middle do not see the edges. Traditional philosophy goes the way of civilization; it becomes a cut-out put into a collage, and philosophers who do not become artists are simply clerks in antique stores. But Buddhist philosophy is not Western philosophy. Western philosophy takes itself seriously and lacks a Zen sense of humor; it is confident in its power to explain everything and serve as the apologetics for the scientific method. For these Western philosophers, Buddhist philosophy is dismissed as "not really philosophy, but just religion." Not all philosophers are so simple-minded, and certainly Wittgenstein knew better; but both Wittgenstein and Heidegger appreciated that they were the end of Western philosophy. They felt the dislocation, they sensed the displacement of civilization, the shift out of *matter*. They knew, along with scientists like Heisenberg, that we do not live *in* reality, we live in a *description* of reality. And the map is not the territory. Of course, we do need maps sometimes when we are lost, but as we make our way home, we come precisely to the place where we no longer need a map. The definition of *home* is precisely the place where we do not need a map. Philosophy can provide us with the furniture of existence, but it cannot turn the furniture into a home. That transformation takes a different kind of understanding in which an object becomes a presence. It was precisely this kind of feeling that enabled Rusty to see the earth as *home*.

The experience of dislocation is unsettling for Westerners who have been habituated to a strong sense of ego, a strong sense of reality as matter, and a strong sense of a cosmic egohood in the form of a personal God. For Buddhism, however, the experience of dislocation from ego, matter, and egoic constructions in the form of "civilization" or "divinity" is part of the contemplative process of enlightenment. The place of Nishitani's work in a planetary culture is not to take us back to some sentimentalization of medieval Japan, but to take us forward to the truly post-industrial society of an ecological steady-state condition. The transition from an industrial to an ecological world-view is reflected in the shift from the materialistic modes of thought as expressed in the philosophies of Adam Smith and Karl Marx to the re-visionings of the relationship between Mind and Nature as expressed in such thinkers of the Pacific Rim as Gregory Bateson and Keiji Nishitani. This philosophical and cultural movement is what I mean by the term Pacific Shift. Just as once before, Reformation Protestantism was the transformation of Christianity in the shift from medievalism to modernism, so now is Reformation Buddhism part of the transformation from European to planetary culture. Precisely because Buddhism is not, strictly speaking a religion, it is more relevant to the spiritualization of everyday life than the conservative modes of consciousness that are crystalized in Hinduism and the Abrahamic religions. This in no way means that these religions that are appropriate to the level of civilization will disappear, anymore than Catholicism disappeared in the Reformation, but it does mean that they will become the conserving and not the innovating force within the new global ecology of consciousness.

This new planetary culture, this *"planetarisches Denken and planetarisches Bauen"* that Heidegger called for in his *The Question of Being*, is not simply a meeting of East and West. It is beyond the old dichotomies of East and West. When you look at the photographs of the earth that Rusty Schweickart just showed us, where is East and where is West? Where is up and where is down? And where is the *ground* when the space shuttle is so positioned that it looks as if you are under the earth rather than on top of it?

One cannot use the old frames, the old horizons, the old solidity of matter. And so Buddhism, which seemed to us in the old days of empires, a heathen religion from the land of the rising sun, takes on a whole new relevance, much as Christianity took on a whole new relevance after the break-up of the Roman Empire. The great Irish mystic A.E. (George William Russell) said that in every passionate conflict there is an exchange of opposites. And so in the Pacific War that preceded the Pacific Shift, we fought. And now look at the United States and Japan. You took Henry Ford and now have Detroit; we took Dogen and now have Zen monasteries. I know that you are being blamed in the newspapers for the bad American trade balance, and that you are being celebrated as the world's best businessmen, but I think if you look at it from a thousand-year point of view, we Yankee traders got the better deal. I will take Dogen Zenji over Henry Ford any day.

In the philosophy of mind of Gregory Bateson, information is not triggered by an *impact*, a materialistic chain of collisions, but by a recognition of *difference*. Information is an event of consciousness and not an impact of matter. The world-view that follows from this is that the universe is not made out of stuff, but patterns; in this Bateson follows Heisenberg to see the universe as made out of music not matter.

The philosophy of Gregory Bateson is a good example of the Pacific Shift, for Bateson in his own lifetime made the transition from Eurocentric thinking to the California world of cybernetics and Buddhism. In his recognition of the pattern that connects minds to nature, he realized that mind was not a substance or secretion locked inside the skull, but that the pathways of Mind extended outside the body. Nature is the unconscious, the *processes* of information and not the *products* of sense perception that flash across the limited screen of consciousness to become the building blocks of our human world of culture and conscious purpose.[3] Another word for this kind of unconscious, this wildness of Mind, is Gaia.[4]

Bateson's work was to challenge the simple materialism that drove the engines of the industrial revolution. He challenged the basic assumptions that humans could dominate nature with an agenda of conscious purposes. This project of challenging the very *ground* of industrial civilization has been continued in the work of Francisco Varela, for Varela's refutation of the notion of *representation* is more than a critique of neurophysiology, it is a dissolution of the *ground* of our materialistic world-view.[5] From the empiricism of Locke we in the West have inherited the idea that the mind is the brain and the brain is basically a template struck by the impacts of matter. Photons and molecules impact upon the skin and the retina, and suddenly we reassemble an image of an eagle on the little movie screen that is hidden in the back of our skulls.[6] Outside is wild and disordered *matter*; inside our skull is ordered perceptions and ideas about perceptions. In his *Two Treatises on Government*, John Locke developed his theory of mind into a theory of society, and thus showed us that all epistemologies have political implications. Locke said that it was the act of taking something out of the *commons* that began a piece of property. The social act of adding labor to the commons produced *property*. Looking back with 20-20 hindsight, we now can see that Locke is basically looking at nature through the lens of the Enclosure Acts which took land out of the medieval commons and turned it into private property, to the benefit of the lord and the dismay of peasant and cottager. Long before England leaped into its eighteenth-century industrial revolution, it prepared for the industrialization of nature by destroying the medieval sense of the agricultural community and elaborating the new economic cents of private property. Nature was the wild, the primitive *commons*, but the taking out of *property* created the new *commonwealth*. In the transformation of *commons* into *commonwealth*, the world-view was transformed from *patterns* of relationship to *objects* of quantitative weight and measurement. The Enclosure Acts told the peasant and villager that he could no longer put his cow into the commons; he could no longer hunt or collect firewood, for the land was no longer a pattern of ecological and communal relationships; it has become *property*.

We have continued on with this notion of property all through the centuries of industrial "development." Eighteenth-century Jefferson continued seventeenth-century Locke's political challenging of the divine rights of kings in the elaboration of the rights of property by moving away from the commons of British oral Common Law to a written constitution. Rights are writs, and a constitution is a form of fencing in of custom into the definitions of written laws. In *The Declaration of Independence*, Jefferson assured his contemporaries that all *men* are endowed with certain inalienable rights, and he *spelled* them *out*. I can alienate my right to be free and become an indentured servant for a time, but I cannot alienate my right to breathe, for then I cannot even serve as a slave.

If we stop to consider the historical context of the Lockian idea of *property*, we can see that Bhopal in India is literally the last gasp of the concept of private property. The industrialist has looked upon the atmosphere as a *commons*, a wild that can be taken and, through labor, turned into property. Property then creates wealth, and in the *commonwealth* it is believed that these new riches will trickle down from top to bottom to create jobs for the unemployed. Nature is commons and can be turned into property, but people are also wild commons that can be turned into property through employment. And yet these distortions of conscious purpose, these representations of a fictional reality, are clearly false; for we can see in the fullest developments of industrialization the contradictions that were not so obvious at the beginning. The atmosphere is not a property, and the individual cannot alienate his right to breathe in exchange for the goods of the Commonwealth.

So goodby Locke, Newton, and Jefferson, and hello Bateson, Nishitani, and Varela. If the Earth is the unconscious, then it is the activity of consciousness and not labor that is productive of value. What we are all involved in is not a Commonwealth but a Commonlife. In a materialistic world-view, I may have *objects* in separating *space*; I may have mansions of Union Carbide's wealth in Connecticut and factories and poison in Bhopal, but in a world-view of interpenetrating *presences* in the groundlessness of Buddhist Emptiness there is no space for these samsaric illusions. If we are all involved in the codependent origination of our Commonlife together, then we can no longer afford the luxurious illusions of the Lockeian Commonwealth.

If consciousness is the activity that produces value, then even the industrially unproductive have value: the unemployable, the old, the young, the senile and the dependent. Even a retarded human being or a senile person has the capacity to turn light into language and unconscious into conscious, and so they must be of value in our Commonlife. And, indeed, in traditional, preindustrial cultures, such people were valued.

So, by now, you can see "the pattern that connects" Bateson to Varela and Varela to Nishitani. It is not simply a question of a new epistemology but of a new world-view. It is an epistemology with political implications, a Gaia Politique. It is not the apologetics for reaction, for a return to the divine right of kings of feudalism, and it is not an apologetics for the industrial domination of nature in Capitalism and Marxism. It is the political exploration for a truly metaindustrial planetary culture.

The transition from the materialistic culture of the industrial nation-state to the planetary culture of a global ecology will take time, but given the speed of technological change and the implosive power of electronic forms of communication, the transition will be much faster than the shift from medievalism to industralism. We will, of course, have the disruptions and catastrophes attendant upon any transition. When you move from one world-view to another, you do have periods of denial, rigidity, crystalization, and violence. In the Renaissance there was an emergence of modernism in banking and art, and a shift from the Romans to the Greeks as the new favored ancestral culture; but this challenging of the power of the Roman Church also triggered the Inquisition. As the modern era comes to an end, its culture is being compressed and miniaturized in hysterical movements of fundamentalism. Essentially, personalities as different as Mishima, Reagan, and Khomeini are all expressive of the nativistic movements attendant upon a change in the *deep structure* of human culture. So you will have extremist Right Wing movements in Japan, just as we have them in the United States, but I doubt if you will become a samurai kingdom again, and I doubt that the United States will become "the Aryan Nation." Extremist groups are a form of paranoia, but *paranoia* means to know beyond and to the side, so there is often a poetry to the caricatures of the paranoid. It is indeed the period of the end of "the Great White Race," and Los Angeles is now a world-city of Hispanics and Asians, so the nativistic movement of "the Aryan Nation" should be looked upon as the Ghost Dance of the rednecks.

The American Indians were not able to stop the railroads, and the rednecks will not be able to stop the new aerospace and cybernetic technologies; they will not be able to lock the United States into the Protestant values and culture of the Reformation. They will, of course, be able to do a lot of damage, to create little eruptions of pus and hate in the American body-politic, for there is always this release of heat in a phase-change. But I do not believe they will be able to stop the emergence of the new planetary culture; nor will the Shiites of Islamic fundamentalism, nor will the monetarists of industrial fundamentalism. As Teilhard de Chardin pointed out so brilliantly and prophetically in his description of "the planetization of mankind," the very efforts of the nation-states to preserve their sovereignty in systems of global defense only brings them closer together. With satellites and aerospace-cybernetic economies, an isomorphism of national structures begins to emerge. The unconscious begins to link the USSR together, for the enemy is the Batesonian "difference" that drives the system. The United States could lose Maine or North Dakota and still remain intact, but if it lost its enemy, the whole economic structure of its society would collapse. The danger of conflict comes not simply from destruction, but from the unconscious transformation in which we become what we hate; so, as the United States and the USSR become intimate enemies, there is always the danger that the two empires will become identical *structures* camouflaged with the superficial *contents* of mere ideologies. We can see this all too clearly now from the history of the conflict between Japan and the United States in World War II. Out of that Pacific War has now emerged the Pacific Shift of the world; had we the contemplative wisdom of Buddhism, we might have been able to move from mindless, passionate conflict to mindful, compassionate balancing; but Americans did not read Nishitani in the forties.

I grew up along the edge of the Pacific Rim, as did Francisco Varela, and all during our youth we kept turning our back on the Pacific to face toward Europe. With the zeal of adolescent intellectuals, we wanted nothing more than to live out our fantasies and hang out in cafés in Paris. It took a long time and quite a bit of hard work before we were finally able to philosophize in the cafés of Paris, but we have, and sometimes even together. It is a curious world, a place where intellectuals complain about the domination of American corporations as they smoke *Marlboros*, a world where knowledge does not have to be realized in the body, a Cartesian world of abstractions. In California, the intellectuals do not smoke, they jog, write books with computers, and eat tofu; in Paris, the intellectuals write with fountain pens on café napkins, gesture with cigarettes as if they were in a movie playing the role of Sartre or Camus, and eat and drink the most outrageous foods that are perfectly designed for causing diseases of the liver. In short, the French are very much like the Japanese, and that is why you are so fond of one another. But for all his style and glory, the European intellectual, be he disciple of Derrida or Habermas, is like a bloodhound who has lost the scent and is going around in circles in a fury of activity lest his master discover that he does not know where to go next. It is time to use new senses, new perceptions; it is time to move on into a new space. It will not work anymore to let the fashionable Left disparage the sacred as a "mystification," for this form of imperial modernization is little more than an act of cultural thievery. It is not the mystics who have trashed the planet. Those who have really "mystified" their abuse of culture and nature are the materialists, be they communists or capitalists.

It is, therefore, small wonder that the open agenda of this international conference is the affirmation of traditions of the sacred *in* an acceptance of electronic technologies of communication. In many ways, the electronic technologies are, as McLuhan predicted, working to reverse some of the deleterious effects of industrial modernization. McLuhan called this "retribalization in the Global Village." My tribe is the Irish. We were the first Third World to feel the impact of imperial modernization. What the English did to the Irish, the Americans did to the Hawaiians. We came in and said "Your *kahunas* are witch doctors. Your culture is inferior; let us modernize you with pesticides and automobiles. We will make Honolulu just like Los Angeles." For Americans, it is a "miracle of modern medicine" if you can create an artificial heart. Cleaning up the air would not seem technologically advanced to Americans, and, indeed, they would be happy living in artificial lungs, if they could be designed to look like Cadillacs.

But slowly, very slowly, we are beginning to understand that the *kahuna* or the "witch doctor" present at this conference, Dr. Credo Mutwa of the Zulu, is not primitive, and that, in fact, his view of mind and body is more advanced than the media hustlers of artificial hearts. Looking back on the 1970s, we can now begin to see that what he was about in general, and what transpersonal psychology was about in particular, was the planetization of the archaic. Yoga, Zen, Tibetan Buddhism, sufism, Kabbalah, shamanism: all the ancient *ways* were made tributaries to the immensity of the sea. That project has now been accomplished. Now it is time for the "New Age" to become truly "new" and to move on. In its blend of "Technology and Tradition," this conference may actually serve to help us move on.

What we are moving into is not simply a new outlook on the world, but a new mentality with which we look out and in. You can begin to appreciate the importance of this new mentality when you look back to consider those times when humanity passed out of one Mentality into another. Interestingly enough, these Mentalities are also associated with certain historical geographies. The relationship between a historical geography and a Mentality constitutes what I prefer to call a "Cultural-Ecology." The story of "Western Civilization" is basically a movement through four cultural-ecologies: (1) The Riverine, (2) The Mediterranean, (3) The Atlantic, and (4) The Pacific-Aerospace. The Riverine geography is the landscape of the first civilization of the Euphrates, Tigris, and Nile. For "Eastern Civilization," the Riverine Civilizations would be those of the Indus and Yang-tze. The second historical geography of our Western Civilization was bound up with the Mediterranean. This is the classical period. The emergence of the modern world involved a projection outward to the Atlantic, and such Western countries as Spain, Portugal, the Netherlands, and England became formative of this new oceanic cultural-ecology. After World War II, world power shifted, and the Pacific Rim became the focal point of the new cultural-ecology.

Now, each of these cultural-ecologies witnessed the emergence of a new polity: (1) City-state, (2) Empire, (3) Industrial nation-state, and (4) our contemporary *enantiomorphic* polity in which opposites are in unconscious political collusion. Each of these four cultural-ecologies, witnessed the emergence of new economies, as Marx pointed out in his progression of (1) Asiatic economies, (2) Feudalism, (3) Capitalism, and (4) Socialism; and each of these witnessed the emergence of new forms of symbolic communication, as McLuhan pointed out in his progression of (1) Script, (2) Alphabetic, (3) Print, and (4) Electronic. If we review the literature characteristic of each of these periods, we can see that both the narratives of imaginative literature and mathematics are structurally organized within a dominant mode of integrating objects, persons, and events. This mode is what I mean by the term "Mentality." The Riverine Mentality is organized around enumeration, and the prevailing mode of narration is the list: the list of the *me's* taken by the Goddess Inanna from Erech to Eridu, the catalogue of the ships that came to the invasion of Troy, the lists of the genealogies of men and gods, and the lists of goods stored within the temple. In the shift from the Riverine Mentality into the Mediterranean one, there was a shift from the mode of enumeration to geometrizing. The appreciate the difference, one only has to contrast Hesiod to Pythagoras or Plato.[7]

To appreciate the next shift from the Mediterranean world to the modern one, contrast Galileo to Plato. Motion for Plato is sinful; motion is the locus of the fallen world. The eternal world of forms is a world of pure geometry and perfect circles. But for the modern world, motion itself—something that was inconceivable in Zeno's paradoxes—becomes the fascination, and Plato's perfect circles transform into Kepler's elipses of planetary motion. Galileo studies the motion of falling bodies, and Leibniz and Newton work out a calculus of infinitesimals. And for the painters, the sky is no longer an iconic gold of sacred radiance but a sky of dynamic movement. Think of the skies of Ruysdael and Rembrandt, and you will appreciate that for the modern world, the Mentality is one of dynamics.

In the nineteenth century, dynamics begins to modulate into transformations. From the thermodynamics of Carnot to the evolutionary changes of Darwin, "transformation" is the basic narrative idea in science, literature, and art. Evolution is a story of ape to man, and novels are stories of rags to riches.[8] In our century, this fascination with transformation has become so intense that we have moved from the simple narratives of dynamics to catastrophe theory. For us Enumeration, Geometrizing, and Dynamics are becoming cumulatively integrated into new forms of morphologies in a form of visual thinking that is being stimulated by computer animation and video synthesizers. If you stop to consider contemporary video art, in either its avant-garde forms with works like Jaap Drupsteen's *Hyster Pulsatu* or in pop art forms like The Cars' music video, "You Might Think I'm Crazy," it is clear that art is not at all mimetic and that "reality" is clearly a fabrication. Video synthesizers are simply democratizing the contemplative insights of zazen, and the epistemology that seems elitist and esoteric in the work of Varela is rendered obvious in works of video art. As it is now for scientists and artists of the new mentality, so it was at the beginnings of science with Huyghens and Rembrandt, or later with Carnot and Turner.

It is easier to talk about these things here in Japan, for you have had articles in your popular press about the "superiority of the Japanese brain" due to the influence of ideographic thinking. So, if I now speak about the return of hieroglyphic thinking, or the development of catastrophe theory into processual morphologies, you are in a better position to imagine what I am talking about. Western scholars of Asian languages, like Sam de Francis, dismiss "the myth of ideographic thinking," and are outspoken apologists for modernization through an imperial enforcement of alphabetic thought for Japan and China. But since Professor de Francis does not seem to understand the cultural history of alphabetic thinking, as described in the Toronto School of Innis and McLuhan, I tend to see his analysis of the Chinese language as ethnocentric.[9] It is itself a product of the mentality of the third cultural-ecology, and not the fourth that we are now moving into. Since Innis and McLuhan have shown us how the emergence of abstract thought was intimately bound up in the cultural history of the emergence of the alphabet for the Phoenecians and the Greeks, we should suspect that the emergence of electronics, computers, and video synthesizers are also intimately bound up with the emergence of new forms of right-brain, visual thinking. To monitor the emergence of this new mentality, simply watch the artists, and pay particular attention to new genres in which musical composition is wed to computer assisted video. In these new art forms, mysticism and science come together. A good example of this kind of mythopoeic art would be the pioneering work of Walt Disney in *Fantasia*, especially in his blending of cosmogony with Stravinsky's *Rite of Spring*. I was five years old when I first saw

Fantasia, so I learned to think in terms of music and visions before I knew how to read. It formed me, for I still think in music and visions. Such people are called "mystics" in industrial culture, but they are simply normal in electronic culture.

As you can see from my brief fly-over of the historical landscape of Western Civilization, the so-called opposition between art and science is spurious. Mountain and valley people may not get along, but when you look down on them with the eye of a pilot or an astronaut, you can see that they are both part of a common watershed. Lord Snow was wrong when he divided up the world of the mind into the sciences and the humanities. When I was teaching the humanities at M.I.T., I was told by the registrar that the engineers tended to take their elective courses in economics and political science, but that scientists tended to take their elective courses in the arts and the humanities. If there are two subcultures, they are not split between the sciences and the humanities, but between Archimedean and Pythagorean modes of imagination.

For the cultures of the West, there has always been a great gulf between the sacred and the profane, between God and *matter*, and this gulf has been carried on into the opposition between "pure" science and applied science. One is the realm of politics and atom bombs, the other is the empyrean of pure theory; but what electronics has done is to bring the opposites closer together by democratizing technology. Before, in the metallurgy of the artisan, the sword was only for the samurai, but now with television, personal computers, and laser-disc *Sony Walkmans*, the technology is for Everyman. In the dislocations from "civilization" attendant upon these technologies, the old reifications of "matter" and the transcendent "God" are no longer appropriate, and it is for this reason that the epistemology of Buddhism has taken on a new meaning in the context of the *groundlessness* in the neurophysiology of Varela. We are witnessing not simply a sequence of "causes" in a cultural transformation but a cybernetic system of emergence in which both recognizeable patterns and non-cognizeable "noise" are interacting with one another to stimulate the shift from one cultural ecology into another.

In the narratives of Western Civilization, phenomena are taken out of their total ecological context and turned into "causes." For Marx, the means of production *causes* a change in the superstructure of ideology; for McLuhan the alphabet *causes* a change in the nervous system. This is too simplistic, and thanks to physics, cybernetics, and Bateson's pioneering work in *Naven*, we can now begin to think in terms of synchronous nets of causes and effects.

The narratives of Western Civilization have always been simplistic and reductionist, for very often they have been simply part of the historical apologetics for Empire. I was raised, even in California, on a narrative that did not tell me anything about the "witch doctors" of the Dogon or the Rishis of India. The maps on the classroom wall were all pink with the colonies of the British Empire. The classroom was a time-warp; I could have been living in the nineteenth century. But when I walked out of the environment of the classroom into the more open world of choice in a bookstore, I came upon the *Bhagavad Gita* and the *Tao Te Ching* in cheap paperback editions. Because of the interacting forces of capitalism and communications technology, I was presented with a larger and more open environment than in the closed and controlled world of the Roman Catholic parochial school classroom. I found these classics of the East on my own; no teacher, either in Catholic school or public school, told me to read *The Bhagavad Gita* and *The Tao Te Ching*. At school I was being told the old narratives of "civilization," but the environment I was living in was no longer that of Western Civilization. I was growing up in a world that was already planetary, and so in reading these Eastern classics at the age of fifteen, I parted company with the world of my teachers.

There is always this lag in education, for the new technologies of communication constitute a new world, while the classroom seeks to maintain the old one. So now that we are in an electronic world of planetary culture, the fundamentalists of the American Moral Majority are seeking to stop history and lock reality within the world-view of the Protestant Reformation. But it would be a mistake to think that religion is always wrong and science and technology always right, for the mode of our religious experience changes along with the transformation of our technologies.

In the ancient Riverine cultural-ecology, the mode of religous experience was Momentary Possession, either in shamanic trance or the *hieros gamos*, the sacred marriage of man and the Goddess, Dumuzi and Inanna. In the imperial cultures of the Mediterranean Cultural-Ecology, the mode of religious experience became Surrender to Authority. And when civilization became too crystalized in the figure of the High Priest, surrender to authority was challenged by prophetic figures who celebrated pastoral and pre-civilized ways of life. Moses would challenge Pharaoh, or Samuel would challenge Saul. What the prophet represents is a radical affirmation of the value of the individual. It is no longer the temple that holds value; the individual can be an epiphany of the Divine. This is a radical and revolutionary notion for a priesthood or a traditional culture, and this Old Testament tradition of prophecy and individuation is still difficult for a Japanese person to understand. But, as you can see, our traditions of individuality do not simply go back to Thomas Jefferson and *The Declaration of Independence*, they go back to the world of the Hebrew prophets.

With the Reformation and the expansion of Europe into the new Atlantic cultural-ecology, the mode of religious experience became Commitment to Belief. Religion was no longer simply a matter of ethnic identification, of the descent of the body, it was a matter of the *mind* and its forms of knowing expressed in doctrine. The structures of the modern world are based upon documents, on Luther's bible and Jefferson's *Constitution*. They are based upon systems of belief in literate doctrines and laws in which Rights are Writs. This is the world McLuhan characterized as *The Gutenberg Galaxy*.

And now we have left that Atlantic world behind in the Pacific Shift. Now we enter a period of planetary implosion in which the individual is brought back into involvement with the ecology of the whole. Religion becomes holistic, and the mode of religious experience becomes a symbiosis of group consciousness. This is something that you Japanese can understand more readily than we Westerners. In this new Pacific Shift of consciousness, the cybernetic net of synchronous events teaches us to recognize that Truth cannot be expressed in an ideology, whether that ideology is capitalist, Marxist, or Islamic, that Truth is that which is above the conflict of opposed ideologies. If one thinks that the Truth can be expressed in an ideology, and that that ideology can become the personal possession of an *ego*, then that ideology gives one a license to kill. If I am a Shi-ite in Lebanon or a Catholic in Northern Ireland, my ideology gives me a license to murder. So the whole mode of religious experience in Commitment to Belief passes away in a transitional period of crystalization, rigidity, and violence. But what one can see in the larger horizons of Rusty Schweickart's space photographs is the world-view above these ancient fundamentalist hostilities. In this world-view, opposites can coexist symbiotically, just as the organelles exist symbiotically within the cell. As we begin to realize that the Earth is a living cell, so we begin to see that the cell is a world of many different organisms, and we begin to understand through a new science of compassion, to tolerate the "aliens" within us and without us. Our medicine changes, and we no longer have John Wayne doctors trying to zap the aliens with powerful weapons. We begin to understand that our bodies are awash with thousands of interpenetrating beings, and that it is often the hysterical response of our own immunological systems that makes us sick.[10] We begin to see that from our bodies to our body-politics, our systems of defense can kill us. As we grow into this new science of compassion, everything changes at once: the narratives of mathematics, of art, of medicine, of religion, and of politics. This is the world of change in which we all are living now.

As our mode of religious experience changes, so, of course, does our way of seeing Good and Evil. If for the Riverine cultural-ecology, Momentary Possession was Good, then pride and self-assertion was Evil. Dumuzi falls because of pride and self-assertion. But pride and self-assertion announce the next level of religious experience, the level at which the individual is able to challenge authority, the world in which Moses challenges Pharaoh. Moses gives us Mosaic law, and commitment to belief in the Torah makes us Good. If Commitment to Belief is Good, then ecstatic transcendence is Evil; it is an escape from the culture into dubious cults. But ecstatic transcendence means moving beyond limits and rediscovering the group consciousness. It is a noise that is a signal. In our culture now, collectivization is evil, and noise is evil. We see demonic polities in which people are brought together through terror and compression. And yet, in a strange way, these collectivizations, like rock festivals and fascist states of war, are temporary noetic polities. They are evil and signals of the emergence of the next level of historical order. What is good for Moses is evil for Pharaoh; what is good for Luther is evil for the Pope, and what is evil for us may be part of an emerging good that "civilized man" cannot begin to fathom.

Now you can begin to see why I choose to speak of cultural-ecologies instead of civilizations. I do not wish to operate within the doctrinal systems of any particular civilized ideology, for I observe as an artist and a historian that there is an isomorphic relationship between evil and pollution for any particular culture, and that this relationship is invisible to the people living within their own civilization. The shape that evil and pollution take for a culture is not simply random and accidental; rather, it is a systemic description of the culture, both in its conscious and its unconscious life. So if you describe a civilization as a cultural historian, you often simply present a list of its heroes, its battles, its inventions, and its works of art. But the list is not the system, so the cultural-ecologist must look under these lists to see the unconscious life of the civilization as presented in its characteristic forms of pollution and noise. For the Riverine cultural-ecology, the form of pollution is soil-loss; but soil-loss shows that the city cannot be defined by its wall, and that the true phenomenology is territorial. This territoriality is the sign of emergence to the next level of historical order in the shift from city-states within walls to empires bounded by geographical limits. The characteristic form of pollution for empires is deforestation, as the trees are turned into maritime vessels and conquering navies. But deforestation is not simply the movement of an object, as in soil-loss; it is the alteration of the climate. This atmospheric change announces the next level of historical order in the shift from empire to world-economy.[11] For our world-economy, the characteristic form of pollution is atmospheric damage in such phenomena as acid rain and the Greenhouse Effect. But these forms of pollution express the shift from a world-economy to a planetary culture. So now we have a global pollution that is our civilizational unconscious, and we have forms of collectivization that are beyond reason. The teenagers who go to rock concerts understand that noise is the new form of identification with the group. A recent rock concert by the group U2 was so loud that it registered as an earthquake on the seismographs of the University of Amsterdam. I have a young nephew who is a musician in a heavy metal group in Los Angeles; he is losing his hearing from playing in the group, but, as he says, "That's just the price you pay." If you are willing to lose the membrane of your biological integrity to play with a group, or join your body to the new body-politics in a rock concert, then what you are demonically signaling is the emergence of the next level of historical order, the shift from literate civilizations to . . . what shall we call them? Noetic polities? Noetic plasmas?

As you look back and notice the isomorphic relationship between societal forms of pollution and cultural forms of evil, you will notice something that the mystics have often talked about, an esoteric observation that is unsettling for doctrinal moralists; namely, that evil seems to be part of the total ecology. Judas cannot betray Jesus until Jesus himself performs a shadow eucharist in which he gives Judas a sop of vinegar that enables the spirit of the devil to enter into him so that the apostle can betray him and the crucifixion can be consummated. Historically, I have described this pattern as one in which the Roman engineers build the roads for conquest and the Christian missionaries use them for conversion. This is an ancient insight from alchemy and Taoism, the principle of reversal, the principle of the *enantiodromia*. But it is not really an esoteric or occult phenomenon. When I lived in the Sangre de Cristo Mountains of southern Colorado, I would notice that in the morning when the sun came up the shadows would cover the entire San Luis Valley. Then the relationship between dawning light and extensive shadows was confusing; but as the sun came up higher, you could begin to see the true relationship between light and dark. The mountain would begin to take in its shadow until, at high noon, the shadow would be entirely under it. And so it is with us in illumination: we no longer project our shadow outward on our neighbors, but we begin to draw it into ourselves. Some of the gurus of our age have cast very large shadows as they stood between their disciples and the light, but now in the period of democratization we have come to the end of the age of gurus and the light is high and available for everyone to see.

I began my talk with Nishitani, so now let me close with Dogen-zenji. In the age of the illusions of *matter*, we sought to conquer and control, and we sent out missionaries and soldiers. But as Dogen says: "To practice and confirm all things by conveying one's self to them, is illusion; for all things (*dharmas*) to advance forward and practice and confirm the self, is enlightenment." What we see now happening in the world is not simply traditional and not simply technological. Ultimately, the Pacific Shift to a new science of compassion is no other than this shift from illusion to enlightenment.

NOTES

1. Keiji Nishitani, *Religion and Nothingness* (University of California, Berkeley, 1982), p. 285.

2. See Russell Schweickart, "No Frames, No Boundaries" in *Earth's Answer: Explorations of Planetary Culture at the Lindisfarne Conferences* (New York, Harper & Row/Lindisfarne, 1977), pp. 3-13.

3. See Gregory Bateson, "Effects of Conscious Purpose on Human Adaptation" in *Steps to an Ecology of Mind* (New York, Ballentine, 1972), pp. 440-447; and *Mind and Nature: A Necessary Unity* (New York, Dutton, 1979), p. 32.

4. See James Lovelock, *Gaia: A New Look at Life on Earth* (Oxford University Press, New York & Oxford, 1979).

5. See Francisco Varela, "Living Ways of Sense-Making: A Middle Path for Neuro-Science" in *Disorder and Order*, ed. P. Livingston (Stanford University Press, Stanford, 1985).

6. See Humberto Maturana and Francisco Varela, *El arbol de conscimento* (Editorial Universitaria, Santiago, Chile, 1984), p. 89.

7. The material that is merely sketched here is treated in greater detail in my book, *Pacific Shift* (San Francisco, Sierra Club Books, 1986), chapter three.

8. For a discussion of the relation between Carnot and Turner, see Michel Serres's brilliant essay, "Turner traduit Carnot" in *Hermès III: La Traduction* (Paris, Edition de Minuit, 1974), pp. 233-244. For a discussion of the relationship between the narratives of evolution and the English novel see Gillian Beer's *Darwin's Plots* (London, Routledge Kegan Paul, 1983).

9. See Sam de Francis, *The Chinese Language*, (Honolulu, University of Hawaii Press, 1984).

10. See Lewis Thomas, "At the Mercy of Our Defenses" in *Earth's Answer*, *op. cit.*, pp. 156-169.

11. See Immanuel Wallerstein, *The Modern World-System: Capitalist Agriculture and the Origins of the European World-Economy in the Sixteenth Century* (New York, Academic Press, 1974), p. 347.

12. As quoted in Nishitani's *Religion and Nothingness*, p. 107.

CHAPTER FIFTEEN

Space-Age and Planetary Awareness: A Personal Experience

RUSSELL L. SCHWEICKART, PH.D.

I'd like to take all of you on this trip with me because the experience itself has very little meaning if it is an experience only for an individual or a small group of individuals isolated from the rest of humanity. I was asked if I had integrated my experience. I think part of what this is all about is the process of integration and it is not my process; it is our process, and I want you to face that process with me now.

To do that, we'll have to go back a bit in history. I don't want to go back too far, but let me go back to 1969 and paint a picture and start from there. In early 1969 I was preparing for my flight on Apollo 9. Apollo 9 was to be the first flight of the lunar module, the first time we would take that spacecraft off the ground to expose it to that strange environment and try to see if it was going to be ready to do the job.

The setting was fairly interesting: in December of 1968, Frank Borman, Jim Lovell, and Bill Anders circled the moon on Christmas Eve and had read Genesis and other parts of the Bible, in a sense to sacramentalize that experience and to somehow transmit what they were experiencing to everyone back on earth, the "good green earth," as Frank called it. Those are people that you know, they are not heroes out of books, they are next-door neighbors. Your child and their children play. They are out there around the moon and

239

reading from the Bible in a way you know means a great deal to them.

And then the next day, in the *New York Times* magazine section came one of those incredible insights. Archibald MacLeish wrote an essay about the step that humanity has now taken, that somehow things rather suddenly have changed and that man no longer sees himself in the same way as he saw himself before, that we see the earth now as it truly is, bright and blue and beautiful in that eternal silence where it floats and men as riders on the earth together on that bright loveliness in the eternal cold, brothers who know now that they are truly brothers. As you are preparing to go up into space yourself, that's a heavy trip because you realize that it's not just a physical thing you're doing but that there's a good bit more to it. So, in all the other preparation that you make, you somehow incorporate preparation for that experience as well.

All this forms the background for that very, very busy foreground, the foreground that involves simulation after simulation, lying on your back in a simulator, sometimes in a spacesuit and sometimes not, looking at the hundreds of dials and switches and controls, going through launch after launch, launch aborts, memorizing all those millions of procedures which are required to save your life and the lives of your fellows if you run into this problem or that problem. You spend another hundred hours or more practicing rendezvous, how to bring two cosmic vehicles together out there in space, which is no simple task. Incredible numbers of meetings going over procedures, detailed checklists, techniques, mission rules, thinking about everything that can possibly happen, everything that can break or go wrong, and then ahead of time, around the conference table, debating, arguing, deciding, documenting what you will do in each case so that when the time comes, you don't then, in a time-critical life or death situation have to go through the debate but you carry out what you've already decided. Those are mission rules.

Hour after hour in classrooms you struggle to keep awake while the instructor leads you through miles and miles of wiring diagrams so that you can understand all the systems that go into that spacecraft that you'll have to fly, and it will keep you alive or kill you if you don't know what you are doing. Stabilization and controls and communication systems, guidance and navigation, waste management, environmental control, radar, on and on and on; all those things that are part of that spacecraft. You take part in testing the spacecraft, not a simulated spacecraft but a real one. And those tests go on and on and on for years ahead of the flight itself for each spacecraft that goes up. You have systems verification tests and integrated systems tests and combined integrated systems tests, attitude chamber tests and countdown demonstration tests, and so on, until you feel as though the spacecraft is going to be worn out before it ever gets a chance to perform up there where it was designed to work.

And then finally comes the morning when you get up, predawn; some people are just starting to come to work; outside the window three or four miles away, you look out there to the north and there is a brilliant white object standing vertically on its tail with searchlights playing on it, and it is somehow a white symbol sitting there on the beach ready for its trip into space, and it's the most awe-inspiring thing you've ever seen. Beautiful. You go down the hall and have the last of what seems like an infinite series of physical examinations; you eat breakfast and then you go down the hall in the other direction and put on your suit with the help of all those technicians.

You've done it a hundred times before. It's exactly the same except somehow this morning it's a little bit different. You go down the elevator with your two friends, you get into a transfer van and you go out to the pad, you go up that tower and you look out across that countryside, the sea in one direction and the rest of the country in the other direction and all your friends back there in the launch control center, and you realize all those years and years of work— five years, six years, seven years—that have gone into this moment. It's a touching thing. And then you get in the spacecraft, you jostle around, you joke and play up in the white room as you're getting in; you put signs on the back of the guy that helps you get in the spacecraft so that everyone on TV sees this ridiculous sign. And then you lie there on your back. They close the door, and you're right back in the simulator. You've done it a hundred times. During the countdown you may doze or catch some sleep, wake up when you're called on to take a reading or something. Then they count backwards down to zero and off you go.

Somehow it's anticlimactic. It's much more exciting from the beach watching it, seeing all that smoke and fire and feeling the power in that concentration of energy that's taking those three people up into space. You feel that and it causes your whole soul to oscillate with the throb of that sound. But you inside now are going up and everything looks very much like it does in simulation and you've done this a hundred times. The only difference is that it's all working correctly; things aren't going wrong; dials read what they should read instead of some joker outside throwing in a problem which you now have to handle. So you go into space, you're lying on your back, you can't really see out until the launch escape tower gets jettisoned partway up and then your window is clear. As you pitch over, getting near horizontal, you get the first glimpse of the earth from space. It's a beautiful sight. Are you scared in that process? No.

You look out the window and you make a comment—everybody has to make a comment when they see the earth the first time— you make your comment and it's logged, duly noted, and then it's to work because you don't have time to lolligag, look out the window, and sightsee. You're up there in March of 1969 and the goal is to put a man on the moon and get him back to the earth before the end of the decade and that's coming up very fast with an incredible amount to do.

On with the job; you get up into orbit, you separate from the booster and you turn around to dock with the lunar module, the first time it's ever been done, the first time the lunar module has ever been flown. You have a little problem doing that because a couple of the thrusters got shut off during the launch and you can't understand why you can't control the vehicle, so there's a moment of panic. You madly go around checking switches, throwing switches, trying anything until somebody notices a little flag that's the wrong way. You throw the right switches and you dock, you extract the limb and now you have to change orbits. You go through all those procedures, you take out the checklists, you read down the lists, you leave nothing to memory, everything is done a step at a time, and you change the orbit, you light the main engine of the command module with the lunar module on the nose now for the first time and you wonder whether maybe it will break apart but it doesn't. You were part of the design, you knew it wouldn't; now you really know.

And so that first night you eat, you doff your suits, stow them under the couches, put them away, climb into the sleeping bag, go to sleep. Up the next morning, eat breakfast for what it's worth, don the suits, and now you've got a full day of checkout again because this time you are making three major maneuvers the next day and you're testing the system that held together the first time you lit the engine but now you're not just going to light the engine, you're going to play games. You're going to wiggle the engine on the back, to test the stress and strain of that tunnel between the command module and the limb to make sure it will really hold together when it's needed. You go out to the edges of the design envelope and see that it really works and holds together and you know it will, but after you've done it, you really know.

So, you've had a busy day and again it's eat, doff the suits, and now you go to bed with a bit more confidence. Next morning it's the same process and you haven't quite gotten enough sleep but it's up and hurry up because you're late. You go back to work and eat fast and get the suits on—in fact, eat while you get the suits on—open up that tunnel and now you go into the lunar module for the first time, a brand new spacecraft and no one's been in it before. It's an amazing sight out the windows of that lunar module because they're much bigger windows. Again, you don't stop, you don't have time for that, and so out with the checklist and down through the day checking out all the same systems that you know so well from paper but now you're there, now you're throwing the switch, you're not just watching on paper what would happen if you did throw that switch. You check out the guidance and control systems, the navigation and communications and environmental control systems and on and on. By the end of the day you're ready for the grand finale of the day when you're actually going to light up the main engine on the bottom of the lunar module that will take one of your friends to the surface of the moon if everything goes right. You have to demonstrate that the engine will work and that you can push both the lunar module and the command module around in case one day that has to be done, little knowing that only the next year that will have to be done to save the lives of three of your friends. You light off that engine and it works, just the way it did in the simulator. It's amazing but it's just like it was in the simulator. You go back into the command module and you're a little behind again, so you hurry up and eat and take the suits off, get back to sleep again because the next day's a big day.

It's up again the next day and back through the cycle. Today's the day you check out the portable life support system, the backpack that will be used to walk around the surface of the moon. It will allow people to live and work and observe, to be human in the hostile environment. You put on the suit that morning, knowing you are going to go outside. You get in the lunar module and you go through all those procedures that you've done a hundred times on the ground but now there's no gravity and you're floating. Things are so much easier when you're floating. You check out the portable life support system and everything seems to work. You strap it on your back and you hook all the hoses and connections and wires and cables and antennas to your body, and now you transfer from the spacecraft which has become home to you. You know it. Your umbilical to that mother is real and it works and you've lived on it. Now you sever that and go on to this one you are carrying on your back. You let all that precious oxygen flow out the door of the lunar module and now you are living in your own spaceship.

You go out the door. Outside on the front porch of the limb you watch the sun rise over the Pacific, an incredible sight, a beautiful, beautiful sight. But don't look at it because you really don't have time. You've really got to get moving. That flight plan says you're behind again. You've only got 45 minutes out there to do all those things you have to do. You collect thermal samples and you start taking photographs and then a stroke of luck occurs because across the way in the command module where your friend is standing also in his spacesuit taking pictures of you while you take pictures of him, his camera jams, and so now he has to fix that camera. We have then just a moment to think about what it is we're doing. But then he gets it fixed and we're off again.

We're back inside the spacecraft. Again, you really need to get moving and get everything back together again and get everything taken care of, put away, and eaten, the suits off and stowed, back to sleep, because the next day is the big test. The next day you have to prove and demonstrate that everything else now has been performing well. You now know the backpack will support you in case you have to be outside the spacecraft. You've demonstrated that. We know that all systems work, the propulsion system works. Now, the big moment is to prove in fact and demonstrate that we can rendezvous, we can take those two spacecraft and separate them and bring them back together again after four or five hours and moving apart a couple of hundred miles. One of them doesn't have a heat shield, so it can't come back without the two getting back together.

The next day you go through all the preparation again, you get in the lunar module which has now become a friend and you go through all the preparation for that rendezvous and you separate. It's like taking a ball in your hand and as you stretch out your arm and your elbow locks, you let go of the ball and the ball floats away, except it's a little different because that's the way it's supposed to work. You're on the ball, by the way! As that arm stretches out, the fingers don't let the ball go and so you get to the end of the stroke on the docking mechanism and it goes clank, you look back and forth and say, "What was that? That wasn't in the simulation." About the time you're wondering what it was and maybe discussion is the better part of valor and you ought to come back in here and start over again, your friend goes clunk and opens up the fingers. You say, "Well, we'll find out in five hours whether it's all OK." So, off you go.

Five hours later, everything has worked right again. It's been a long five hours and you've gone through a lot of tests but everything has worked. Here you come and you're coming back together again. There's no reunion like that reunion, not only because it's your heat shield back there and that's the only way to get home, but because that's your friend over there, Dave Scott, he's your next-door neighbor. He was never a neighbor like he's a neighbor now. So you dock and get back together. You open the tunnel and there's a reunion that can't be topped. You get everything done and get back in the command module and you're tired, absolutely exhausted, you haven't had enough sleep or had a good meal, in fact, you probably haven't eaten that day. You sit there, you've taken off your suit and you have just a piece of that lunar module left sticking on the nose of the command module. You throw a switch and it's gone. There's a piece of you that just floats off. It's a machine, but so are we. It goes away, floats off into the distance, having done its job. Now your thoughts turn to things like a shower and a bed to sleep in and all those things you realize you haven't been thinking about for those five hectic days that you've just been through. But all that is five days away because the flight plan shows that now we can go for ten days. We show that we can go the whole mission, the endurance part. So, for the next five days while you think about a steak, a shower, a bed, you float around the earth doing other tests.

Now for the first time you have a chance to look out that window. You look out at that incredibly beautiful earth down below and you reach down into the cabinet alongside the seat and you pull out a world map. You play tour guide. You set up a little trace on top of the map which has your orbit traces on it. You look ahead to where you're going and what countries you're going to be passing over, what sights you're going to see; and while the other guys are busy you say in ten minutes we're going to be over the Mediterranean again. You look forward to that.

You go around the world, around and around and around, performing these tests. Every hour and a half, you go around the earth. You look down at it. Finally, after ten days, 151 times around the world, 161 sunrises and sunsets in ten days, you turn around and light that main engine again for the last time and you slow down just enough to graze that womb of the earth, the atmosphere.

Down you come into the atmosphere. As you come back in, you experience that deceleration, the inverse of what you experienced to get out, and it seems as though you are under an incredible pressure. You know that you are experiencing at least four G's, four times the force of gravity. You say, "Jim, what is it now?" and he says, "Two-tenths of a G." By the time you reach four or five G's you begin to sense the burden that man has lived under for millions of years. As you look out the window you see your heat shield trailing behind you in little bright particles, flaking off, glowing, the whole atmosphere behind you glowing, this glowing sheath corkscrewing back up toward space.

Finally, you slow down enough where all of the bright light out the window, the fireball that you've been encapsulated in, has now dissipated and you're now subsonic. You're coming down into the heavy part of the atmosphere and there's just a couple of things left. You cross your fingers because all through the flight you've been throwing switches and various pyrotechnic devices, explosive devices that have sealed one fluid from another, one portion of the spacecraft from another. You throw these and the thing goes pop or bang, depending on where it is, how loud it is. You have a couple more of those to go and those are the ones that control your parachutes. You throw the switch for the next to the last time and it goes pop and the drag chutes come out. You say, "It worked," as you slow down to a couple hundred miles an hour.

You throw one more switch and pop, out comes the main chutes and they work. You realize that the last explosive device, the last switch that you've had to throw, the last surge of electrons through all the wiring has had to work and it worked. Now everything is behind you and splash, you're on the surface of the Atlantic. There are people circling around in helicopters and ships. You're back in humanity again, an incredible feeling.

What has it all meant? Will man now, after that experience, be able to set foot on the moon and return to earth by 1970? Yes. All those things that had to work and be proven have worked and been proven. You've been a part of it and you've done a tremendous job.

But there are more significant benefits. You've played a part in a changing concept of man and what life is all about. A relationship that you have assumed all these years, and not just you but man, humanity. The whole of history has assumed a relationship to a planet—a relationship that has now changed. You now know it because it's a part of your gut, not a part of your head. You wonder, you marvel that Archibald MacLeish somehow knew. How did he know? That's a miracle. But up there you go around every hour and a half, time after time. You wake up usually in the mornings and just the way the tract of your orbits go, you wake up over the Mid-East and over North Africa. As you eat breakfast you look out the window as you're going past and you look at the Mediterranean area, Greece, Rome, North Africa, the Sinai, and you realize that in one glance what you're seeing is the whole history of man for years, the cradle of civilization. Think of all that history you can imagine, looking at that scene. You go around, down across North Africa and across the Indian Ocean and look up at that great subcontinent of India pointed down toward you as you go past it, Ceylon off to the side and Burma, Southeast Asia, out over the Philippines and out over that monstrous Pacific Ocean, that vast body of water. You never realized how big that is before. You finally come across the coast of California and you look for those friendly things, Los Angeles and Phoenix, and on across El Paso and there's Houston, there's

home, there's the Astrodome. You identify with that, it's an attachment.

You go on across New Orleans and then there's the whole peninsula
of Florida laid out. All the hundreds of hours you spent flying across
that route, down in the atmosphere, all that is friendly again. You
go out across the Atlantic and back across Africa. You do it again
and again. You identify with Houston and then you identify with
Los Angeles, Phoenix, and New Orleans. The next thing you recognize
in yourself is that you are identifying with North Africa. You look
forward to that, you anticipate it and there it is. That whole process
begins to shift as to what you identify with.

When you go around the earth in an hour and a half, you begin
to recognize that your identity is with that whole thing. That makes
a change. You look down and you can't imagine how many borders
and boundaries you cross. That wake-up scene the year before, there
you are, hundreds of people killing each other over some imaginary
line that you are not even aware of, you can't even see it. From
where you are the planet is a whole and it's so beautiful and you
wish you could take each individual by the hand and say, "Look at
it from this perspective. Look at what's important."

And so, a little later, your friend goes out to the moon and now
he looks back and he sees the earth not as something big where he
can see the beautiful details, but as a small thing out there. Now
that contrast between that bright blue and white Christmas tree
ornament and that black sky, that infinite universe, really comes
through. The size of it, the significance of it—it becomes both things.
It becomes so small, so fragile and such a precious little spot in that
universe that you can block it out with your thumb. You realize that
on that small spot, that little blue and white thing is everything that
means anything to you. All history, music, poetry, art, war, death,
birth, love, tears, joy, games, all of it is on that little spot out there
that you can cover with your thumb.

You realize with that perspective that you've changed, that there's
something new there. That relationship is no longer what it was.
Then you look back on the time when you were outside on that
EVA and those few moments that you had—because a camera
malfunctioned—to think about what was happening. You recall standing out there and the spectacle that went before your eyes. Now
you are no longer inside something with a window looking out at

a picture. You are out there and what you've got around your head is a goldfish bowl and there are no boundaries. You are really out there over it, floating, going 25,000 miles an hour, ripping through space in a vacuum and there's not a sound. There's a silence the depths of which you've never experienced before. That silence contrasts so markedly with the scenery of what you're seeing and the speed at which you know you're going intellectually. That contrast, the mix of those two things, really comes through.

You think about what you're experiencing and why. Do you deserve this, this fantastic experience? Have you earned this in some way? Are you separated out to be touched by God to have some special experience here that other men cannot have? You know the answer is no, there's nothing you've done to deserve this. It's not a special thing for you. You know very well at that moment, and it comes through to you so powerfully, that you're the sensing element for man. You look down and you see the surface of the globe that you've lived on all this time and you know all those people down there. They are like you, they are you, you represent them. You are up there as the sensing element, that point out on the end. That's a humbling feeling. It's a feeling that says you have a responsibility, it's not for yourself. You have to see, the eye that doesn't see does not do justice to the body. That's why it's there. That's why you're out there. Somehow you recognize that you're a piece of this total life and you're out in the forefront and you have to bring that back. It becomes a rather special responsibility and it tells you something about your relationship with this thing we call life. That's a change, that's something new and when you come back there's a difference in that world now, there's a difference in that relationship between you and that planet and you and all those other forms of life on that planet because you've had that kind of experience and it's so precious.

All through this, I've used the word *You*. Because it's not I, it's not Dave Scott, it's not Dick Gordon, Pete Conrad, John Glenn, it's you, it's us, we, life, that had that experience. And it's not just my problem to integrate, it's not my challenge to integrate, my joy to integrate, it's yours, it's everybody's.

I'd like to close with a poem by e.e. cummings that became a part of me somehow out of all this and I'm not really sure how—and he says:

i thank You God for most this amazing day: for the leaping greenly spirits of trees and a blue true dream of sky; and for everything which is natural which is infinite which is yes

Based on a talk originally presented at the Lindisfarne Foundation in June 1974.

CHAPTER SIXTEEN

Near-Death Experiences: Implications for Human Evolution and Planetary Transformation

KENNETH RING, PH.D.

About a decade ago, the world began to hear about a curious but irresistibly intriguing phenomenon. Called the *near-death experience* (now often abbreviated as NDE) by its chief popularizer, psychiatrist Raymond Moody (1975, 1977), whose books proved to be international best sellers, this moment of transcendental radiance, occuring when individuals reach the apparent threshold of imminent death, somehow fascinated and captured the attention of millions of people around the world. Indeed, one wonders whether, aside from the sexual orgasm, there has ever been an experience whose duration is so brief—many near-death experiences appear to last less than a minute—that has stimulated so much reflection and commentary.

In this connection and in the wake of this pioneering work,[1] many books and articles examining near-death experiences and their implications have now been published both in the United States and elsewhere. Numerous professional conferences in the United States, Europe, and Asia, have likewise dealt with this experience; and an international organization—the International Association for Near-Death Studies (IANDS)[2]—has emerged as a vehicle for disseminating the findings of NDE research around the world. Such attention appears to have triggered a deep and growing absorption with this tiny sliver of life—its apparent last moments—on a very wide scale.

So pervasive is this interest that, at least in the United States, the near-death experience has achieved the status of a *cultural* and not just a clinical phenomenon. Not only have hundreds of radio and television talk shows featured discussions on the subject in addition to countless articles about it in the print media, but also one can scarcely find anyone who has not encountered such an experience in a Hollywood film, a television soap, a short story or novel, or even in a cartoon of a fashionable magazine. If one is sensitized to their existence, they seem to be as ubiquitous as convenience stores and just about as well known. In the United States alone, literally millions of people are now known to have had near-death experiences; this means that many millions of us are directly acquainted with one or more individuals to whom this kind of experience has happened.

Consequently, the near-death experience hardly appears to be a passing fad[3] but is a salient fact of our time and one which continues to exert a very powerful hold on our collective consciousness. In addition to its popular appeal, in recent years it has begun to be appreciated as a phenomenon with the potential for affecting human consciousness and thus life on earth in a very profound way. Some have speculated that it is already beginning to do so (Flynn, 1986; Grey, 1985; Grosso, 1986; Ring, 1984, 1987). But before we can meaningfully explore the deeper implications of near-death experiences, specifically those concerned with human evolution and planetary transformation, we must first examine the experience itself more closely, for it is obviously the foundation stone on which our conclusions must rest.

CONTENT AND PATTERNING OF THE NDE

What is it exactly that someone experiences who reports having survived an NDE? Perhaps the best way to grasp this (through the written word) is for you to imagine that this is something that is happening to you. There are, however, two important qualifications. First, though they tend to follow a single common pattern, near-death experiences vary greatly in terms of the number of experiential elements that serve to define the prototypic pattern. In short, some are more complete than others. Second, as one gets deeper into the experience, there are several different "branches" that one may follow after experiencing the basic NDE "stem." For our purposes, you should imagine a fairly full NDE, which will progress along one of the most common branches.

Suppose you are driving in your automobile at a high rate of speed along a crowded highway when suddenly a truck pulls in front of your car, forcing you to jam on the brakes—but too late. In the next instant there is a terrible, sickening collision and then. . . . If you are typical of the thousands of people researchers have interviewed who have reported NDEs, what would you experience?

Probably the first sensation you would be aware of would be a feeling of extreme peace and tremendous well-being. You would feel no pain—nor indeed any bodily sensation of any kind. You might be aware of a kind of crystalline, pure silence unlike anything you have ever experienced before. You would probably have the direct awareness that whatever this was, you were absolutely safe and secure in this all-pervading atmosphere of peace.

Then you would begin to have a kind of visual awareness of your environment. The first thing you would notice is that while you— the real you—appear to be watching everything from above, your *body* is "down there" surrounded by a knot of concerned individuals. You are watching all the frenetic activity below you with a feeling of detached objectivity, perhaps even with a sense of slight amusement. "Why are they making such a fuss about that body?" You might think *"I'm* perfectly fine." Indeed, you have never felt better in your life—your perception is extremely vivid and clear, your mind seems to be functioning in a hyper-lucid fashion and you are feeling more fully alive than you can ever remember. You watch the scene below you, noting your crumpled car flipped over on its belly by the side of the road, and you observe that off in the distance an ambulance is trying to weave its way through the stalled traffic. . . .

Suddenly your attention is drawn to an inviting, velvety blackness and you find yourself moving through this blackness—without a body but with an unmistakable sense of motion—and, as you do, you are aware that this blackness has the configuration of a tunnel. That is, the black space is bounded (though vast) and cylindrical and you seem to be propelled through it as if you are headed for a definite, but still unknown destination. Although you are travelling through this tunnel with a sense of increasing, indeed extraordinary, speed, you do not feel afraid. You just accept what is happening to you, knowing that everything will be all right.

As you approach what appears to be the end of the tunnel, you become aware of what is at first a pinpoint of light. This light quickly grows bigger and brighter and becomes more effulgent. It is an extremely brilliant light—golden-white—but is absolutely does not hurt your eyes at all. You have never experienced a light like this— it seems to be sourceless and to cover the entire vista before you. As you move closer to the light, you begin to be overwhelmed with the most powerful waves of what can only be described as pure love, which seem to penetrate to the very core of your being. There are no thoughts at all now—only total immersion in this light. All time stops; this is eternity, this is perfection—you are home again in the light.

In the midst of this timeless perfection, however, you become aware that somehow associated with this light there is a definite *presence*. It is not a person, but it is a *being* of some kind, a form you cannot see but to whose consciousness your own mind seems now to be linked. A telepathic dialogue ensues. The presence informs you that you must make a decision whether to remain here or to go back. Even as this thought is communicated to you, you are suddenly seeing, as though a million simultaneous yet precise and sharp images, everything that has ever happened to you in your life. There is no sense of judgment—you are watching all this like a spectator—but as this patterned fabric of your life unravels before you, you grasp the essential meaning of your life and in the moment of that realization, you see with absolute clarity that you must go back, that your family, especially your children, need you. . . .

That is the last bit of transcendental awareness you have. The next thing you know is that you are in excrutiating pain in what is clearly an altogether different and heart-breaking human environment that you eventually recognize to be a hospital room. It is three days later, you are enmeshed in tubes and IVs in an intensive care unit, unable to talk but able to remember every last detail of what happened to you when your body lay on the roadside and you hung suspended between life and death.

In reflecting on your near-death experience—though you would probably not label it thus—what is clear to you is that this was no dream or hallucination. Nor was it something that you simply imagined. This was compellingly real and absolutely objective: it was more real than life itself. You wish you could talk to somebody about it, but who could understand, even if you found words adequate to describe it? All you know is that this is the most profound thing that has ever happened to you and that your life—and your understanding of life—will never again be the same.

So much for a fairly common *deep* near-death experience and its immediate aftermath. In any event, this is what many people have said "it is like to die." Of course, the bare recital of such an experience only raises a multitude of empirical and interpretative questions; it does not provide any firm answers (except, possibly, to those who have the experience) concerning what occurs at death, much less what, if anything, takes place *after* biological death. However, considerable research has recently been conducted into these experiences and we now know a great deal more about them.

PARAMETERS AND INTERPRETATIONS OF THE NDE[4]

Among the first questions usually asked about this phenomenon is, how often does it actually occur? If one were to take one hundred consecutive cases of patients who clinically died,[5] how many of the survivors would related NDEs?

Early research (Ring, 1980; Sabom, 1982) suggested that the answer might be about 40%, and this estimate has also been supported by the results of a Gallup poll (Gallup, 1982), which was based on a much larger and more representative sample of people who have been close to death.[6] The body of research on near-death experiences is consistent in showing that most people remember nothing as a result of a near-death crisis, but that a very high percentage of those who claim to have some conscious recall report experiences that conform, at least in part, to the prototypic NDE we have already considered. A scattered number will report idiosyncratic experiences that usually seem to be halluncinatory in character; likewise, a tiny fraction of all cases appear to be negative experiences.

If one extrapolates from Gallup's sample base to the population from which it was designed to be representative (160 million adult Americans), it is possible to estimate how many people living in the United States have already had an NDE—about 8 million! This number has astonished many people (including some researchers) and should be carefully noted since it plays a key role in the thesis to be advanced later in this article.

Another question that is often asked is, does the way one nearly dies affect the experience? Investigators have examined a diverse array of conditions associated with the onset of death: combat situations, attempted rape and murder, electrocutions, near-fatal falls, near drownings, vehicular crashes, freezings, hangings, as well as a great range of strictly medical and surgical conditions. Overall, the pattern seems quite clear-cut: by whatever means a person comes close to death, once the NDE begins to unfold, it is essentially invariant and has the form described earlier. In addition, research on suicide-related NDEs (Greyson, 1981; Ring and Franklin, 1981–1982) has shown that these experiences likewise tend to conform to the prototypic pattern. In short, so far as is now known, situations covering a wide gamut of near-death conditions appear to have a negligible effect on the experience itself.

If situational variables do not significantly influence the experience, what about personal characteristics? Are certain people more likely to have such an experience because of social background, personality, prior beliefs, or even prior knowledge of near-death experiences? Once again, the research to date is consistent in finding that individual and social factors appear to play a minimal role. Demographic variables such as gender, race, social class, or education, for example, have been shown not to be connected with NDE incidence and form. Similarly, it is evident that there is no particular kind of person— defined by psychological attributes—who is especially likely to have a near-death experience. It might be thought that people who have a preexisting or strong religious orientation or who already believe in some form of post-mortem existence would be more prone than others, but this is not so. Atheists and agnostics are no less likely to recount prototypic near-death experiences than religious people, though their interpretation of the experience is apt to be different. Finally, prior knowledge does not seem to increase the probability of having one.

Thus, despite persistent inquiry and recently renewed interest into the question, we are obliged to conclude that the near-death experience seems to "select" its recipients in a random manner. At any rate, if there is any type of person who is an especially good candidate, we have not yet succeeded in identifying the characteristics.

When we come to the question—and it is an all-important one—
of *universality*, we must admit that this is an area of research that
is still lamentably underdeveloped.[7] Nevertheless, we do at least
have a fair amount of data from various cultures that afford us some
tentative answers concerning the extent to which the NDE is a culture-
free phenomenon.

We already have enough information to assert confidently that in
England and in continental Europe near-death experiences take the
same form as in the United States (Giovetti, 1982; Grey, 1985; Hampe,
1979). This is hardly surprising since these countries share a Judaeo-
Christian heritage. In the IANDS archives and in a few scattered
articles (Counts, 1983; Green, 1984; Stevenson and Williams, in press),
there are fragmentary data from a diverse number of cultures whose
traditional beliefs are quite different from those of the west. Included
here are cases from India, Japan, South America, Melanesia, and
Micronesia, among others. In general, these cases show some obvious
parallels to the classic pattern, but often involve elements that deviate
in specific ways, especially in the deeper stages where more archetypal
imagery comes into play. At this point, then, the prudent conclusion
must be that, in Western cultures, our data are simply too fragmentary
to permit any firm judgement concerning the universality of the
prototypic NDE model.

Nevertheless, from the body of cross-cultural data that we do have,
it seems plausible to infer that despite some degree of cultural
variation, there may be certain universal constants such as the out-
of-body experience, the passage through a realm of darkness toward
a brilliantly illuminated area, and the encounter with "celestial"
beings. Only further research, however, can substantiate this hypothesis as well as settle the question of the universality of the
prototypic near-death experience as a thanatological phenomenon.

Finally, we must address the issue of the general interpretation of
the NDE. As many considerations of this formidable matter have
already established (Grey, 1985; Greyson and Flynn, 1984; Grosso,
1981; Moody, 1975; Ring, 1980; Sabom, 1982), there exist a plethora
of theories and a minimum of consensus about them. The interested
reader is advised to consult the literature in near-death studies for
the specifics of the theory, over which debate continues to be heated.
These theories tend to fall into three broad classes: biological, psychological, and transcendental, though many interpretations do not

confine themselves to a single perspective. The biological theories tend to be reductionistic and antisurvival in tone whereas those with transcendental emphases tend to be empirically untestable but compatible with a survivalistic interpretation. Naturally, the psychological theories are intermediate in most respects.

We must emphasize that a decade of research on the near-death experience has utterly failed to produce any kind of generally accepted interpretation, even among those who have spent years carefully examining it. Moreover, I have recently tried to show (Ring, 1984) that the surrounding interpretative issues are even more complex than many theorists have apparently appreciated. At the present time, then, the question of how such an experience can be explained—or, indeed, whether it even can be—remains shrouded in a cloud of obscurity and contentiousness. The irony is that this entire question may well prove to be entirely irrelevant to the issue of its importance to humanity at large.

The larger significance of the near-death experience turns not so much on either the phenomenology or the parameters of the experience but on its *tranformative* effects. For it is precisely these effects that afford us a means of merging it with certain broad evolutionary currents that seem to be propelling humanity toward the next stage of its collective development. To understand the basis of this linkage, we must now explore the ways in which a near-death experience tends to change the lives, conduct, and character of those who survive it.

TRANSFORMATIVE EFFECTS OF NDES

The most recent work in near-death studies (Bauer, 1985; Flynn, 1986; Grey, 1985; Ring, 1984) has been increasingly focused on the aftereffects of the NDE, and it is concordant in revealing a very provocative set of findings. First, it appears that just as the near-death experience itself seems to adhere to a common pattern of transcendental elements, so also there seems to be a consistent pattern of transformative after-effects. Second, this pattern of changes tends to be so highly positive and specific in its effects that it is possible to interpret it as indicative of a *generalized awakening of higher human potential*. To see how this could be so, and to lay the groundwork for its possible evolutionary significance, let us now review the findings of my own study of aftereffects, described in my last book, *Heading Toward Omega* (Ring, 1984).

This investigation, whose findings rest on the statistical analysis of specially designed questionnaires as well as qualitative data from personal interviews, examined three broad categories of aftereffects: (1) changes in self-concept and personal values; (2) changes in religious or spiritual orientation; and (3) changes in psychic awareness. Wherever possible, the self-reports of respondents were compared to assessments provided by individuals such as close friends or family members who had known the experiencer well both before and after his or her near-death experience. For most statistical analyses, data from appropriate control groups were also available for comparative purposes. What, then, is the psychological portrait that can be drawn from this study?

First, in the realm of personal values, people emerge from this experience with a heightened *appreciation of life*, which often takes the form not only of a greater responsiveness to its natural beauty but also of a pronounced tendency to be focused intently on the present moment. Concern over past grievances and worries about future problems tend to diminish. As a result, these people are able to be more fully present to life now, in the moment, so that an enhanced attentiveness to their environment and a freshness of perception follow naturally. They also possess a greater appreciation of themselves in the sense that they have greater *feelings of self-worth* generally. In most cases, it is not that they show signs of ego inflation, but rather that they are able to come to a kind of acceptance of themselves as they are, which they will sometimes attribute to the tremendous sense of affirmation they received "from the Light."

Perhaps one of the most evident changes that follows a near-death experience is an *increased concern for the welfare of others*. This is a very broad and important domain with many different aspects to it. Here I will only be able to briefly summarize its principal modes of expression—increased tolerance, patience, and compassion for others, and especially an increased ability to express love. Indeed, after a near-death experience, people tend to emphasize the importance of sharing love as the primary value in life. In addition, they seem to feel a stronger desire to help others and claim to have more insight into human problems and more understanding of other human beings. Finally, they seem to demonstrate an unconditional acceptance of others, possibly because they have been able to accept themselves in this way. In a sense, one might characterize all these changes as exemplifying a *greater appreciation of others* and, as such, it may represent still another facet of what appears to be a general appreciation factor that the near-death experience itself serves to intensify.

As there is an overall increase in the aforementioned values, in other values there is a clear and consistent decline. For example, the importance placed on material things, on success for its own sake, and on the need to make a good impression on others, all diminish after individuals undergo a near-death experience. In general, people-oriented values rise while concern over material success plummets.

Finally, one more change in the realm of personal values should be noted. These people tend to seek a deeper understanding of life, especially its spiritual or religious aspects. They tend to become involved in a search for increased self-understanding as well, and appear more inclined to join organizations or engage in reading or other activities that will be conducive to achieving these ends.

Incidentally, with respect to these value changes—as well as to other categories of aftereffects—it appears that these self-reports may well reflect changes in behavior. Though we clearly need more corroborative evidence than is available in *Heading Toward Omega*, statements by close friends and family members tend to provide support for the behavioral changes these people describe in themselves.

Moving to the area of religious and spiritual changes, it will come as no surprise to learn that there are far-reaching aftereffects here, too. In general, however, such changes tend to follow a particular form to which the term *universalistic* might most appropriately be applied. In characterizing this universalistic orientation, it will be helpful to distinguish a number of different components that together make up the model spiritual world-view of those who have experienced a near-death crisis.

First, there is a tendency to describe themselves as more spiritual, not necessarily more religious. By this they appear to signify that they have experienced a deep inward change in their spiritual awareness, but not one that made them more outwardly religious in their behavior. They claim to feel, for example, much closer to God than they had before, but the formal, more external aspects of religious worship often appear to have weakened in importance. They are also more likely to express an unconditional belief in "life after death" for everyone and to endorse the conviction that not only will there be some form of post-mortem existence, but that "the Light" will be there for everyone at death, regardless of one's beliefs (or lack of them) about what happens at death.

Interestingly—and this is a finding also suggested by my earlier research in *Life at Death* (Ring, 1980) as well as Gallup's (1982) survey—a greater openness to the idea of reincarnation is often expressed. It is not that they find themselves ready to subscribe to a formal belief in reincarnation, but rather that it is a doctrine that makes more sense to them than it did prior to their near-death experience. My impression is that this increased receptivity to rein-carnational ideas is part of a more general friendliness to and ac-quaintance with Eastern religions and with some of the more esoteric and mystical variants of Christianity and Judaism.

Finally, the near-death experience draws people to a belief in the idea known to students of comparative religion as "the transcendent unity of religions," the notion that underlying all the world's greatest religious traditions there is a single and shared transcendent vision of the Divine. In espousing this view, people will sometimes aver or imply that they came to this realization directly through their own near-death experiences. Similarly, they are more inclined than others to admit to a desire for a form of universal spirituality that by embracing everyone would exclude no one. This is not a naive hope or wish that the multitudinous and incredibly diverse religious traditions throughout the world might somehow melt into a single "universal religion," but only that individuals of different and seem-ingly divisive religious faiths might one day truly realize their unity with one another.

The last domain of aftereffects explored in *Heading Toward Omega* dealt with changes in psychic awareness. Not only my finding but those of others (Greyson, 1983; Kohr, 1983) tend to support the hypothesis that the near-death experience serves to trigger an increase in psychic sensitivity and development—that following their expe-rience subjects become aware of many more psychic phenomena than had previously been the case. For example, they claim to have had more telepathic and clairvoyant experiences, more precognitive experiences (especially in dreams), greater awareness of synchron-icities, more out-of-body experiences, and a generally increased susceptibility to what parapsychologists call "psi-conducive states of consciousness" (that is, psychological states which seem to facilitate the occurrence of psychic phenomena). Although the data on apparent increases in psychic awareness lend themselves to various interpretations, it does seem clear that a heightened sensitivity to psychic phenomena follows a near-death experience (which, of course, may well include subjectively convincing paranormal features in its own right).

Having now reviewed the findings on some of the major aftereffects of near-death experiences, we must seek a coherent framework to place them in so that their implicit patterning may be brought into relief. I believe it is possible and plausible to regard the near-death experience as playing a critical *catalytic* role in personal development. Specifically, it seems to serve as a catalyst to promote the *spiritual awakening and growth* of the individual because of its power to thrust one into a transcendental state of consciousness whose impact is to trigger a release of a universal "inner programming" of higher human potentials. There may be in each of us a latent spiritual core that is set to manifest in a particular form if only it can be activated by a powerful enough stimulus.[8] In the near-death experience it appears that the stimulus is the light, and the similarity and consistency of the spiritual changes following a near-death experience point to what may be a common "spiritual DNA" of the human species. In these people, the pattern of changes in the consciousness and conduct bears a marked similarity to what Bucke (1969) long ago claimed for his examples of "cosmic consciousness" and to which the modern psychiatrist, Stanley Dean (1975), has more recently called our attention, A near-death experience certainly tends to stimulate a *radical spiritual transformation* in the life of the individual, which affects his self-concept, his relations to others, his view of the world *and* his world-view, as well as his mode of psychological and psychic functioning. But how does any of this—profound as these changes may be—speak to the weighty issues of human evolution and planetary tranformation?

IMPLICATIONS OF THE NDE FOR HUMAN EVOLUTION AND PLANETARY TRANSFORMATION

I believe only a very partial understanding of the significance of the near-death experience can be attained from a strictly psychological perspective, that is, one that concentrates on the *individual's* experience and its effects upon him. A more complete appreciation is available, however, if we shift the level of analysis from the individual plane to the sociological where the meaning of the transformative pattern will be more apparent. We must look at the near-death experience from this broader perspective in order to discern the possible deeper significance for humanity at large.

Recall, first of all, that it has already been projected that perhaps as many as *eight million* adult Americans have experienced this phenomenon—and we know that American children also report such experiences (Bush, 1983; Gabbard and Twemlow, 1984; Morse, 1983; Morse, Connor, and Tyler, 1985). Although we do not have even a crude estimate of how many people in the whole world may have had this experience, it certainly does not seem unreasonable to assume that additional millions outside the United States must also have had them. But the point is not simply that many millions will know this experience for themselves but also *how the NDE will transform them afterward*. We have already examined how people's lives and consciousness are affected and what values come to guide their behavior. To begin to appreciate the possible planetary impact of these changes, we must imagine these same effects occurring in millions of lives throughout the world, regardless of race, religion, nationality, or culture.

From various studies of transcendental experiences (Bucke, 1969; Dean, 1975; Hardy, 1979; Hay, 1982; Grof, 1985; James, 1958), we know that the radical spiritual transformation which often follows a near-death experience is by no means unique to that experience alone. Rather, as Grof (1985) has recently implied, transcendental experiences, however they may come about, tend to induce similar patterns of spiritual change in individuals who undergo them. In short, the near-death experience is only *one* means to catalyze a spiritual transformation, but many others, which seem to reflect the same underlying spiritual archetype, have unquestionably been triggered by something other than a near-death crisis.

Is there any way to estimate the extent of such transcendental experiences in general? Probably not with any real hope for acceptable accuracy, but we do have at least a basis for a rough sort of guess for English-speaking countries. In national surveys in the United States, England, and Canada, for example, up to *one-third* of those polled admit that they have had some kind of powerful spiritual

experience (Hay, 1982). Of course, from these data only, it is impossible to claim that such experiences necessarily induce the kind
of transformative pattern I have previously delineated. Nevertheless,
it does seem warranted to infer that many more people must undergo
these transformations by means other than a near-death experience.
Thus, if these other transformations are added to the presumed
millions of near-death experiences, we immediately see that we are
dealing with a far more pervasive phenomenon than one might have
first assumed.

A third consideration in this argument pertains not simply to the
number of people in the world who may have experienced a major
transformative awakening, however it may have been occasioned,
but to the rate of increase in such transformations. In the case of
near-death experiences, of course, it is mainly modern resuscitation
technology that is responsible for creating such a large pool of
survivors. Before the advent of cardio-pulmonary resuscitation, for
example, most would have died; now many not only are saved but
go on to live drastically changed lives because of their close encounter
with death. With resuscitation technology likely to improve and to
spread in use around the globe, it appears inevitable that many more
millions will undergo and survive near-death experiences and thus
be transformed according to this archetypal pattern.

Similarly, although there are not, as I have indicated, any systematic
studies of the incidence of transcendental experiences in general,
various students of higher consciousness (Ferguson, 1980; Grof, 1985;
Russell, 1983; White, 1981) have speculated that such experiences
are widespread, at least in the Western world, and that their number
may be growing exponentially.

Such intriguing possibilities fit neatly with the next observation
needed to complete the foundation for my argument based on recent
theories concerning the spread of behavioral properties throughout
a population. I am thinking here particularly of the theory of the
young English biologist, Rupert Sheldrake, whose book, *A New Science
of Life* (1981), has fanned widespread interest and controversy in
scientific circles ever since its publication. In his book, Sheldrake
propounds a hypothesis of what he calls "formative causation," which
states that the characteristic forms and behavior of physical, chemical,
and biological systems are determined by invisible organizing fields—
morphogenetic fields, in Sheldrake's phrase. Although I cannot review

here the author's evidence in support of his hypothesis,[9] Sheldrake's basic idea is that once such fields do become established through some initial behavior, that behavior is then facilitated in others through a process called *morphic resonance*. Thus, for example, once an *evolutionary variant* occurs in a species, it is likely to spread throughout the entire species.

Sheldrake's ideas are similar to (but certainly not identical with) the theme of the currently very popular "hundredth monkey effect," whose empirical authenticity now appears entirely without foundation, but whose appeal as a framework for conceiving social contagion phenomena is almost irresistible. This seemingly apocryphal tale describes how a new behavior, potato washing by monkeys, spread to all monkeys on a certain Japanese island as well as to monkeys on adjacent islands when an imaginary "hundredth monkey" indulged in the new ritual. In principle, once the hundredth monkey engaged in this new behavior, that was all that was needed to create a strong enough field for morphic resonance to occur, thus turning innovation into custom. In this case, the hundredth monkey presumably established the critical mass necessary to transform the eating habits of the entire colony.

What is the relevance of all this to the near-death experience and to the issues of the evolution of consciousness and planetary transformation? There is a possible connection stemming from the following observation, which has previously been made by a number of others besides myself. We do not know the limits of Sheldrake's hypothesis. If it is correct—and it is at present the subject of much excited interest and experimental work—it is distinctly possible that it may apply to states of consciousness as well. This extrapolation has, in fact, been made by science writer Peter Russell (1983), whose commentary will make explicit the connection between our concerns here and Sheldrake's work.

> Applying Sheldrake's theory to the development of higher states of consciousness, we might predict that the more individuals begin to raise their own levels of consciousness, the stronger the morphogenetic field for higher states would become, and the easier it would be for others to move in that direction. Society would gather momentum toward enlightenment. Since the rate of growth would not be

dependent on the achievements of those who had gone
before, we would enter a phase of super-exponential growth.
Ultimately, this could lead to a chain reaction, in which
everyone suddenly started making the transition to a higher
level of consciousness. (Russell, 1983, p. 129)

Although Russell's own formulation may seem somewhat hyper-
bolic and simplistic, it does have the virtue of suggesting both a
hopeful and larger vision of the inherent potential of the near-death
experience and of other similar transcendental experiences. If we
now consider the high base rate of all transcendental experiences
generally thoroughout the world, the likelihood of their increasing
incidence, and the possible mechanism by which the effects of such
states may spread across a population, we may finally discern the
possible global significance of the near-death experience.

May it be that this high rate of transcendental experience *collectively
represents an evolutionary thrust toward higher consciousness for humanity at large?* Could it be that the near-death experience is itself
an *evolutionary mechanism* that has the effect of jump-stepping individuals into the next stage of human development by unlocking
previously dormant spiritual potentials? Indeed, are we seeing in
these people, as they mutate from their former personalities into
more loving and compassionate individuals, the prototype of a new,
more spiritually advanced strain of the human species striving to
come into being? Do these people represent the "early maturers" of
a new breed of humanity emerging in our time—an evolutionary
bridge to the next shore in our progression as a species, a "missing
link" in our midst?

These are heady and provocative questions, but they are not entirely
speculative ones. Many thinkers before me have dreamed and written
of the coming to earth of a higher humanity and have attempted to
describe the attributes of such people. Although these visions of a
higher humanity are subjective, the transformations I have outlined
in this article have happened to real people, and they are among us
now. And we can at least ask: How well do these visions of a new
humanity match the characteristics of these people?

For one representative portrait of this new humanity,[10] let me draw
on the views of the well-known author, John White (1981), who has
helped to popularize the term *Homo noeticus* in this connection. In

reading his description, bear in mind that it was *not* intended as a characterization of someone who had experienced a near-death crisis, and that it is similar in many ways to accounts provided by other evolutionary thinkers who have addressed the same issue.

> *Homo noeticus* is the name I give to the emerging form of humanity. "Noetics" is a term meaning the study of consciousness, and that activity is a primary characteristic of members of the new breed. Because of their deepened awareness and self-understanding, they do not allow the traditionally imposed forms, controls, and institutions of society to be barriers to their full development. Their changed psychology is based on expression of feeling, not suppression. Their motivation is cooperative and loving, not competitive and aggressive. Their logic is multi-level/integrated/ simultaneous, not linear/sequential/either-or. Their sense of identity is embracing-collective, not isolated-individual. Their psychic abilities are used for benevolent and ethical purposes, not harmful and immoral ones. The conventional ways of society do not satisfy them. The search for new ways of living and new institutions concerns them. They seek a culture founded in higher consciousness, a culture whose institutions are based on love and wisdom, a culture that fulfills the perennial philosophy. (White, 1981, p.14)

Although this is an idealized description, the transformative process that the near-death experience tends to set into motion certainly appears to lead to the development of individuals who approximate the ideal type White posits as the prototype of the new humanity.

Even if my own ideas about the seeding of a new humanity through the spread of near-death experiences and other transcendental experiences are found to have some plausiblity,[11] their implications for planetary transformation admittedly allow for a variety of short-term scenarios. I am not one who foresees the emergence of a new, cooperative planetary culture as a necessary consequence of the kind of evolutionary shift in consciousness I detect. Rather, I see that shift as a potential of the human species that is beginning to manifest, but whether it takes hold and transforms the earth depends on many factors; not least is the extent to which many of us consciously align with these trends and seek to awaken.[12] Clearly, nothing in the collective human potential emerging from the spawning grounds of transcendental experiences precludes the possibility of our planet's self-destructing. Nothing is assured or inevitable. No one living in the last years of the twentieth century—unarguably the most horrific in history—could deny for a moment that our prospects for surviving intact into the next millennium are shrouded in black uncertainty.

At the same time, human beings live in hope as well as fear and this recent curious phenomenon—the near-death experience—seems to be holding out a powerful message of hope to humanity that even, and perhaps expecially, in its darkest moments, the Light comes to show us the way onward. It is up to each of us whether we shall have the courage and the wisdom to follow where it beckons.

NOTES

1. To be sure, others had researched the phenomenon long before Moody—and another physician, Elizabeth Kübler-Ross, was already a highly visible international figure who spoke compellingly about the NDE—but it was really Moody's book which, by *labelling* the phenomenon, rooted it in the soil of contemporary Western culture.

2. IANDS' address is Box U-20, University of Connecticut, Storrs, CT, 06268.

3. Raymond Moody has said that after his first book, *Life After Life*, came out, he expected that the interest in the NDE that it generated would run its course within just a few months (personal communication, 1981).

4. A more detailed consideration of these issues will be found in my recent book, *Heading Toward Omega* (1984), especially in Chapter 2.

5. In fact, many individuals who have "only" been close to death but seemingly not "clinically dead" (i.e., without vital signs such as heartbeat and respiration for a short time) have related that they, too, have had NDEs. A broader consideration of the conditions under which individuals may undergo NDEs or similar experiences will be broached later in this article.

6. Actually, Gallup's figure is approximately 35%, but there are methodological reasons for thinking this may be a slight underestimation of the population parameter.

7. Near-death studies is that branch of thanatology which is especially concerned with the study and understanding of the NDE.

8. In preparing this paper for publication, I discovered that Stanislav Grof in his most recent book, *Beyond the Brain* (1985), had independently arrived at a similar conclusion based on his work of nearly three decades with psychedelic therapy and other forms of deep experiential work. In this connection he writes that

According to the new data, spirituality is an *intrinsic* property of the psyche that emerges quite spontaneously when the process of self-exploration reaches sufficient depth. Direct experimental confrontation with the [deep] levels of the unconscious is *always* associated with a spontaneous awakening of a spirituality that is quite *independent* of the individual's childhood experiences, religious programming, church affiliation, and even cultural and racial background. The individual who connects with these levels of his or her psyche automatically develops a new world-view within which spirituality represents a natural, essential and absolutely vital element of existence. (Grof, 1985, p. 368; my italics)

9. I have discussed some of it briefly elsewhere, however, see Ring, 1984, pp. 261–262.

10. By using this phrase, I of course do *not* mean to imply that NDErs and others who have undergone similar transformations represent a new *biological* species—that would be absurd. Rather, I am suggesting that such persons may be signalling a rapid shift in the overall level of spiritual awareness in Homo sapiens; that is, that humanity at large may be about to move into a higher stage of its inherent evolutionary capacity. The extent to which there may be actual changes in human biological parameters is an open question that will need to be addressed empirically.

11. Interestingly enough, another near-death researcher, Margot Grey (1985), has recently independently arrived at conclusions almost identical to mine on the basis of her own research on NDEs. In addition, Rupert Sheldrake, without having had an opportunity to review my work in detail, has told me (Sheldrake, private communication, 1985) that my extrapolation of his ideas seems legitimate to him.

12. Toward that end, a colleague of mine, Alise Agar, and I are establishing a new foundation, to be called the Omega Foundation, to further scholarly inquiry, professional research, and public involvement through the arts and media concerning the ways in which individuals may better align with and help to realize our collective evolutionary potential.

REFERENCES

Bauer, M. (1985). Near-death experiences and attitude change. *Anabiosis, 5,* 39–47.

Bucke, R. (1969). *Cosmic consciousness* New York: E. P. Dutton.

Bush, N. (1983). The near-death experience in children: Shades of the prisonhouse reopening. *Anabiosis, 3,* 115–135.

Counts, D. (1983). Near-death and out-of-body experiences in a Melanesian society. *Anabiosis 3,* 115–135.

Dean, S. (1975). Metapsychiatry: The confluence of psychiatry and mysticism. In S. Dean (Ed.), *Psychiatry and mysticism* (pp. 3–18). Chicago: Nelson-Hall.

Ferguson, M. (1980). *The aquarian conspiracy.* Los Angeles: J. P. Tarcher.

Flynn, C. (1986). *After the beyond.* Englewood Cliffs, NJ: Prentice-Hall.

Gabbard, G., and Twemlow, S. (1984). *With the eyes of the mind.* New York: Praeger.

Gallup, G., Jr. (1982). *Adventures in immortality.* New York: McGraw-Hill.

Giovetti, P. (1982). Near-death and deathbed experiences: An Italian survey. *Theta, 10,* 10–13.

Green, J. (1984). Near-death experiences in a Chammorro culture. *Vital Signs, 4,* 6–7.

Grey, M. (1985). *Return from death.* London: Routledge & Kegan Paul.

Greyson, B. (1981). Near-death experiences and attempted suicide. *Suicide and Life Threatening Behavior, 11,* 1016.

Greyson, B. (1983). Increase in psychic phenomena following near-death experiences. *Theta, 11,* 26–29.

Greyson, B., & Flynn, C. (Eds.). (1984). *The near death experience.* Springfield, IL: Charles C. Thomas.

Grof, S. (1985). *Beyond the brain.* Albany, NY: State University New York Press.

Grosso, M. (1981). Toward an explanation of near-death phenomena. *Journal of the American Society for Psychical Research, 75,* 37–60.

Grosso, M. (1986). *The final choice.* Walpole, NH: Stillpoint.

Hampe, J. (1979). *To die is gain.* Atlanta, GA: John Knox.

Hardy, A. (1979). *The spiritual nature of man.* New York: Oxford University Press.

Hay, D. (1982). *Exploring inner space.* Middlesex, England: Penguin Books.

James, W. (1958). *The varieties of religious experience.* New York: Mentor.

Kohr, R. (1983). Near-death experiences, altered states and psi sensitivity. *Anabiosis,3,* 157–174.

Moody, R., Jr. (1975). *Life after life.* New York: Bantam.

Morse, M. (1983). A near-death experience in a 7-year old child. *American Journal of Diseases in Children, 137,* 959–961.

Morse, M., Conner, D., and Tyler, D. (1985). Near-death experiences in a pediatric population. *American Journal of Diseases in Children, 139,* 595–599.

Ring, K. (1980). *Life at death.* New York: Coward, McCann & Geoghegan.

Ring, K. (1984). *Heading toward omega.* New York: William Morrow.

Ring, K. (1987). From alpha to omega: Ancient mysteries and the near-death experience. *Anabiosis,* Vol. 6, Nr. 1.

Ring, K., and Franklin, S. (1981–1982). Do suicide survivors report near-death experiences? *Omega, 12,* 191–208.

Russell, P. (1983). *The global brain.* Los Angeles: J. P. Tarcher.

Sabom, M. (1982). *Recollections of death.* New York: Harper & Row.

Sheldrake, R. (1981). *A new science of life.* Los Angeles: J. P. Tarcher.

Stevenson, I., and Williams, E. (in press). Near-death experiences in India: A preliminary report. *Journal of Nervous and Mental Diseases.*

White, J. (1981, September). Jesus, evolution and the future of humanity. Part I. *Science of the Mind,* pp. 8–17.

CHAPTER SEVENTEEN

The Omega Project

KENNETH RING, PH.D. AND ALISE AGAR

During the past two decades, there has been a great deal of attention given to a range of transcendental experiences that collectively have suggested a new vision of human possibilities and cultural renewal. The transformative power of such experiences has been appreciated throughout history in the legacies of the ancient mysteries. The so called "counterculture" of the 1960s first made many persons familiar with the capacity of psychedelic agents to induce states of expanded awareness. However, it soon became evident that these heightened states of consciousness were not the product of the drugs per se, but were inherent attributes of the human psyche. As such, they can be brought about in many different ways or can even occur spontaneously.

We now live in an era where the means to effect such states— the many spiritual disciplines, contemporary forms of psychotherapy, and the various psychospiritual technologies—are well-known and commonly used. As a result of these influences and others, such as continuing psychopharmacological investigations and medical resusitation techniques, millions of people now have direct first-hand knowledge of transcendental states of awareness, whether through meditative practice, shamanistic rituals, psychedelic substances, near-death crises, spiritual healings, radical psychotherapy, holotropic breathing, or other avenues which lead to similar domains of experience.

With the spread of, and increasing acquaintance with, such experiences, many observers have begun to speculate on the potential cumulative impact of this cultural phenomenon. Of the many different kinds of interpretations that have been advanced regarding the significance of these experiences, the one with which the Omega Project is especially concerned deals with its possible evolutionary import.

May it be, for example, that all of these experiences of expanded awareness are part of an evolutionary unfolding of the human species toward higher consciousness and with it the emergence of a new form of planetary culture? At the present time, of course, it is not possible to answer this or similar questions in any definitive way, in part at least because we lack a solid research foundation for the systematic and comparative study and understanding of transcendental experiences and their effects.

Accordingly, the Omega Project—a forum for the exploration and critical examination of these fundamental questions of higher consciousness and human evolution—has been designed with these three principles in mind:

1. To encourage and seek support for research on transcendental states of awareness, which for ease of reference we will call simply *Omega experiences*. By this phrase we mean to denote experiences which point toward the ultimate evolutionary potential of human consciousness.

Omega experiences include such states as mystical and religious awakenings, however they may occur; near-death and other out-of-the-body experiences; and communication with "higher-order" beings. These experiences bring one's awareness into a realm that completely transcends the ordinary sensations of space and time and radically alter our sense of who we are and what our purpose is. Our aim is to seek a deeper understanding of such states.

Among the basic questions to be studied are: What are the common phenomenonological properties of such states? What is their neurological basis, or at least their correlates? What are the most reliable and effective ways of inducing Omega experiences?

2. To encourage and support research directed at documenting and understanding the *transformative effects* of Omega experiences.

Obviously, if Omega experiences have any evolutionary significance, they must leave persons who undergo them in a changed state, which expresses itself both in character and conduct. What are the changes that Omega experiences bring about? How lasting are they? Are different varieties of Omega experiences equivalent in producing and sustaining such changes?

3. To encourage discussion and further exporation of these ideas in science, philosophy, and in the arts and humanities in general.

Although the Omega Project seeks to provide a firm research basis for the study of transcendental experiences and their aftereffects, it is by no means "just another research foundation." Its larger purpose is to interest gifted persons whose work has direct influence on broad-scale cultural trends to contribute to the development of these ideas by dealing with them within the context of their own creative endeavors. We seek the co-explorations not only of scientists and other scholars, but also of writers, film makers, television and print journalists, artists, musicians, poets, and all of similar creative spirit.

We believe each person has some special part to play in illuminating the evolutionary design which now seems to be thrusting itself more insistently into our collective consciousness. Working together and in concert with one another, perhaps we can more effectively align with these great evolutionary forces for the betterment of all.

Recently, the Omega Foundation has been established as a nonprofit organization to further the ideas outlined here. The foundation will publish a periodic newsletter to be followed eventually by a journal. It will also sponsor both large scale conferences and small invitational seminars, in order to stimulate interest in Omega experiences and their evolutionary implications. Those interested in the Omega Project can receive more information at the following address: Omega Foundation, P.O. Box 2263, Orinda, CA., 94563.

CHAPTER EIGHTEEN

Death, The Final Stage of Growth

ELISABETH KÜBLER-ROSS, M.D.

It is a great honor to be here in Japan. I was here fifteen years ago with my children in the hope of showing them the differences in different countries, different cultures, different traditions. And fifteen years later when I return here, I begin to realize that there are no differences whatsoever. The only things that are different are the external forms. The clothes, the costumes, the houses may be different, but the individual human being is absolutely the same.

What I saw in this conference on the first few days was something that reminded me very much of home. Home being, really, all different parts of the world. When I watched the Zulu healer, he talked the same language, radiated the same kind of healing energy, and is the same kind of human being that my Eskimo healers in Alaska present—using the same kind of language. When I watched the purification of the four corners with the arrow, it was the exact same ritual with different colors, different tools, perhaps, that our own American Indians use in the Medicine Wheel. The only things that differ are the external forms. The internal human being has not changed over thousands of years, and the one thing that has not changed is birth and death.

Ask where our science and technology are taking us, and you probably all are aware that we are in a tremendous transition at this present time. The world is indeed in a transition from a world of science and technology to a world of true spirituality. And the

Presented at the Ninth Conference of the International Transpersonal Association entitled *Tradition and Technology in Transition*, April 1985, Kyoto, Japan.

question is how can we assure that this future is going to be better than our past. Yesterday, I spent the day in Hiroshima, and I did need to go to Hiroshima before talking here today. When I talk about death in the United States or in Europe, I am reminded of Nazi Germany where my work with dying patients started. I was a young girl from Switzerland, an island of peace, a country that has had very few windstorms in life, a country that has no unemployment, no race problems, no wars for hundreds of years. And growing up in a country like this you are not prepared for life. But life prepared me in its own way in that it made me born as a triplet. We were three girls; one of my sisters and I were identical, the remaining one was not. To be born as a triplet is something I would not wish to my enemy. We had absolutely everything materially. We had pretty dresses, pretty shoes, gorgeous home, nice garden, all the material things in the world. But we had absolutely nothing, because if I had died at the age of two or six or eleven, there was an absolute clone duplicate of me; I am not even sure that I am not my sister standing here. You grow up having everything and having to share everything, but you have nothing if there is not one human being who knows you as a person and who knows that he is talking to you and not your triplet sister. We tried everything in school in the hope that our teachers would know the difference. We were very good or very bad in school. My sister and I together would have made a genius, and the teachers did not care enough to find out who was who. In order to be fair, they gave us straight Cs through the whole of our school years. And do you understand what that does to a child?

To a child it means that nobody really cares. And when my sister had her first date as a teenager, she became very sick and nobody knew how sick she was. It was at this time that I saw her absolute despair in her fear of losing her boyfriend if somebody else were to go out with him. And I told her: "If you really can't go on that date, I'll go for you. He will never know the difference." And we hoped desperately, naturally, that somebody would know the difference. I even asked her how far she went, and I do not mean that geographically. Children are very honest people. They are perhaps the only honest people left in the world, besides dying patients. I did go on that date for her. When I got home, I realized that he did not know that he had gone out with her sister. That was probably the first windstorm in my life.

I became aware that you can have absolutely everything materially, but you have absolutely nothing if you do not have love and do not have individual recognition as a unique human being. And that was the biggest gift life gave to me, because I was forced to leave home at a very young age. Then I went to see life; life in Germany, war-devastated cities like the picture of Hiroshima. I went to Maidanek concentration camp where 960,000 children were put into gas chambers. I saw trainloads of babies, shoes of murdered children, and carloads of women's hair that were shipped to Germany to make cloth for winter coats. But my question and my interest were not in death and dying. My question was, "How can grown-up people, like you and me, kill 960,000 innocent children and on the same day worry about their own child at home who has chicken pox?" And a young Jewish girl gave me the answer. She looked at me and she shared that her parents and grandparents, brothers and sisters were killed in the gas chamber. Then, they tried to squash her in, but there was not enough room so she was removed after having already been put on a death list. She swore that she would not leave this place of horrors, of man's inhumanity to man, until she had lived long enough to tell the whole world of all the atrocities. When the liberation army came, it actually dawned on her that if she did that, she would not be any better than Hitler himself because she would be spending her life planting seeds of hate instead of seeds of love and compassion. Then she said to me, "You, too, would be capable of doing that." And I wanted to say very quickly, "Oh no, not me!" But it suddenly dawned on me that I could not say that, because as the American Indian saying goes: "Do not judge and criticize your fellow man until you have walked in his moccasins for a mile." A few days later, when I was on my way back to Switzerland, I did not have any food in my stomach for several days, and I suddenly realized that if a child would walk by me with a piece of bread, I would be very capable of stealing that bread out of that child's hand. That is where my work with death and dying started.

We have since worked with thousands of dying grownups and, in the last ten or fifteen years, almost exclusively with dying children. It is very important to realize that we all know everything and that the only important thing we have to learn is how to get in touch with all our knowledge inside. Singing, poetry, and dance is the universal language that my dying children use when they try to share with another human being their inner knowledge of their impending death. And they also share with you their unfinished business that may lead later on in life to violence or, for children in the United States, very often to suicide. Suicide is the third cause of death among children in the United States between the ages of six and sixteen. I do not know the statistics in Japan, but it is also very bad. Twenty-five percent of our grown-up population is raised with incest, twenty-five percent with physical and sexual abuse, not to speak of emotional abuse. It is impossible to become spiritual if you are traumatized to this extent.

What we are learning from dying patients is what to do before you are on your death bed. Because many of my patients say, "You know, Dr. Ross, I've made a good living, but I've never really lived." And they die with resignation, sadness, bitterness, and very often a very prolonged and extended dying process. If you want not to be afraid of dying, you cannot be afraid of living. And if you live fully, it will not matter to you if you die at age ten, fifty, or one hundred and five. Our task is to raise the next generation of human beings who do not know Maidanek and Auschwitz, who do not know Nagasaki and Hiroshima anymore except from history books, who do not know all the tragedies we are facing in this decade, like AIDS—which we will understand maybe twenty-five years from now—another windstorm of life which is brought to mankind to open your eyes and to open my eyes.

Windstorms of your life are one of the things that you will remember at the moment of your death. There will be only two things that will be important at the moment of your death that you will think about. They are the beautiful moments and the windstorms. The special moments are all too few for most people—our memories of having connected with another human being who has loved us unconditionally, who did not say, "I will love you if you bring good grades home," "I will love you if you get into the right school," "God, would I be proud of you if you finished high school," "I would really be proud of you if I could say, 'My son, the doctor.'" That word "if" has destroyed more lives than any nuclear weapon. It is a slow lingering death, because people who grew up with "I love you if . . .," with conditional love, will try to shop for love for the rest of their lives and will never find it, because you cannot buy love in any form.

If we listen to dying patients, we will see that human beings consist of a physical, emotional, intellectual, and spiritual quadrant. We have heard from earlier speakers how important the physical quadrant is in early life. The so-called primitive cultures have known that in getting their babies in their pouch or on their back. Physical contact is absolutely essential to raise a next generation of children that do not know destruction, war, and negativity anymore. If a baby has a lot of physical contact, that will be the foundation of the house and it will be solid.

What I am saying of newborn babies is equally true of dying patients. It is essential to keep them physically comfortable, and this means oral pain medication around the clock, without false pity. If you give them the Brompton mixture, the oral medication, regularly and calculate exactly how much they need, you can keep your terminally ill patient conscious and pain-free. And then, only after the physical quadrant is taken care of, can you be concerned about the emotional quadrant. This is the problem in our society at this time because, for some strange reason, we are turning all the human babies who are all born perfect and natural into unnatural grownups. We do not know that there are only five natural emotions. We turn them all into unnatural emotions before children get to first grade.

People have many, many fears and phobias—they are terribly unnatural. They will drain your energy and prevent you from living in harmony among the four quadrants. We do not allow children to cry. We tell them: "You are a sissy again," "Big boys don't cry," "If you don't stop crying, I'll give you something to cry about." This will shut you up very fast. You will end up a very distorted grownup with a lot of problems, with shame, guilt, and self-pity. And all unnatural emotion, which we call unfinished business, will have its physical consequences. Repressed grief will have a lot of effect on your pulmonary system, on your GI system. If you are not allowed to be angry and say, "No, Mom," and you get spanked and punished, you too will develop into Hitler. Whether a little Hitler or big Hitler does not matter. You will end up being full of rage, revenge, and hate later on.

Jealousy is a natural emotion. It helps children learn how to play the flute, dance, to read. If we grownups turn it into something ugly, it will go into competition, which is something very negative and ugly. Love is the biggest problem in our society, because it is no longer unconditional love. And people who are full of guilt and conditional love also do not understand this aspect of love that has the courage to say, "No! No, I am not going to tie your shoelace. I have all the confidence in the world that you can do it on your own." This is the birth and beginning of self-confidence, self-trust, and your own inner authority. You have no unfinished business, no unnatural emotions which develop between the ages of one and six—this is when you get your basic attitudes which ruin you for life.

If you are raised with natural emotion, you are allowed to cry, you are allowed to be angry—which, in its natural form only takes fifteen seconds—then you will grow up and develop your intellectual quadrant at about age six. And in adolescence, your spiritual, intuitive quadrant begins to emerge. Once this quadrant emerges, then you will know where you have to go, what you want to be, and you will follow your own inner drama, your own inner voice. It would no longer matter at what age you die, and you would be prepared for anything and everything life brings to you. You would have no anxiety, no doubts; you could walk into a room of a dying patient and you would not think, "What should the patient be told?" "What am I going to say when he says this or that?" You would listen to your own intuition and you would know that your own intuition is always correct.

Many wonderful things happen when your spiritual quadrant opens up. You will suddenly understand that what the different religions teach is really true. I personally believe that they teach all the same thing using a different external form or different languages. You will know that if you need something, you have to ask. And if you need it, you will be given it. You will not be given it if you only want it.

My briefest and best example of this occurred after I had been lecturing for several days in California. I was in the airport waiting for my plane to take off to go to Europe the next morning. As people got ready for boarding, a young woman pulled my blouse and said, "Dr. Ross!" I wanted to say, "No! My name is Mary Smith." I did not say that, but I remained quiet and not open at all. And she said very desperately that in October she and her husband lost their nine-year-old son from cancer. Two weeks after his funeral, they were informed that their eleven-year-old daughter was full of cancer, beyond any treatment, beyond any possibility to make it. What she really said, not in any symbolic language, but in plain English was, "We really, really need your help!" I had the difficult task of making the choice between catching my plane and getting to Europe or helping this one couple. And in my despair, I thought to myself, "Oh, God! If I only had one hour, right here, right now." And the moment my thought was finished, I heard over the loudspeaker, "Flight 83 is delayed one hour."

I am not exaggerating, but your life will totally be this way if you get in tune with your own spiritual quadrant and if you learn the humility to ask when you need help.

Why is this so important when you work with dying patients? The beauty about man is that man was given two things. One was a universal language that was true all over the world. You can talk to the Australian Aborigines, to Eskimos, to Hindus, to Muslims, to Buddhists, to Jews, to Catholics, even to wishy-washy Protestants. It is a totally universal language. This is the part you are born with that is your eternal, immortal part, that has all knowledge.

If a child dies before he or she is grown up—for example, develops leukemia at age three and dies at age nine—or loses sight, he or she will be given something that in the long run will be more precious than what he or she loses. This is a universal law. Children who die at a young age develop an intuitive, spiritual quadrant early on in life. And this is why dying children not only know that they are dying but are willing to share it with you, if they sense that your own intuitive, spiritual quadrant is open, that you do not play games and that you do not lie to them.

Children are teachers. Children are the best teachers in the world of the symbolic language of dying patients. I have been seeing a five-year-old dying boy who is very close to death and has had near-death experiences. He does not intellectually understand the meaning of a brain-stem tumor, but he knows he is dying of a brain tumor. He tries to tell us what it is like when you die. He sent me a picture that—just as poetry, dance, or music—represents a message in a universal language. It showed a rainbow with a beautiful castle at the end of the rainbow, and next to it sunshine with a smiling face. When he came back from his near-death experience, he told his mother, "This is God's Crystal Castle and the smiling, dancing stars that told me 'Welcome back home.' " This is the language of a five-year-old, if you are ready to hear it.

After his near-death experience, he was no longer afraid to die, but he had one piece of unfinished business. He called me up rather urgently and said, "Elisabeth, I absolutely need to know if Quasar is going to wait for me when I die." Quasar was his dog, who had died two weeks earlier. You are not trained in medical school to answer questions like this. But from my experience with dying children, I told him that all I know is that you get what you need, not what you want. And if you really need Quasar to be there for you, ask and he will be there. A few days later, he had another near-death experience, and he called me up, very excited, and said that not only was Quasar there but he wiggled his tail.

I hope you understand that working with dying children is not depressing. It teaches you a lot about how we could live so that we are not afraid of death, of dying, or of living. The other thing we are given with birth is free choice. We can use free choice as a gift or a curse. We have seen what happens to mankind with competition, with materialism, with the illusion that we can buy love, love of other countries, support for more weapons and wars; but we also see what happens when we use our power of free choice for the benefit of mankind. When you study dying children and dying patients for years, you ask yourself what death is, what happens to all these beautiful children. What happened to the children of Maidanek? What happened to the children of Hiroshima and Nagasaki? My research of what happens started, unknowingly, when I went to the wooden barracks to see where the children spent their last nights. I not only saw messages to mommies and daddies that they scratched into the wooden barracks walls, but what I found all over the concentration camps were little symbols of butterflies scratched into the wooden barracks walls.

I did not know in those days what the meaning of a butterfly was. I was very touched by one poem, which said that man does not understand butterfly and butterfly does not understand man. That is where I was in 1945. In the next twenty-five years, man will understand butterfly and butterfly will understand man.

We use the symbol of the butterfly when we work with dying children and they ask us what happens when they die. We do not tell them that you go to sleep. We do not tell them that you go to heaven. We use the universal language and tell them that you are not really what you seem to be. Your body is like a cocoon and when this cocoon gets damaged beyond repair, what happens is that it simply releases the butterfly that is much more beautiful than a cocoon.

It is very important that those of us who do research in death and life after death find a universal language, because the subjective experience of birth and death is a universal human experience, totally independent of your cultural and religious background. If people become spiritual, they will no longer differentiate between the religions. As you probably know, the Christian religion has twenty thousand subgroups. To me, that is not even Christian. What we need to learn in the future is that we are all human beings, all consisting of physical, emotional, intellectual, and spiritual quadrants. We need to learn not to judge and criticize each other, but to try to help our fellow man, to open up our own spiritual quadrant, our own inner knowledge, so that we know where we are going, where we belong, and to contribute to the benefit of mankind—which most people understand only after death, when it is somewhat too late.

I will summarize briefly my finding from studying twenty thousand people in their near-death experience from all over the world. When your physical body is destroyed by whatever means, it will simply release the "butterfly." In the second stage, there is psychic energy, still manipulative, but you will have all awareness. And in very practical language, that means if you get killed in an accident, your eternal, immortal part will be released from your body. Your body may be trapped in a car, but you will float a few feet above the accident; and you will not only know what people are saying, but you will be able to know how many blow torches were used to extricate you out of the car. But awareness is a step higher and also means that you will be aware of the thoughts of the drivers who drive by and use excuses why they should not stop at the scene of the accident. In this second stage, you will be whole again.

The first thing my multiple sclerosis patients who have been paralyzed and in wheel chairs say is that they were able to sing and dance again. You verify this with the help of science and technology and your intellectual quadrant that still has a need to verify all these thing. The only way I know how to verify that you are whole again is to ask blind people who had absolutely no light perception for ten years or more. I asked them what they were able to see. And they will tell you the color of your sweater, the design of your tie, what kind of jewelry you wear. You cannot tell me that this is due to oxygen deprivation.

In the second stage, you will not only be perfect again, but you have to be aware that this is real but not reality, just like you see in your dreams with your eyes closed. It is very real but not reality. In this stage, you will also know that human beings can never die alone. You can send a man in a rocket to the universe and miss the target; the moment his physical body cannot be alive, he can no longer be alone. You will always be able to move any place in the universe that you think of. If you die in the United States and think of your parents in Tokyo, with the speed of your thought, you will be in Tokyo or Kyoto or wherever you think of.

The other reason you cannot die alone is that those who preceded you in death will be waiting for you. If you are a Californian and you have had nine wives, you do not have to worry, because the only thing that counts outside of this physical energy field is love. In real love, unconditional love, you will always meet the ones you have loved the most—a grandma, grandpa, mother, brothers, or sisters. After you have had your reunion, then you get into the area where man can no longer manipulate. Man can ordinarily manipulate physical and psychic energy. Because we were given free choice, it can be positive or negative. Near-death experiences can only go up to here.

At the time of this permanent transition, if you have a near-death experience, you may see a light at the end of something; for you that means transition. It can be a tunnel or bridge or gate. But at the end you see the glimpse of a light. Any human being who has seen this light knows that this is spiritual energy which comes from God and cannot be manipulated. In this conditon, you will have all knowledge. Near-death experiences can only reveal a glimpse of this. You could not tolerate more, and you would have to come back. If you die, the connection between the "cocoon" and the "butterfly" is severed. This veil is closed and it is in the presence of this light which different people from different continents give different names. It is called love, light, God, Christ—whatever you call it. In this presence, you will be totally wrapped in love, compassion, and understanding. Negativity is not possible here. And here you begin to appreciate that every human being is born perfect with all the knowledge that you need to have and that the sum of your individual personal life is nothing else than the sum total of every choice you make every moment of your life.

What I mean by choice is not only your deeds, but also your words and thoughts. It is sad that we have to lose children before we learn what is important. It is tragic that our children have to commit suicide before we can change our priorities. It is tragic that mankind as a family needs to go through Nazi Germany, through Nagasaki, through Hiroshima, through Vietnam, before we open our eyes. We do seem blind and need to be shaken up before we learn to see.

And now we have AIDS. I do not know if it is a tragedy here yet, but it will be. We have thousands of AIDS patients in the United States. The prisons are full of AIDS patients. The city hospitals in New York have sixty three-year-old children who are dying of AIDS, their parents dropping them in city hospitals, unaware that they delivered babies with AIDS due to the long incubation period. They are dropped in city hospitals and the parents disappear because they are unable to care for them.

My dream is to start a hospice for three-year-olds with AIDS, but that does not solve the problem. The biggest lesson I have probably learned in the last six months is to overcome my own fear of AIDS and to make a workshop for AIDS patients.

In the midst of pain, anguish, and tragedy of thirty-five young men who were dying of AIDS in different stages, one man was totally beaming, not artificially but from his heart. And I asked him at the end of the workshop, "How can you beam?" He said that it took this horrible disease to make him finally aware of what unconditional love is all about. He shared how he came from a very fundamentalist Christian family in the south of the United States, very punitive, very judgmental, very much against his lifestyle. He condemned them, they condemned him, and he left home with nothing good to say. He went from bad to worse, and he ended up a very young man in a city hospital in San Francisco dying of AIDS. In the last moment, he did what all human beings do, and there is no difference. He thought about the windstorms of life which are meant to prepare you for life. And he had many of them. But he also thought of the moments when the father takes time out to take his son fishing; or when a mother threatens to spank you and grandma quietly holds you in her arms and gives you a hug. And these are the moments. And he suddenly realized that he had had many moments in his life.

He asked the doctor if he would not mind giving him a weekend pass before he died, which was expected to happen any day. For God knows what reasons, this doctor had the courage to give him a weekend pass. This young man called home to North Carolina where he had not seen his parents for many years and said, "Mom, I am dying of cancer (that was the only white lie he told). I need to come home and say good-bye to you." The mother did not get hysterical. She said very calmly, "We are looking forward to seeing you one more time." Then he described how he walked across the meadow toward the log cabin with the beautiful porch in front, and the mother steps out on the porch, the father a few feet behind (he is always a few feet behind). The mother still wears the same apron, and she steps toward him with her arms outstretched. And his last big fear: "Oh, God, if she sees the holes in my checks, my big purple nose, my ugly, almost repulsive face, she will stop and not touch me." But he has learned because of the windstorms of his life to take life as a challenge, not as a threat. He walks towards his mother and his mother towards him. As she hugs him, she stays cheek to cheek with her son. She whispers in his ear, "Son, we know that you have AIDS and it's okay with us."

To me, that was probably one of the most profound experiences. If man can learn what unconditional love is and not judge and not criticize, and practice this kind of love, then the future of the world will be beautiful. Then, we will begin to understand that we are all parts of this, and that we are—in the most literal sense—brothers and sisters. And as I said at the beginning, the things that differ are the external things, but the internal things are basically the same. So I wish you not an easy life, but a life full of windstorms and plenty of moments.

Contributors

ALISE AGAR is a psychologist currently investigating the evolutionary implications of transcendental experiences. She is interested in the relationship between cosmic intelligence and mythic imagination. She is Associate Director of the Omega Institute in Orinda, California (with Kenneth Ring).

MARIE-LOUISE VON FRANZ, PH.D., is one of the most prominent theoreticians of Jungian psychology today. She was born in Munich, but spent most of her life in Zurich, Switzerland. There she worked directly with Carl Gustav Jung for thirty-one years and was one of the founders of the Jung Institute in Kuessnacht near Zurich. An analyst in private practice, she also works as training analyst at the Jung Institute. Among her publications are numerous articles and the books, *Number and Time*, *The Grail Legend* (with Emma Jung), *C.G. Jung: His Myth in Our Time*, *Dream and Death*, *Time, Rhythm, and Repose*, and *Projection and Re-Collection in Jungian Psychology*.

JAMES GARRISON, PH.D., is currently Administrative Director of the Esalen Soviet-American Exchange Program. His dissertation at Cambridge University was a Jungian exploration of the relationship between the Judeo-Christian prophecies of the end of time and problems of the nuclear age. He currently lectures and writes on the scientific, political, psychological, and theological aspects of nuclear technology and the global crisis. He is the author of the books, *From Harrisburg to Hiroshima* and *The Darkness of God*.

287

STANISLAV GROF, M.D., PH.D., is a psychiatrist with over thirty years' experience in research pertaining to non-ordinary states of consciousness. Formerly Chief of Psychiatric Research at the Maryland Psychiatric Research Center and Assistant Professor of Psychiatry at The Johns Hopkins University in Baltimore, MD, he is currently Scholar-in-Residence and Member of the Board of Trustees at the Esalen Institute in Big Sur, California. He is one of the founders and pioneers of transpersonal psychology and founding president of the International Transpersonal Association. Among his publications are over eighty articles and the books, *LSD Psychotherapy, Beyond Death* (with C. Grof), *Beyond the Brain: Birth, Death, and Transcendence in Psychotherapy,* and *The Adventure of Self-Discovery.*

JACK KORNFIELD, PH.D., is a clinical psychologist, teacher of Vipassana meditation in the United States and Europe, and founder of the Insight Meditation Center in Barre, Massachusetts, as well as the Insight Meditation Center West in California. He received traditional training in Western psychology and has been able to integrate it with broad practical and theoretical knowledge of the Eastern spiritual disciplines. His meditative experience includes many years of life as a Buddhist monk in South Asia. He is the author of the books, *Living Buddhist Masters, Still Forest Pool,* and *Seeking the Heart of Wisdom* (with J. Goldstein).

ELISABETH KÜBLER-ROSS, M.D., is a Swiss-born psychiatrist who has gained world-wide fame for her pioneering work with terminally ill patients and for her theoretical explorations in the realm of death and dying. She has dedicated her life to psychological assistance to adults and children dying of cancer and, more recently, to patients dying of AIDS. Her theoretical interests include human spirituality, phenomenology of near-death experiences, and survival of consciousness after death. Among her publications are many articles in scientific journals and the books, *On Death and Dying, Questions and Answers on Death and Dying, Death, the Final Stage of Growth, To Live Until We Say Goodbye, Working It Through, Living in the Death and Dying, Remember the Secret,* and *On Children and Death.*

RALPH METZNER, PH.D., is a psychotherapist in private practice, professor of East-West psychology and Dean at the California Institute of Integral Studies in San Francisco. A pioneer in psychedelic therapy and transpersonal psychology, he lectures and conducts seminars throughout the world. Among his publications are numerous professional articles and the books, *The Psychedelic Experience* (with T. Leary and R. Alpert), *The Ecstatic Adventure, Maps of Consciousness, Know Your Type,* and *Opening to Inner Light.*

JOHN W. PERRY, M.D., is a Jungian psychiatrist in private practice who was instrumental in founding the C.G. Jung Institute in San Francisco. He is a pioneer in modern understanding of the psychotic process in psychological terms and founder of Diabasis, an experimental treatment facility supporting individuals in severe transpersonal crises. Among his publications are many professional articles and the books, *The Far Side of Madness, Lord of the Four Quarters, Roots of Renewal in Myth and Madness: The Self in the Psychotic Process,* and *Individuation in Evolution.*

KENNETH RING, PH.D., is Professor of Psychology at the University of Connecticut and past president of the International Association for Near-Death Studies (IANDS). A pioneer in the fields of thanatology and transpersonal psychology, he is the author of about forty professional articles in these fields and of the books, *Life At Death: A Scientific Investigation of the Near-Death Experience* and *Heading Toward Omega: In Search of the Meaning of the Near-Death Experience.*

RUSSELL L. SCHWEICKART, PH.D., is an American astronaut who participated in the Apollo 9 mission. While performing a "spacewalk" and other astronautical feats during this mission into space, he had important personal experiences that deeply affected his perception of the earth and all that lives on it.

KARAN SINGH, PH.D., is a noted scholar of political science, philosophy, music, poetry, and cultural history. Former Regent of Jammu and Kashmir, he was a member of the Indian government for many years and held ministerial posts in the Cabinet. He received his Ph.D. from the Delhi University after completing a thesis on the political thought of Sri Aurobindo. He is a superb scholar of the ancient Indian scriptures and a charismatic speaker. He has written books focusing on various topics in the fields of political science and philosophy, translated folk songs, composed original poems, and published two volumes of his personal and political memoirs, *The Heir Apparent.*

BROTHER DAVID STEINDL-RAST, PH.D., is a Benedictine monk, philosopher, and internationally known scholar of religion. His writings
explore the original mystical message of Christianity and its relationship to the great spiritual philosophies of the Far East. He was
born in Vienna where he also studied art, psychology, and anthropology, and he received degrees from the Vienna Academy and the
University of Vienna. He has lectured on various aspects of contemplative life in the United States, Europe, and Asia and is the author
of the books, *The Listening Heart* and *Gratefulness, the Heart of Prayer.*

WILLIAM IRWIN THOMPSON, PH.D., is an internationally known cultural
historian, philosopher and writer addressing in his works issues of
planetary relevance. He is the founding director of the Lindisfarne
Association, a ground-breaking educational community. Among his
books are *At the Edge of History, Passages About Earth, The Time
Falling Bodies Take to Light,* and *Pacific Shift.*

FRANCISCO VARELA, PH.D., is an important representative of the
Chilean school of biology. He has developed creatively the ideas of
Gregory Bateson and has done pioneering work in the area of artificial
intelligence and the study of neurobiological and cybernetic mechanisms of perception and cognition. He is the author of many articles
in the field and of the books, *Principles of Biological Autonomy* and
Autopoiesis and Cognition (with H. Maturana).

FRANCES VAUGHAN, PH.D., is a psychotherapist in independent practice in Mill Valley, California, former President of the Association
of Transpersonal Psychology and current President of the Association
of Humanistic Psychology. She is one of the pioneers in transpersonal
psychology, a field in which she continues to practice therapy, lecture,
teach, and offer consultations. She is the author of *Awakening Intuition, Accept This Gift* (with R. Walsh), and *The Inward Arc: Healing
and Wholeness in Psychotherapy and Spirituality,* and co-editor (with
R. Walsh) of *Beyond Ego: Transpersonal Dimensions in Psychology.*

ROGER WALSH, M.D., PH.D., is Associate Professor in the Department
of Psychiatry and Human Behavior at the University of California
in Irvine. He is one of the pioneers of transpersonal psychology with
special interests in the areas of philosophy of science, Buddhist theory
and practice, and psychological aspects of the global crisis. In addition
to many articles in professional journals, he has written the books,

Beyond Ego: Transpersonal Dimensions in Psychology (with F. Vaughan), *Beyond Health and Normality* (with D. Shapiro), *Meditation: Classic and Contemporary Perspectives* (with D. Shapiro), *Accept This Gift* (with F. Vaughan), and *Staying Alive: Psychology of Human Survival*.

JOHN WHITE is an author and editor in the fields of consciousness research and higher human development. Among his books are *What is Enlightenment?*, *Frontiers of Consciousness*, *Pole Shift*, and, for children, *The Christmas Mice*. His writing has appeared in *The New York Times*, *Saturday Review*, *Reader's Digest*, *Esquire*, *Science of Mind*, *Omni* and *Science Digest*. Formerly the Director of Education for The Institute of Noetic Sciences, he lives in Cheshire, Connecticut.

MICHAEL E. ZIMMERMAN is Professor of Philosophy at Newcomb College, Tulane University. Author of *Eclipse of the Self: The Development of Heidegger's Concept of Authenticity*, Zimmerman has also written numerous essays on Heidegger's philosophy. In addition, he has published articles on the nuclear arms race, environmental ethics, and the role played by feminism in changing humanity's conception of its place in Nature. He also serves as Clinical Professor of Psychiatry at LSU Medical School, and Clinical Professor of Psychology at Tulane University Medical School. He has written extensively on the role of philosophy in medicine and psychotherapy.

Index

Abinash Chandra Bose, 149
Actualization, tendency, 4
A.E. (George William Russell), 223
Aggression, integration of, 34
Alchemy, philosophers' stone, rose-colored blood, 27, 28
Allport, Gordon W., debasement, 5, 9
American Indians and rednecks, 227
American Moral Majority, 233
Amnesty International, 43
Anthropôs, 25
    archetype of man, 26
    Figure, Christ-Beserk, 26
    and personal love, 33
Antichrist
    challenge of, 173
    at end of Christian aeon, 26
    nonrecognition of, 169
Archaic identity
    Anthropôs, divine man, 31
    differences among people, 31
    participation mystique, 30
Archetype(s)
    Anthropôs, 26
    of Antichrist, 165
    beserk, 34
    Eros, 30

Jungian, and transpersonal
    experiences, 71
    of Self, 81, 165
    Wotan, 161
Arrien, A., 42
Assuras, 52
Athanasius, Saint, God becoming
    human, 174
Atharvan, great seer, 149
Atharva Veda, Bhumi Suktam, Hymn to
    the Earth, 149
Aurobindo, Sri, 147
    evolution of consciousness, 3
    higher humanity, 123
    journey toward perfection, 121
Austin, Mary, mystical experience, 99
Avidya (Indian), 44
Awareness
    exercise in, 46
    self-, exercise in, 43

Basic Perinatal Matrices (BPM), 63
    amniotic universe
        characteristics, 64
        intrauterine, existence, 64
        nature of experiences, 64
    cosmic engulfment

and hell, 64
   nature of experiences, 64, 65
   death-rebirth experience, nature of, 66
   death-rebirth struggle, nature of, 65
Bateson, Gregory, 72, 205, 222, 223, 224, 233
Becker, Ernest, symbol of hero, 178
Behavior, collective, global symptoms, 2
Being, 12
Being-amid-becoming, 12
Beserk
   as dark aspect, 27
   in Klaus's vision, 26
   visible image of invisible authority, 33
Bertine, Eleanor, on Christianity, 164
Bhagavad Gita, 147, 233
Biology
   Gedanken experiment, 206
   as autonomous cognitive system, 207
   illustrating attitude and framework changes, 208
   and internal representation of physical environment, 207
   logic of coherence, 205
   logic of correspondence and logic by coherence, 208
   and perception, 207
   new, 205
      autonomy and transformation, changes of emphasis, 214, 215
      source of metaphors, 215
Bluebeard, 42
Bodhisattva, Manjusri, 142
Bohm, D., 73
Boy George, 221
Brandt, W., 1
Brhadaranyaka-Upanishad, verse, 22
Brother Klaus. *See* Fluë, Niklaus von
Bucke, R.M., *Cosmic Consciousness*, 123, 124
Buddha, (Siddhārtha Gautama), Right Thought, 133, 137

Campbell, Joseph, *The Hero with a Thousand Faces*, 184
Capra, Fritjof, physics, 72, 93
Cars, The, *You Might Think I'm Crazy*, 221

Castanada, Carlos, Don Juan, 48
Chardin, Pierre Teilhard de. *See* Teilhard de Chardin
Chekhov, Anton Pavlovitch, principle of dramaturgy, 191
Christ. *See also* Jesus Christ
   a becoming, 125
   event, significance, 152
   and Hiroshima, 167
   as messiah, 124
   shadow aspect of, 26
Christ-figure
   and medieval alchemists, 27
   unofficial development of, 26
Christianity
   Armageddon, 132
   and building bridges, 130
   Eleanor Bertine on, 164
   emergence, 132
   metanoia, 131
   othonoia, 131
   other teachers, 133
   paranoia, 131
   Second Coming, 132
   today, 130
Christian mysticism, 107
Jesus Christ
   appeal to common sense, 113, 114
   baptism, 129
   and the church, 117
   conversion, 110
   cross, historical interpretation, 115
   emphasis on community and senses, 113
   and Gospels, 114
   and Jesus Christ, 107, 108
   proclamation of Kingdom of God, 108
   Kingdom of God, defined, 109, 111
   parable, definition and example, 111, 112, 113
   resurrection, 115
   salvation, 110
   Shroud of Turin, 116, 117
   teaching method in parables, 108, 111
   and trouble, 114
Chuang-tzu, 33
Concept(s), 12
   Einsteinian physics, 144
   Golden Rule of Confucius, 89

Heisenberg's Uncertainty Principle, 144
individuality, 91
messiah, 91
perinatal matrices, 67
quantum mechanics, 144
Stanislav Grof's extended cartography of psyche, 144
Conflict, inner, perspectives, 49, 50
Confucius (K'ung Ch'iu), 20
and *Jen*, virtue (force), brotherly love, 89
on perfect knowledge and perfect virtue, 89
Consciousness
and change, 16
collective, 2
Cosmic, 6, 123, 124
crisis in, 119
development of, 3
ego, 24
integrated levels of, 10
and matter, 57
and mechanistic science, 57
nonordinary, 57
nonordinary state, conditions, 68
optimal states of, 9
ordinary state, conditions, 68
perennial philosophy, 5
psi-conducive states of, 262
research, and psyche, 57
self-exploration of, 120
universal, 6
Council of Unterwalden, 19
cummings, e.e., 249, 250

Davies, P., 72
Day After, The, 145
Death
abuse, physical and emotional, 277
and AIDS, 284, 285
American Indian saying, 276
and birth, universal human experience, 282
and butterflies, 281, 282
children as teachers, 280, 281
confrontation with, in experiential sequences, 62
deeds, words, and thoughts, 284
fears and phobias, 278

inner knowledge of, 277
lack of caring, child's view, 275
learning from dying patients, 277
love, the problem, 279
Maidanek concentration camp, 276
man and universal language and law, 280
and near-death experiences, 282, 283
personal intuition, 279
persons and four quadrants, 278
physical pain, 278
practice of unconditional love, 285
and rebirth, perinatal level, 63
repressed grief, 278
and the spiritual need vs. want, 279
suicide, 277
and sum of individual life, 284
and unconditional love, 283
universal language of dying children, 276, 277
and windstorms of life remembered, 277
Declaration of Independence, The, 225
de Francis, Sam, 231
De Lauer, Richard, Undersecretary of Defense, 188
Denial and negation, and nature of lying, 45
Derrida, 220, 228
Devil
in Christian paintings, 47
and demons, 51
and denial, 45
and excretion of sinners, 47
and Martin Luther, 47
Disney, Walter Elias, *Fantasia*, 231
Dōgen, Zen Master, 136
Dorn, Gerald
cosmic man, 29
on philosophers' stone, 28
Drive, single instinctual, aspects, 25
Drupsteen, Jaap, *Hyster Pulsatu*, 231
Duality
good/bad, 36
good and evil, 47
and integration, 37
spirit and matter, 37
Dyson, Freeman, on defensive shields, 192

Eastern Church, Philokalia, 48
Eastern culture
  mythology, demons, 52
  pluralistic view of good and evil, 52
Ecosystem (Earth), 1
Edinger, Edward, *Ego and Archetype*,
    180
Ego
  -annihilating encounter, 37
  ideal, 50
  super-, 43
Einstein, Albert, 144
Elgin, D., 3
Elimination, of evil, alternatives, 47
Eliot, T.S. (Thomas Stearns), Judaeo-
    Christianity, 174, 175
Enclosure Acts, 224, 225
Enlightenment
  defined, 12
  development of consciousness, 5
Eros
  differentiation of, 35
  from *homo totus*, the cosmic man, 29
Errico, Rocco, the coming of Christ, 132
Evil
  concealment of, 43
  as entity of wrongness, 37
  face of, masks, 43
  judgmentalism with violent rage, 51
  occurrence of, Kabbalah, 38
  part of total ecology, 237
  processes of transformation, 38
  propaganda of, 40
  recognition and identification of, 43
Evolution, 3
  in consciousness, 133
  Cro-Magnon and Neanderthal, 120,
    121
  development of consciousness, 3
  dying species and new breed, 122
  emerging species and resistance, 121
  and higher humanity, 123
  Homo noeticus, characteristics, 123
  inner, 33
  and liberation or enlightenment, 134
  moral, 121
  mutant humans, 122
  and nature's resistance to extinction,
    120
  and New Age, 134

  and noetics, 123
  and survivolution
    description, 122
    species gap, 120
Evolution and brain
  commonsensical understanding, 209
  conception of imaginary beings, 208
  evolutionary change, aspects, 211
  evolutionary thinking, defined, 209
  genetic change, 211
  job of evolutionist, 209
  knowledge and action and ethics,
    basis of, 215, 216
  letting go of certainty, antedote, 216
  natural drift, defined, 211
  natural selection, 210
  neuroscience
    adaptation and operational closure,
      differences, 214
    neurobiology, and sensory
      perception, 212, 213
    representationism and, 211, 212
    retina, 213, *213*, 214
  optimal adaptation, 210
  population genetics, study of, 209
  proscriptive vs. prescriptive rule, 210
  search for optimization, 209, 210
Excretion, as basis for judgment in
    child, 46
Existence, primary goal of, 5
Experience(s)
  Basic Perinatal Matrices (BPM), 63–67
  cosmic engulfment and hell, 64
  death and rebirth, perinatal level, 63
  death-rebirth struggle, 65
  dislocation, 222
  mystical, 94
  peak, 75
  perinatal, 62
  psychotic visionary, 90
  shared, 14
  transcendence of limitations, 68
Experiential research
  insights and possibilities, 75
  and neutralized perinatal forces, 75
Experiential therapy
  confrontation with death, 62
  inner process transcendence of
    biographical level, 61

physiological manifestations,
   unconscious level, 61
and recollective-biographical level of
   psyche, 60
self-exploration and emotional and
   physical pain, 61

Faust, Johann, Mephistopheles, 161, 162
Fluë, Niklaus von (Brother Klaus)
   and beserk, 34
   birth, 18
   and Christ-figure, 27
   counselor, political, 20
   and frightening vision, 24
   great vision, 20, 21
   and Heiny am Grund, 19
   hermit's cell, 19
   judge, 19
   marriage, 19
   and political incident, 19
   religious mendicant pilgrim, 19
   settling of quarrel, 20
   visionary states, 19
Fraser, J.G., times of interregnum, 31
Freud, Sigmund
   denial and repression, 44
   personal unconscious, 24
   repression, 42
   struggle between id and ego, 45
Fromm, Erich, malignant aggression, 75
Fry, Christopher, *A Sleep of Prisoners*,
   100
Fuller, Robert, 198

Gaia, 244
Gallop, G., Jr., poll, 255
Gandhi, Mohandas Karamchand. *Called*
   Mahatma
   force of truth, 140
   power of love, 140
Genetic memory (human), speculation
   on, 49
Global consciousness
   and *Bhagavad Gita*, 147
   Cartesian-Newtonian-Marxist
      paradigm collapse, 144
   evolutionary thinkers, 147
   human predicament, 145
   imperative move toward, 146

MAD, Mutually Assured Destruction,
   146
new philosophy, 147
   concepts into mental structure of
      mankind, 147
   halting nuclear arms race, 148
   individual search for inner peace,
      148
   revival of sanity, 148
   worldwide network, 148
philosophical underpinning, 147
search for new model, mankind, 144
terricide, 146
transition to, 147
vedas, 147
Vedic seers, AUM, 146
Global crises
   evolutionary catalyst, 3, 4
   psychological roots, 73–78
   solution to, with inner transformation,
      78
Global symptoms
   collective behavior, 2
   collective consciousness, 2
God
   abandonment and acceptance of, 170,
      171
   of all possibilities, 152
   becoming human, Athanasius, 174
   -conscious, 126
   Cosmic Creator, 154
   denial of, 45
   eye of, 43
   glory of, revealed, 126
   heaven and hell, 128
   and higher consciousness, 127
   and humanity, 170
   in plutonium, 169
   sovereign over history, 155
   in suffering servant, 169
   as symbol, 159
   ties to, 126
   unity with, 126
   Yahweh, 154
Goethe, Johann Wolfgang von, *Faust*, 44
Govinda, Lama, turning about in
   deepest seat of consciousness,
      126
Green, Alyce, 9
Green, Elmer, 9

Grimmir (Wotan), 22
Grof, Christina, 59
Grof, Stanislav, 9, 144
Grund, Heiny am, 19

Habermas, 228
Harman, W., 6
Heidegger, Martin, *The Question of Being*, 222, 223
Heisenberg, Werner Karl, 144, 222
Hell, experience of, 65
Heraclitus, 195
  and *polemos*, 198
  war of opposites, 50
Hitler, Adolf, 39
  and Germans, 39
  as prophetic phenomenon, 167
  and rationalization of expression of rage, 51
  and Wotan, 161
Holocaust, and concealment of evil, 43
Human being. *See* Man
Human evolution. *See* Evolution
Humanity, and welfare of planet, 10
Human relationship(s)
  of individuated persons, 33
  transpersonal view of, 10
Huxley, A., 5

I Ching, creative principle, 33, 34
Ideals, use of, 4
Identity, true, 6
Image(s) and imagery
  Hiroshima, 169
  and Brother Klaus's vision, 22
  portrayal of world-situation today, 197
  shadow and schizon, 46
  of spiritual center, archetype of Self, 81
Imagination
  and devil, 53
  and distortion of mythology, 177
  and shadow, 50
Individuality
  in America, 91
  and balance with societal concerns, 91
  image of spiritual center, archetype of Self, 81

myth and ritual approach, 80
Individuation
  distorted heroic myth, Americans, 182
  distorted mythic symbol, Marxism, 181, 182
  ego, shadow, Self, defined, 178
  eternal child, 183
  first half of life, 178, 179
  German shadow, 181
  integration of the anima, 179
  meaning of symbols, 180
  primitive peoples, 181
  second half of life, 179
  self-made man myth, Americans, 183
  Western symbols, 181
Innis, 231
Integration, of shadow, 39
Intelligence, predator, prey, 50
International Association for Near-Death Studies (IANDS), 251
International Transpersonal Association (ITA), 148
Ipuwer, Egyptian wise man, 88
Isaiah, 154

Jalāl ad-Dīn ar-Rūmī. *See* Rūmī, Sufi
James, William, 6
Jaweh, 26
Jesus Christ
  and cosmic consciousness, 127
  incarnation and resurrection, significance, 127
  meaning of injunction, from perspective of metanoia, 128
  metanoia, 125, 126
  realization of higher intelligence, 124
  Son of God, 124
  and unclean spirits, 46
  and way to Kingdom, 128
Jesus of Nazareth. *See* Jesus Christ
John, Saint (the Divine), 165
  Book of Revelation, 166
  recorded words of Jesus Christ, Patmos, 130
Journal of Transpersonal Psychology, purpose, 9
Judgment(s)
  of evil, and fear and condemnation, 47

good/evil, superimposed on other dualities, 36, 37
good/bad and good/evil, differences, 38
power of, 38
Jung, Carl Gustav
agnoia, 10
Answer to Job, 27, 158
and Antichrist, 163
on Apocalypse, 26
appearance of atomic bomb, 166
archaic identity, 30
archetype of Self, 81, 165
avoiding war, 35
centrality of consciousness in human development, 10
Christ-figure, 26
on Christianity, 162
on Christian symbols, 165
coincidenta oppositorum, 36
devil, 53
ego, shadow, and Self, 178
eternal secret, 32
on evil, 163, 164
fragmentary man into wholeness, 173
Germany, Wotan, 160
Hitler and Germans, 39
idea of Christian charity, 29
integration of anima, 179
love, 30
man is problem, 163
Niklaus von Flüe, patron saint of psychotherapy, 33
objective love, 22
pairs of opposites, 18
relationship, core of all problems, 32
rose mysticism, 29
on St. John, the Divine, 165
Self, 22
shadow, described, 39
taking back of projections, 31
on vision of beserk, 23
Wotan, 161
Wotanic experiment, World War II, 27

Kabbalah, occurrence of evil, 38
Kabir, mystic and poet, 97, 98
Kapleau, P., 6
Khunrath, Henricus
alchemist, on rose-colored blood, 28

intracosmic Christ-figure, 29
Kissinger, Henry, China, 196
Klaus, Brother. *See* Flüe, Niklaus von
Knowledge
and awakened mind, 13
perfect, Confucius, 89
and selective perception, 13
Krishna, Pandit Gopi, higher humanity, 123, 133, 147
K'ung Ch'iu, *called* K'ung Fu-tzu. *See* Confucius
Kyoto School of Philosophy, 218

Laing, R.D., the divided self, 41
Lao-tzu, 34, 133
Law, William, personal Cain and Abel, 49
Lifton, Robert Jay
psychic mutation, 158
psychic numbing, 193
Locke, John, *Two Treatises on Government*, theories of mind, 224
Lorenz, Konrad, aggression, 34
Love
blind, 30
emanation of, 28
greatest revenge, 127
objective, 22
personal, 33
unconditional, God, 126
unmentioned dynamic, 92
Lucas, George, *Star Wars* trilogy, 184

Machado, Antonio, on the path, 216
MacLeish, Archibald, *New York Times*, 240
Mc Luhan, Herbert Marshall, 230, 231, 232
The Gutenberg Galaxy, 234
retribalization in Global Village, 228
Mc Waters, B., 3
Macrocosm and Microcosm
events from, and transpersonal experiences, 72
implications of events from, 72
Mad Bear, 143
Magritte, René, 221
Mahavira, 133

Man
    anamnesis of original, 26
    and call from cosmos, 129
    cosmic, described, 29
    fragmentary, into wholeness, Jung,
        173
    inner states, 51
    problem, 163
Mark
    conversion, 109
    reactions of common people, 114
    summary of teaching of Jesus Christ,
        108
Marx, Karl, 222, 230, 232
Maslow, Abraham H.
    metapathologies, 4
    peak experiences, 75
    self-actualizing people, 14
Materialism, world-view of, 6
Matthew, Saint
    Christ never left humanity, 132
    take my yoke upon you, 129
Maturation, psychological, 3
Mechanistic science, portrayal of
        consciousness, 57
Mencius
    goodness, 90
    selflessness, 89
Metacosmic Void, 69
Metapathologies, 4, 5
Midrashim, 42
Minos, King, 42
Mohammed, 133
Moltmann, Jurgen, rejection of Jesus,
        described, 170
Moody, Raymond, 251
Moses, 133
Müller, Max, madhu-honey, 22
Mumford, L., 5
Mutwa, Credo, of the Zulu, 229
Mystics and mysticism
    inner Christ, 22
    mystic awareness, 94
    mystic as prophet, 106
    mystical experience
        alienation/belonging and sin/
            salvation, struggle, 98
        awareness, 97, 105
        and beginning of religious
            traditions, 101

        belonging, 96
        communion, 97
        communion with Ultimate Reality,
            99
        definition, 96, 97
        ethics, morality and moralism, 103
        example, 95
        exploration into God, 100
        fearfulness vs. commitment, 103,
            104
        rediscovery of God, 99
        and religious tradition, 106
        and religion, 101
    rose, 29
    symbolization of cross, 106
Myth(s) and mythology
    aspects of Star Wars, 183, 184
    bear, 23
    Bluebeard, 42
    Cain and Abel, rivalry, 49
    Churning of Milky Ocean (Samudra-
        Manthana), 144, 145
    demons, 51
    demons, Buddhist and Hindu, 52
    distorted myths
        Marxism, 181, 182
        self-made man, 183
        by imagination, 177
    explanation of myth, 177, 178
    hero
        importance of, 178
        process of individuation, 178
        slaying of, 178
    heroic myths, distortions, 180, 181
    Hundu, and origin of evil, 47
    Judaic-Christian, and judgment, 37,
        38
    King Minos, 42
    light and dark, 50
    Star Wars, mythic symbol, 184
    Wotan, 22

Nanak, Guru, 133
National characteristics, German, being
        beserk, 23
Nature, true, awakening of, 6
Nazis
    and archetypal possession, 160
    and racial purity, 47

Near-death experiences (NDE)
  belief in life after death, 261
  as catalyst in personal development,
    262
  categories of aftereffects, 258, 259
    appreciation of life, 259
    greater feelings of self-worth, 259
    increased concern for welfare of
      others, 259, 260
    search for deeper understanding of
      life, 260
    search for increased self-
      understanding, 260
  changes in psychic awareness, 261
  cultural phenomenon, 252
  described, 253, 254
  desire for universal spirituality, 261
  frequency of, 255, 256
  and general interpretation of, 257,
    258
  hold on collective consciousness, 252
  increased susceptibility to psi-
    conducive states of consciousness,
    262
  moment of transcendental radiance,
    251
  personal characteristics, 256
  and promotion of spiritual awakening
    and growth, 262
  random selection, 256
  reflections on, 254, 255
  and transcendent unity of religions,
    261
  transformative effects, 258
  type of, 256
  universality of, 257
  variety of experiential elements, 252
Needham, Joseph, systems theory
    approach, 82
Neumann, Erich, modern mass
    movements, 181
New Testament
  make all one Christ, 125
  unclean spirits, 46
Nicholas of Cusa, *coincidentia
    oppositorum*, 36
Nietzsche, Friedrich Wilhelm
  friendly enemy, 198
  higher humanity, 123
  medicinal nihilism, 220

Nishitani, Keiji, *Religion and
    Nothingness*, 218, 219, 222
Nixon, Richard, China, 195, 196
Nuclear threat, costs, destruction power,
    2

Old Testament, Cain and Abel, 49
Omega Project
  co-exploration, 273
  contributions from gifted persons, 273
  and cultural phenomenon, cumulative
    impact of, 271
  forum for exploration and
    examination, 272
  principles, 272
  and transcendental states of
    awareness, 271
O'Neill, Eugene, *A Long Day's Journey
    into Night*, 95
Opposites
  co-existence of, 37
  co-incidence of, 36
  divine, 28
  good and evil, conflict, 45
  Hiroshima and Christ, 167
  integration of, 172
  judge-persecutor, 51
  man and woman, love, 32
  metaphoric, 40
  psychic, 18
  reconciliation of, 26
  reconciliation of, and transformation,
    48
  union, 27
  union of irreconcilable, 24
  unity of, 16
Oshua, 42

Pain, emotional and physical in
    experiental self-exploration, 61
Paul, Saint
  Christ as Second Adam, 125
  reality of spiritual body, 129
  redeemed humanity, 174
  renewing your mind in Christ, 126
Perception(s)
  defined, 11
  of knowledge past/future, 13
Perennial philosophy, 6

Perinatal experience, 62
  characteristics, 62
  death and rebirth, 63
  as interface between collective and
      individual unconscious, 63
  process, 62, 63
  significance of concept, 67
Perspective(s)
  evolutionary, 5
  of human evil, 51
  materialistic, 5
  metanoia, 128
  perennial philosophy, 5
  role of denial and negation, 45
  on state of inner conflict, 49
  evolutionary and historical
      antecedents, 49
  on personal/developmental basis, 49
  theological/mythical, 50
Philosopher's stone, and rose-colored
    blood, 27, 28
Philosophy, enlightenment, 12
Philosophy and politics
  aspects, Western, 221, 222
  Bhopal in India last of private
      property, 225
  commitment to Belief, 234
  commonlife, 225, 226
  cultural-ecologist, function, 236
  dynamics into transformations, 230,
      231
  electronics and aerospace, and
      dislocation, 221
  emergence of abstract thought, 231
  Good and Evil, changing view, 235
  gulf between sacred and profane, the
      West, 232
  intellectuals, 228
  isomorphic relationship between evil
      and pollution, 236
  Lockian idea of property, 225
  materialistic culture to planetary
      culture, transition, 226
  Mentalities, 229
  metaindustrial planetary culture, 226
  mode of religious experience, 233,
      234
  Moses, 235
  music video, 221
  new art forms, 231, 232

new science of compassion, 235
Pacific Shift, 222, 227
planetary implosion, 234
planetization of archaic, 229
planetization of mankind, 227
principle of reversal, 237
relationship between Mind and
    Nature, 222
shift of illusion to enlightenment, 237
theory of mind to theory of society,
    Locke, 224
Thomas Jefferson and written
    constitution, 225
traditions of individuality, 234
Truth, 234
two subcultures, 232
universe of patterns, 223
video, as form of vision, 221
video synthesizers and visual
    thinking, 231
void in materialism, 220
Western civilization and four cultural-
    ecologies, 229, 230
Western materialism and Buddhist
    emptyness, 219
Pietsch, H., 73
Planetary awareness, change in man,
    240
Planetary transformation
  and humanity, new, 267, 268
  hundreth monkey effect, 265
  and morphic resonance, 265
  rate of increase of transformations,
      264
  transcendental experiences and higher
      consciousness, 226
  and spiritual transformation, 263
Population explosion, 1
Powers, Thomas, on Russia, 191
Presidential Commission on World
    Hunger, The (1979), 2
Pribram, K., 73
Prigogine, I., 73
Projection(s)
  delusional, in East and West, 40
  taking back of, 31
  withdrawn and relationship, 31
Psyche
  cartography of, and transpersonal
      experiences, 72

complexio oppositorum, 158, 159
  as equal to all existence, 57
  God as a symbol, 159
  locus in, 157, 158
  new cartography of, 59
  new image of, 57
  recollective-biographical level of, 60
  resolution in, 175
  Russian, 190
  traditional model of, 57
  transpersonal dimensions of, 67
Psychedelic research
  basis of data, 58
  drug technique
    motive for use, 58
    nature of, 59
    and transcendence, patients, 59
  nondrug technique
    holistic therapy, process, 59
  participants in, 58
Psychiatry
  need for new model, 59, 60
  and new image of psyche, 57
Psychology
  depth, 24
    common unconscious of wide
      national units, 24, 25
    ego consciousness, 24, 24
    group unconscious, 24, 25
    personal unconscious, 24, 24
    universal psychic archetypal
      structures, 24, 25
  enlightenment, 12
  mythic
    evolutionary process of ceremonial
      system, 88
    myth as guideline, 88
Psychopathology
  and importance of transpersonal
    experiences, 73
  and perinatal level of unconscious, 73
Psychotherapy
  new image of psyche, 57
  revelations, imagery paralleling myths
    and rituals, 80
Purification
  as alternative, 47
  need for, 46

Quetzalcoatl, 133

Rama, 133
Reagan, Ronald, and American
  scientists, 186
Reality, new image of, 57
Reich, Wilhelm, character armor, 44, 45
Religion(s)
  Buddhism
    demons, 52
    relevance, 223
  Christianity
    Armageddon, 132
    building bridges, 130
    demon as malevolent, 52
    emergence, 132
    metanoia, 131
    orthonoia, 131
    paranoia, 131
    Second Coming, 132
    today, 130
  dogma, 102
  dogmatism, 102
  element of doctrine, 102
  health and vitality, defined, 105, 106
  instrument for awakening, 126
  Jewish
    influence of cosmic dualism, 50
    wisdom tradition, 174
  Judaeo-Christian tradition, polarization
    of good and evil, 52
  ritual and ritualism, 104, 105
  Taoism, yin and yang, 195
  Zoroastrian, and cosmic dualism, 50
Ricoeur, Paul, evil and the sacred, 37
Ring, Kenneth, *Life at Death, Heading
  Toward Omega*, 261
Ritual(s)
  Chou, sacral king, second dynasty,
    83, *84*
  Chung Kuo, middle Kingdom, 83, *84*
  Confucius and *Jen*, 89
  cosmic axis, 83, *84*
  cultural immaturity, Near East, 90
  democratization in mortuary cult, 88,
    89
  doctrines influencing concept of
    individuality, China, 89
  festivals of reenthronement, Egypt, 82
  figure, Great Man, 81
  Great Individual and diffusion of
    status, 88

Heaven, T'ien, earliest form, 83, *84*
Hsia Dynasty, *Wu-Wei*, exemplars of caring and nonassertion, 88
inner sacral kingship, Buddha, 91
insight of societal harmony cultivated from within, 90
introduction of messianic hero, Egypt, 88
inward realization and internalization of kingship, Israel, 90
Mencius, 89, 90
Ming-Tang, Hall of Light, 86, 87, *87*
Mo-tse, universal love, *Chien Ai*, 90
New Year Festivals, Mesopotamia, 81, 82
parallel of psychotic visionary experience, 90
rise of aristocracy, 88
sacral kingship
    Ancient Near East, 81
    India, 82
    to messiah, Israel, 91
self-contained cosmos, China, 82, 83
shamans, functions and powers, Shang and early Chou Dynasties, 87
Shang and Chou Dynasties, second and first millennium B.C., 83, 84, *85*
Taoists, doctrine of, 90
theme of center, Far East, 81
Ti, at present, 83, *84*
Ti, royal ancestors of Heaven, Bronze Age, 83
Unique Man, Bronze Age, function of, 81
whole world, bronze cosmic mirrors of Han Dynasty, 84, 85, *86*
Robinson, John, *Twelve New Testament Studies*, baptism, 171, 172
Rogers, Carl, 4
Rosicrucian movement, 29
Rumi, Sufi, lower self, 48
Russell, Peter, 265, 266

Sade, Marquis de, 51
Sagan, Carl, *The Cold and the Dark, The World After Nuclear War*, 145, 146
Sartre, Jean-Paul, 220
Satan. *See* Devil

Schell, Jonathan, *The Fate of the Earth*, 2, 145
Schizon
    definition, 41, 42
    image of, 46
    recognizable to others, 42
    splitting-off of, 42
Schweickart, Rusty, 218, 219, 221, 234, ✳ 235
SDI (Strategic Defense Initiative), 183
    alternatives
        bonding together of humanity, 197
        development of new myth, 198
        experience despair, 193
        friendship, 196
        integration of nondualism, 197, 198
        integration of projected shadow, 193
        shift in human self-understanding, 194, 195
        withdrawal of projections, 196
    complexity and testing, problem of, 188
    contrast of Russian and American views, 191
    fears of SP-BMD, 190
    image of world-situation, today, 197
    incomplete mythology, 186
    integration of male and female, new myth, 199, 200
    justification for, 192
    major criticisms, 187, 188
    manifestation of incomplete myth, 187
    new nondualistic myth, 198, 199
    nondualistic thinking, 195
    other objections, 188
    President Reagan and American scientists, 186, 187
    requirements for laser weapons, 188
    Russian psyche, 190
    Soviet Anti-*Star Wars* defense, problem of, 188
    Soviet perceptions of SDI as first-strike initiative, problems, 189, 190
    Star Wars, synopsis, 184, 185
Self
    and beserk, 34
    eye of God, 43

eye of, within, 42
and inner dualism, 33
integration of personal shadow, 28
relationship with, in other person, 32
Self-awareness
    and devil within, 53
    exercise in, 43
Self-destruction
    alternatives to, 16
    race to, 7
Self-discovery, race to, 7
Self-exploration, integration of
        techniques for, 77
Self-healing, capacity for, 13
Shadow
    described, Jung, 39
        integration of, reasons for, 39
        nonrecognition of, 39
Shapiro, D., 10
Sheldrake, Rupert, 72, 73
    formative causation, 264, 265
    A New Science of Life, 264
Shepard, Paul, predator carnivores, 49,
        50
Shroud of Turin, 116, 117
Siddhartha Gautama (Buddha) on
        hatred, 135
Sin(s)
    missing the mark, 126
    original, and purification taboos, 46
Sivananda, Swami, inward battle, 48
Sivard, R., 2
Smith, Adam, 222
Smith, Hedrick, *The Russians*, 191, 192
Smith, Huston
    levels of reality, 12
    theistic metaphysics, 11
Snow, Lord, 232
Social responsibility
    looking at suffering, 139
    openness to experience, 139
    two forces, 140
Social unrest, 4
Socrates, *daimon*, 52
Soul, and battle of evil spirits, 48
Space-Age
    around the world, every hour and a
        half, 246
    into atmosphere and deceleration, 246
    awe-inspiring symbol, 241

camera malfunction, moment to think,
        244
countdown, anticlimactic, 241
docking, 245
first glimpse of earth from space, 242
floating, 244
go for ten days, 246
main chutes out, splashdown, 247
making major maneuvers, 243
meaning
    concept of man, changed, 247
    identity with whole planet, 248
    infinite universe, size and
        significance, 248
    planet, small and fragile is
        everything, 248
    planet whole, invisible borders and
        boundaries, 248
    relationship to planet, changed, 247
    sensing element for man, 249
mission rules, 240
moment of panic, 242
new perspective, 248
one hundred sixty-one sunrises and
        sunsets, 246
preparation for experience, 240
rendezvous, 245
sight through window of lunar
        module, 243
    and with world map, 246
silence and scenery, 249
special responsibility, 249
sunrise over Pacific, 244
testing spacecraft, 241
understanding systems, 240
Spirit and spirituality
    battle of evil with soul, 48
    global, 16
    in global terms, 14
    Holy Spirit, 173
    Holy Spirit today, 174
    process of, 173
    vision of interconnectedness of all
        life, 137
Spiritual practice
    acknowledgment, 142
    beginning of, 141
    Benares, holy city, 141
    Bodhisattva, Manjusri, 142

compassion and near enemy pity and
grief, 136
equanimity and near enemy
unintelligent indifference or
callousness, 136
ghats, 141
impeccability, 138
love and near enemy attachment, 135
and meditation, 138
mindfulness and Love, 143
seeing emptyness, 137, 138
separation, study of, 141
service and responsible action vs.
meditative life, 135
sympathetic joy and near enemy
compassion, 136
Star Wars, 208, 209
Sufis, saying, 137
Supracosmic Void, 69
Svipall, (Wotan), 22
Symbolism of Evil, The, (Ricoeur), 37
Symbols and symbolism
Anthropôs, 25
baptism, 171, 172
bear, 23
beserk-Christ, 30
butterflies and death, 281, 282
cross, 106
God as, 159
hero, 178
inner warfare, 48
meaning of symbol, 180
self-made man, 183
shadow, discovery of within, 40
Star Wars, mythic symbol, 184
Western, 181

Tao Te Ching, 233
Tart, Charles, 9
Taylor, S., 4
Teilhard de Chardin, 147
evolution, 3
higher humanity, 123
noogenesis and Omega point, 121
noosphere, 125
planetization of mankind, 227
Terentius (Roman poet), 37
Thaker, Vimala, 137

Theology
abandonment and acceptance of God,
170
anthropocentricity, 168
anticommunism of West, 163
appearance of atomic bomb, Jung,
166
baptism, 171, 172
book of Revelation, 169, 170
collective guilt, 163
complexio oppositorum, 158, 159
confessional response, 155, 156
discernment of locus, 157, 158
divinity in history, aspects, 155
Emmanuel, 152
existence or nonexistence, 163
and Faust, 161, 162
Gnostic teaching, 165
Godhead revelations, 152
hermeneutic of engagement, 157, 159,
160
Hiroshima
apocalyptic challenges, 157
as apocalyptic phenomenon, 167
and apocalyptists, 153
focus of, 166
numinous, 153
path to wisdom, 151
Hitler as prophetic phenomenon,
167
Holy Spirit today, 174
Holy Spirit of wisdom, 173
humanization of eschaton, 153
ingoddedness, 174
integration of opposites, 172
Isaiah, prophesies, 154, 155
John, Book of Revelation, 166
Judaeo-Christian tradition, 151
Jung, *Answer to Job*, 158
liberation of women, 174
mission of Jesus, 151
Nazis and archetypal possession, 160
new God-image, Hiroshima, 169
nonacknowledgment of unconscious,
162
oppositional parallelism, 168
power of church, 167, 168
power and understanding of Yahweh,
156
prophecies of Deutero-Isaiah, 156

Psalmist, 171
psychotheology, 158
rejection of Jesus, described, 170
resolution in psyche, 175
salvation through Christ, moral
    impact, 167
Significance of Christ event, 152
Spirit, process of, 173
Summum Bonum, 164
symbols in psyche, 159
two sons of God, 165
universal religious nightmare, 172
wisdom tradition, Jewish, 174
Wotan as psychic force, 161
Yahweh, 154
Transcendence
exploration of, 10
of limitations, transpersonal
    experience, 68
Transformation
and ideal-ego, 50
inner, and global crisis, 78
of negative complex, 44
and no, 46
after positive to negative dominance
    of perinatal matrices, 76
recognition of shadow and mask, 43
reconciliation of opposites, 48
self-, and symbol of shadow, 40
technology of human importance, 77
and wise judgment, 51
Transpersonal experience, 11
analysis of, 75
aspects, 70
and cartography of psyche, 72
challenge to Newtonian-Cartesian
    paradigm, 70
cosmic consciousness, 69
of domination by perinatal forces,
    influences of, 74
events from microcosm and
    macrocosm, implications, 72
flow of chi energy, 69
identification with
    body-ego to cosmic identity, 76
    supracosmic and metacosmic void,
        69
importance to psychopathology, 73
and instant intuitive information,
    implications, 71

and integration with scientific
    disciplines, 72
interpretation, 70
and Jungian archetypes, 71
manifestations of spell of perinatal
    domain, 74
perinatal dynamics, imposed strategy
    of, 75
phenomena
    beyond comprehension, 72
    of extrasensory perception, 71
and philosophy of life, 74
positive to negative dominance of
    perinatal matrices, 76
reduction of aggression level, 76
relevancy, 70
specificity of recall, 70
transcendence of
    limitations, 68
    spatial barriers, 69
    time-space continuum, 69
Transpersonal psychology
definition, 10
origin, 9
pioneers, 9
Transpersonal vision
awakening, 17
definition, 11
and illusions, 14
inner source of guidance, 13
Tucker, Robert, Marxism, 181
Tveggi (Wotan), 22

Unconscious
collective, 25
    Anthropôs figure, 34
    and individual, and perinatal
        experience, 74
common, of wide national units, 25
and consciously unacceptable, 41
domain, perinatal, 62
    as interface with individual and
        collective unconscious, 67
group, 25
inhibitions and prohibitions, 44
level, physiological manifestations, 61
nonacknowledgment of, 162
personal, 24
Understanding, 2
development of, 2

self-, of devil within, 53

Van Halen, 221
Varela, Francisco, 224, 227, 228, 232
Vaughan, F., 6, 10
Vedas, 147
Virtue, perfect, Confucius, 89
Vision(s)
  Christ-Beserk, 24
  and ideals, 4
  illumination of, 13
  Niklaus von Flüe's, interpretation of, 22
  truth of existence, 13
  visionmakers and healers, 16
  of world, healed and whole, 15

Walsh, R., 2, 6, 10
Weiman, Henry, on Jesus, 151, 152
Weinberger, Caspar W., Secretary of Defense, 190
Western art
  discovery of matter, 219
  early Renaissance painting, epiphany of sacred, 219
  presence replaced by object, 219
Western culture
  and attributes of devil, 53
  concept of demon, 52
  experience of dislocation, 222
  materialism to nihilism, 220
  music video to dislocation, 221
  one-sided thinking, 30
  polarization of good and evil, 52
  punks vs. yuppies, and nihilism, 220, 221

symbols of painting, 219, 220
White, John
  enlightenment, 12
  Homo noeticus, 266, 267
Wholeness
  accepting of unacceptable, 41
  fragmentary man into, Jung, 173
  freedom from egocentric attachment and, 13
  integrated levels of consciousness, 10
Wilber, Ken, 3, 6, 9
  Atman project, 194
  evolutionary transcendence, 15
  mental-psychic clarity, 14
  origin of murder and warfare, 194
  sense of awareness, 14
  sexuality, 15
  vision/logic, 11
  Western science and perennial philosophy, 72
  Wisdom Culture, 15
Wisdom, source of, 10
Wittgenstein, Ludwig, 222
World hunger, malnutrition statistics, 1
Wotan, 22
  article by Jung, 160, 161
  god of berserkers, 23
  Grimmir, 22
  hrammi, bear's paw, 22
  Svipall, 22
  Tveggi, 22

Yalom, I., 4
Young, Arthur, 73

Zenji, Dogen, 223
Zoroaster, 133